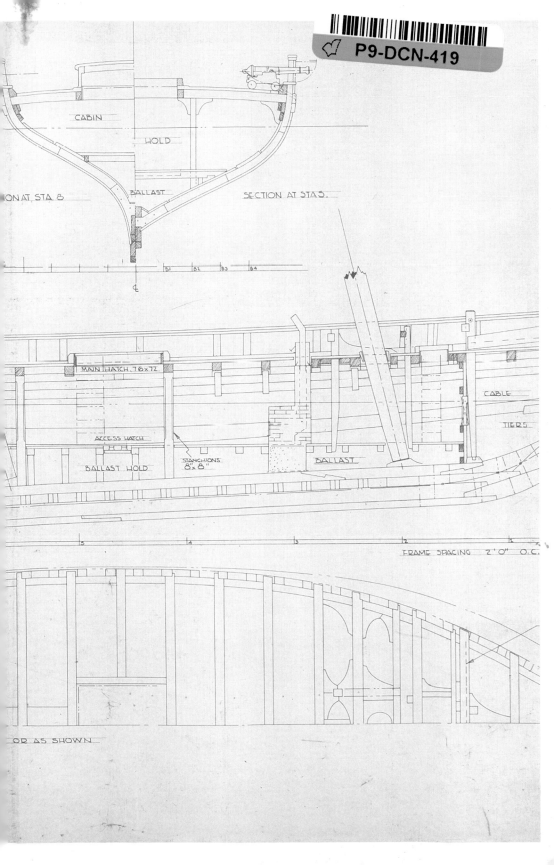

CABIN

HOLD

BALLAST

ION AT STA. 8

SECTION AT STA 5.

B1   B2   B3   B4

MAIN HATCH, 76 x 72

ACCESS HATCH

BALLAST HOLD

STANCHIONS
8" x 8"

BALLAST

CABLE

TIERS

5   4   3   2

FRAME SPACING 2'0" O.C.

OR AS SHOWN

PRIDE

OF THE

SEA

PRIDE
OF THE
SEA

Courage, Disaster, and a Fight for Survival

TOM WALDRON

CITADEL PRESS
Kensington Publishing Corp.
www.kensingtonbooks.com

CITADEL PRESS BOOKS are published by

Kensington Publishing Corp.
850 Third Avenue
New York, NY 10022

Copyright © 2004 Tom Waldron

All Kensington titles, imprints, and distributed lines are available at special quantity discounts for bulk purchases for sales promotions, premiums, fund-raising, educational, or institutional use. Special book excerpts or customized printings can also be created to fit specific needs. For details, write or phone the office of the Kensington special sales manager: Kensington Publishing Corp., 850 Third Avenue, New York, NY 10022, attn: Special Sales Department: phone 1-800-221-2647.

CITADEL PRESS and the Citadel logo are Reg. U.S. Pat. & TM Off.

Designed by Leonard Telesca

First printing: April 2004

10   9   8   7   6   5   4   3   2   1

Printed in the United States of America

Library of Congress Control Number: 2003110769

ISBN: 0-8065-2492-8

For Stephanie

"It is a mighty force that of mere chance; absolutely irresistible."
—JOSEPH CONRAD

PRIDE
OF THE
SEA

CHAPTER 1

Aug. 11, 1985
Aboard the Pride of Baltimore
The Baltic Sea

All Dan Parrott wanted was a couple hours of sleep, but the boat wasn't cooperating. After working half the night, the twenty-three-year-old deckhand had climbed up into his bunk a little earlier and nodded off as the *Pride of Baltimore* sailed south along the Swedish coast. Sleep was sometimes difficult in low-ceilinged bunks that more than one crew member had compared to coffins. But now it was impossible, thanks to the steep Baltic Sea waves that were shoving the ninety-foot schooner into an uncomfortable early-morning roll. During his four months on board the *Pride*, Dan had gotten used to its slow arcing rolls in steep seas. But these were more dramatic than usual, almost violent.

Lying half-awake under a grubby cotton sleeping bag that hadn't been washed in months, Dan was suddenly startled by a splash of water. As the ship reached the bottom of its deepest port roll yet, seawater had sprayed into his darkened bunk. While leaks were common on the *Pride*, this was the first time Dan had experienced water in his bunk. He realized seawater was sloshing so high in the bilges that it had come up and over the thin planks that made up the cabin's interior wall, and down into his bunk. Moments later, the *Pride* leaned once again to port and a second, bigger spray of water splashed on his bed. Parrott gave up on sleeping; he knew he would soon be going back to work.

Up on deck, Jennifer Lamb, the ship's twenty-five-year-old second mate, was in charge of the early-morning watch. About 7:45 A.M., with the weather growing more worrisome, she alerted the *Pride*'s forty-one-year-old captain, Armin Elsaesser, who emerged up the ladder from his cabin at the boat's aft end. The schooner had left the small harbor of Vastervik, Sweden, the day before in a calm fog—appropriate conditions for a crew nursing wicked hangovers after a night of drinking with local sailors. But the weather had quickly turned rougher once the ship cleared the southern end of Oland Island, an ancient chunk of limestone dotted with windmills on Sweden's east coast, and reached the dark open waters of the Baltic. The southwest wind picked up speed and steep waves began to come quickly.

The morning forecast warned of a possible gale from the west and with the skies closing, Elsaesser decided he had no choice but to summon his entire crew. The twelve-member crew was usually divided into three deck watches that alternated shifts, but there were times when everyone was needed to set or strike sail on the *Pride*, a replica of a Baltimore clipper from about 1812. Hearing the all-hands call, Dan pulled back the thin blue curtain that ran along his bed, rolled down from his damp bunk, and got dressed to work in the sixty-degree weather. The hatch leading up to mid-ship from the main cabin was battened tight to keep seawater from splashing in, forcing Dan and other crew members to go through the *Pride*'s cramped engine room and into the aft cabin, where a second ladder led up to the deck through an open companionway.

Climbing up, Dan glanced skyward and saw five sails were set. Even he, a relative newcomer, could tell that this was too many for the brisk wind. Without needing to be told, he headed straight to the hand pump on deck and began using it to clear the *Pride*'s overloaded bilges. The rest of the crew trickled up, including Sarah Fox, the twenty-four-year-old cook, who was generally excused from sail handling. Sarah had gotten up at around five a.m. to make breakfast, but was happy to put aside her galley chores, slip on her bright yellow foul-weather gear, and do some actual sailing.

Armin—as the crew always called him—stood near the tiller and considered his options. He was just over six feet tall, with blue eyes and blond hair swept back from a broad forehead. The handsome son of a prosperous Ohio family had sailed on *Pride* for parts of the last five years. This stint as captain began in London two months earlier and was scheduled to end in Hamburg in September. In the fifth month of a two-year goodwill excursion through Europe—its first time across the ocean—the *Pride* had never been farther from home. It was also Armin's first sail through Europe, and one made more special because he was sharing it with Jennifer, his girlfriend of three years.

With his full crew assembled, Armin instructed them to strike the foretopsail, a rectangular sail that hung far above the deck, to reduce the *Pride*'s exposure to the stiffening winds. Some of the crew climbed high up in the rigging to furl the sail. By the time they were finished, the waves reached eight feet and came in such quick succession that the *Pride* was having trouble pushing through them.

As each wave rushed in from starboard, the *Pride* slid sideways down the wave, its towering masts and wooden yards heeling to port and then back to starboard. Hoping to ease the rolling, Armin ordered the crew to strike the *Pride*'s enormous foresail, shaped like a right triangle with its top corner snipped off.

The crew stumbled on the pitching deck as they struck the foresail and tidied up the spaghetti-like pile of lines left over. The *Pride* sailed on with its mainsail up at the aft end of the ship, and two smaller sails, the jib and staysail, suspended out over the bow. Striking the foresail, however, did little to ease the rolling, and Armin called for the mainsail to be struck. The crew hustled aft and quickly hauled it down, leaving the *Pride* with an unusual sail pattern—only the jib and staysail, two of the forward-most sails.

The wind reached forty knots, or close to forty-five miles per hour, and the *Pride* continued to roll. While much of his crew struggled to lash the mainsail to the varnished, fifty-foot-long wooden boom angling back from the mainmast, Armin considered how to give the ship more power through the waves.

When the mainsail was stowed, he instructed Chris Rowsom, the bearded, curly-headed first mate, to reset the foresail that had been struck only minutes before. Nobody was happy about Armin's reversal but they took their places to work with the big sail. Several crew members quickly untied the brails that held the sail to the *Pride*'s forward mast, and the huge sail unfurled once again.

At the helm, Armin held on to the *Pride*'s long rosewood tiller and watched the ship's progress through the steep waves. As Chris tied off the line securing the foresail to a large wooden cleat on the deck, Armin suddenly realized that the biggest wave of the morning was bearing down on the *Pride* from starboard.

"Hang on!" Armin shouted.

Whoosh! A vicious combination of wind and sea rolled the *Pride* sharply to port and the boat's left side scooped down and under an enormous amount of green Baltic seawater, which cascaded over the deck and drenched the port side from bow to stern. The seven people who had been working with the foresail on the port side were suddenly in water up to their waists. They braced wherever they could to stay on their feet as seawater ran into their boots and lifted ropes, trash, and coffee mugs off the deck. As usual on the *Pride*, nobody wore a life jacket, which was too bulky to work in. And despite the obvious risks, nobody had bothered to put on a safety harness and strap himself to the boat. In the macho culture of the *Pride*, crew members rarely used harnesses.

The *Pride* pushed ahead sluggishly and pivoted tentatively back to starboard. But with much of the deck still under water, Armin's voice suddenly boomed out a second time from the helm: "Hang on!"

Before the first wave drained off, a second one swamped the boat, and this time the ship lurched farther to port, leaning more than forty degrees from vertical—an exceptionally pronounced heel. Out of the water on the starboard side, Jennifer hung on and waited for the ship to stabilize, even as a woozy feeling in her gut told her it might not. She had sailed thousands of miles on the *Pride* and her instincts shouted: *Wrong! It's gone way beyond where it's supposed to go.*

But within a couple of heartbeats, the *Pride* found its balance and eased slowly back to starboard. It wasn't going over.

Even so, the seven crew members on the port side were in trouble. This time, the sea wave packed far too much power. It shoved the seven off their feet and tossed them toward the thigh-high port railing. Its deck awash with the Baltic, the boat was sailing out from under them. At the helm, Armin watched in horror as the sea threatened to sweep away more than half his crew.

Veteran sailors know one rule perhaps better than all others: Don't leave the boat until the boat leaves you. Instinctively, many of the seven grabbed for ropes or anything else as they washed toward the rail. Dan Parrott hooked a thick line known as the foresail safety sheet with the crook of his arm and held fast under the onrushing water, while Rob Whalen, the ship's bosun, hung on by grabbing one of the *Pride*'s heavy cannons. The water flipped veteran deckhand Sue Burton off the deck, but she managed to latch on to the rail before leaving the boat completely. Clinging with both hands to the wooden rail, she craned her face above the rushing water, which flooded over her body and swept off her shirt and bra. Washing backward, deckhand Al Nejmeh extended his arms as far as he could. One hand caught some of the ship's thick wire rigging, the other grabbed hold of a yellow blob streaming toward him, which turned out to be Jeff Simmons, another deckhand. Both grabbed the rail. When the torrent of deck water subsided, Al and Jeff pulled themselves back in, as did Dan, Rob, and Sue.

Five were back on board, but two others were gone. Sarah Fox, the cook and least experienced member of the crew, felt herself being swept into the sea. In the confusion, Sarah was certain the *Pride* was going over on its side and she had one thought: *Get away!* If she didn't get clear, the boat's towering rigging would crash down on her. Fully submerged, Sarah willed herself to swim until she had to stop, suddenly aware of a tangle of ropes around her neck. Terrified of being strangled by ropes attached to the 120-ton boat, Sarah shook free and kept swimming. Fully dressed in the chilly water, Sarah finally sputtered to the surface, popping up through the water like a cork just in time to see that the *Pride* had not capsized but was sailing on without her.

Sarah could also hear someone screaming for help. Locating the sound, she saw that it was Ellen—deckhand Ellen Huebsch, who had been her roommate at Colby College in Maine. As with Sarah, the wave had flipped the twenty-five-year-old Ellen over the rail and into the water. The two friends made brief eye contact as Ellen realized she, too, was caught in a tangle of lines that had washed off the deck; her hands, she discovered, held another jumble of rope.

A second later, the *Pride*'s forward progress pulled the lines taut and Huebsch was being dragged along, leaving Sarah behind. Ellen managed to keep her head above the water as the schooner pulled her through the waves several feet off to port from the stern. In the surreal moment, Ellen figured she had somehow screwed up. *This can't be happening. You're not supposed to leave the boat*, she thought.

Soaked but back on his feet, Al Nejmeh saw what had happened to Ellen, rushed aft and began hauling her in with the tangle of lines. With Ellen almost close enough to be pulled up to the deck, the ropes unknotted themselves without warning, creating slack in the lines, and Ellen dropped back from the boat. But again she held fast to the lines and for a second time the *Pride*'s forward momentum pulled the ropes taut, yanking her with such a jerk that Ellen's sea boots fell off in the water. Hauling gingerly a second time, Al and others managed to get her back to the boat, where she was pulled up and dumped on deck like a giant codfish.

Now alone, Sarah struggled to stay afloat in the waves, rising and falling in the eight-foot swells as the *Pride* headed downwind. She kicked off her leather shoes, but her pants, sweater, and foul-weather top became deadweight pulling her under. The former lifeguard and distance swimmer could barely keep her mouth out of the stormy water long enough to breathe. She spotted a bag of trash that had washed off the deck and worked her way over, thinking it had enough air to keep her afloat. After clinging to the garbage and battling the waves for a moment, Sarah spotted a horseshoe-shaped life ring that crew member Wendelyn Marks tossed overboard during the confusion. She managed to reach the life ring, slip it around her neck, and only then gulp her first deep breath since being thrown from the deck.

On the *Pride*, it was near-chaos. At the aft rail, Sue Burton pointed and screamed at Sarah who was rapidly vanishing, paying no attention to the fact that she was wearing only a pair of shorts and boots. Some of the crew scrambled up the rigging with binoculars to try to keep sight of Sarah, while Ellen, back on deck, joined Sue and pointed too, as the crew had been taught to do in man-overboard situations. Ellen was terrified; she had helped Sarah land the cook's job on the *Pride* when another woman had quit, and now she was overboard. Ellen thought briefly of Sarah's parents, oblivious back home in Massachusetts.

Most stunned of all was Armin, who had helplessly watched the Baltic surge. The usually unflappable captain was terrified he might lose Sarah; crew members could see the fear in his face. "Hang on, Sarah!" he shouted into the wind. "We're coming! We won't leave you behind." The words, of course, weren't for Sarah, who was far out of earshot. Armin was trying desperately to reassure himself.

Armin had run into plenty of storms while sailing—both as a kid on Buzzards Bay in Massachusetts and later as a professional captain—but he had never lost a crew member who went overboard. He knew the boat had to reverse course quickly to find her in the rough conditions, but getting a schooner turned around in a Baltic storm was not so easy. Struggling to keep his composure, Armin ordered the *Pride*'s engine started and called for the ship to come about.

But the three sails that were set, including two extending out forward of the ship, wouldn't allow the boat to swing around in the stiff wind. Armin ordered the sails struck and the crew yanked the jib and staysail down at the bow. They then turned and dropped the foresail in a heap for the second time that morning. After several precious minutes, the *Pride* finally turned upwind but the over-matched diesel engine struggled to counteract the heavy wind and waves.

In the confusion of turning the boat, the unthinkable happened and the crew lost sight of Sarah. Lookouts in the rigging scanned the waves, spotting some of the debris that had washed off the deck, but not the ship's young cook. A dreadful fear that they might not find Sarah hung over the boat. *This turned to shit real fast*, thought Rob Whalen, a laconic, dark-haired *Pride* veteran.

An explosion of tangled lines, sails, and debris littered the deck as the *Pride* fought to motor upwind. The thick wooden jib boom, which angled out from the *Pride*'s bow and secured the jib and other sails, repeatedly speared the oncoming waves. Suddenly, Chris Rowsom, who was up in the rigging with binoculars, spotted Sarah bobbing in the waves. She had managed to reach the life ring and, astonishingly, looked okay. But it was clear that the schooner and its eighty-five-horsepower engine could not overcome the wind to reach her until the storm subsided.

Despite the stormy conditions, Armin decided to send out a rescue party, and the crew scrambled to launch *Rhino*, the inflatable orange dinghy stored on deck. The crew quickly unlashed the small boat and carefully lowered it over the rail. Dan Parrott and Rob Whalen volunteered to man the rescue effort.

Going first, Dan lowered himself into the small boat seesawing in the waves a few feet below the *Pride*'s deck. In a flash, he was in the water, flipped out of the dinghy by the waves. Dan hoisted himself back in. Up on deck, Rob looked down at the heaving boat, took a second to screw up his courage, and climbed carefully down to join Dan. With the dinghy and the great schooner moving in different rhythms in the high seas, several crew members had to use extra caution as they lowered *Rhino*'s one-hundred-pound outboard motor to the two men. Hanging from a thick rope, the motor swung in the wind until Rob grabbed it and attached it to *Rhino*'s stern. The two men hooked up the gas line, and the entire crew took a deep breath as Rob pulled the crank to try to start the notoriously unreliable motor. To everyone's astonishment, it roared to life on the first pull. Accelerating into the wind as it left the schooner, the dinghy suddenly shot up in the air, pushed backward like a Frisbee. For a terrifying split second, the boat looked like it would flip backward, but the bow stayed forward and the dinghy remained upright as it set out over the waves. Reaching each crest, the bow climbed six feet in the air and only its propeller remained in contact with the water.

Sarah was about a quarter mile away, but the two men couldn't see her from the dinghy because of the large swells. Relying on the lookouts on *Pride* to point them in the right direction, they spotted Sarah as they crested a wave. Unbelievably, she was smiling broadly. The men maneuvered close by, and with a burst of adrenaline, hauled her out of the sea and into the inflated boat.

The short downwind ride back to the *Pride* gave the three crew members an unusually revealing look at the sea's raw power—and the ship's vulnerability. Each wave shoved the *Pride* like a toy boat up and out of the water, exposing expanses of green bottom paint. The ship, with its bare masts rising starkly above the deck, threw off great volumes of water and was writhing like a serpent.

Stunned and cold, Sarah was soon handed up to the deck, where Armin greeted her with an emphatic hug. She made her way into the cabin, vomited the seawater she had swallowed and crawled into her bunk to warm up. Ellen went down to change out of her soaked clothes, only to burst into tears. With all twelve crew members finally back on board, the *Pride* turned again to the south and headed once more for its destination, the Polish port of Gdynia.

Before long, the wind eased and the sun brightened, providing some relief to the worn-out sailors as they cleaned up the deck. To everyone's surprise, Sarah emerged later that day and cooked stew for dinner.

Armin, a usually vivid writer, recorded in his captain's log an uncharacteristically dry version that glossed over the accident's distress. It was a just-the-facts account, not surprising since the log would be sent home to the *Pride* office back in Baltimore. In wrapping up his narrative, Armin recounted how the seas finally calmed that evening and the entire crew came on deck to enjoy the sunset and gentle sailing.

"Little is said about the recent events, but privately we are all very thankful to be safe and well," Armin wrote that night with the finality of a Victorian storyteller. "The ship and her crew are fine."

In the days and weeks that followed, the twelve people on board the *Pride* sorted out their feelings about that morning—the worst moment in the goodwill ship's nine-year history. Sarah Fox was grateful to be alive and credited Armin and others with risking their own lives to save hers. Novice deckhand Dan Parrott was astonished by the hair-raising adventure but figured it was all simply part of schooner sailing.

Others were less accepting. Sue Burton called her parents back in Baltimore to recount the drama and admitted she had lost faith in the boat. Al Nejmeh had come across the Atlantic on the *Pride* and had enjoyed the sailing, but coming so close to washing into the Baltic left him with no illusions about the ship's seaworthiness. A musician and poet as well as a sailor, he was shaken enough to put his concerns into a chilling verse he memorized and recited for his shipmates.

One section of his poem read:

'Twas Poseidon ya see,
Took six others and me,
Pushed and pulled us along for a ride,
Up and out and then down, and we come back around,
Before vanishing over the side,
But you cling or you're dead,
To your life on a thread.

Weeks later, after leaving the ship, Al heard from an old friend, Nadine Bloch, who was seeking advice. She had been offered a job on the *Pride* for its trans-Atlantic return to Baltimore in the summer of 1986. But she wasn't sure about the trip, especially in light of the Baltic accident, the news of which rocketed through the world of schooner sailing.

What do you think of the Pride? Nadine had asked.

Al wrote back and made plain his opinion:

Dear Nadine,
The *Pride* was a great experience and I met great people. But Nadine, you're a very good friend of mine. I wouldn't recommend you get on that boat. I don't think the boat is safe.

Nobody spent more time replaying the disaster than Armin himself. So much had gone wrong. He allowed the early-morning watch to be caught with too much sail up as the wind built, and once he was at the helm, he worked the boat into an odd sail pattern that did little to handle the rapid waves. Those were mistakes of judgment or execution, and every sea captain was guilty of those. But the result was unacceptable and the specter of nearly losing a crew member left him anxious about a return to the *Pride*.

Armin loved the ship as much as anyone; the physical sensations of sailing her could be sublime and she had taken him from San Francisco to Stockholm. But the storm had bruised his confidence. The ship's behavior in conditions that were rough but by no means terrifying—the deep roll, the steep heel, and the astonishing blast of water over the deck—left a vivid impression.

Later that year, as he prepared to return to the *Pride* in Spain, Armin poured out his concerns in a letter to Jennifer, who was sailing in the Caribbean. A captain's first duty is to the safety of his crew and Armin could not shake the hard fact that he had nearly failed his most basic responsibility.

"While I look forward to . . . getting to Spain, I'm just not crazy about returning to *Pride*. I feel little of the confidence and trust in her you feel for *Westward* [an educational schooner both Armin and Jennifer had sailed on]—and for good reason. The crew will be just fine . . . But frankly, the experiences last summer have left me feeling very uneasy; they recur to haunt me. The prospect of losing a life fills me with the most horrible dread. And that awful moment surfaces to remind me of just how close I came."

The most awful of moments still awaited Armin and the *Pride*.

CHAPTER 2

Fall 1985

When carpenters began trimming dense Central American timbers to build a Baltimore clipper in 1976, nobody figured it would one day be battling treacherous waves and a forty-knot wind in the Baltic Sea. Rather, the plan was to keep the boat in the calmer waters of the Baltimore harbor as a floating museum—an authentic, cannon-laden throwback to a shining period in the city's maritime history. Even the name, *Pride of Baltimore*, had a historical echo, not to mention more than a little sentiment—a good fit for an unabashedly sentimental city. The problem was that the *Pride*, which came along as the nation rediscovered the glory of tall ships, was just too beautiful to keep tied to a dock. The ship's builder, an artist and sailor enchanted by maritime history, insisted on sailing his creation. The boat, he said, was a piece of living history that nobody had experienced for at least a century.

Never mind that the *Pride* was also modeled on a type of schooner that was all about speed, not safety, and that sometimes disappeared without a trace. Melbourne Smith, who built the boat, acknowledged the risk and warned plainly that the ship could be dangerous if placed in unsure hands. But, he said with a confident smile, that was part of the appeal. Extra risk meant extra reward.

So the boat went to sea, and the reward was indeed great. The city of Baltimore had a marvelous civic treasure. And the *Pride*'s ever-changing crew had the chance to experience old-style, and sometimes fabulous, sailing. When the wind was right, the *Pride* heeled gracefully and glided powerfully along under a vast expanse of dirty white sails. It was unforgettable sailing, like riding bareback at night on a wild black mare, one crew member liked to say. The *Pride* and her sailors developed an intimate relationship with the sea, which was just under them. In even moderate conditions, water washed down the weathered pine decking. When forced to sail close to the wind, the *Pride* crashed through the waves the best she could, the sturdy jib boom leading the way off the bow, plunging again and again through the sea. It was a dramatic sight: the heavy piece of lumber extended forty feet ahead of the ship, laden with lines and heavy furled sails, went under, straining at the sea, and, after a breathtaking moment, sprang free in a foamy geyser. A crew member caught out on the jib boom in such conditions had two options. Climb up out of the way and watch, or hang on to the boom, get dunked one or two times, and take the ride of a lifetime.

One nineteenth-century American mariner suggested that the conservative British would be too afraid to sail Baltimore clippers. Their sail plans were too extreme, their rigs too light. All in all, he said, they sacrificed too much stability in the name of performance. A century and a half later that remained no less true for the *Pride*. While the public understood little about the *Pride*'s inherent vulnerability, any knowledgeable sailor who came on board was sure to notice. Even so, the insular schooner world was full of experienced sailors who grasped the risks but were sure *they* could handle the *Pride*. With the right luck, they figured, the schooner could keep at it for fifty years. Or, if the Baltic was any gauge, it could be lost tomorrow.

With no home of his own, Armin returned from Europe in the fall to live with a cousin outside Baltimore. He went kayaking during the weekends on the reservoirs north of the city or in the tidal marshes of Maryland's Eastern Shore, and spent the week downtown preparing to return to the *Pride*. In January, he would meet the boat in Spain and, after a period of maintenance, take her through the Mediterranean to Malta and Greece. The schedule called for Armin to take a summer break, but return to the *Pride* and bring the ship back across the Atlantic in the fall.

Armin was delighted with the itinerary and the chance to sail through the Greek islands that had produced some of history's most daring sailors. To get ready, he listened to a book-on-tape version of *Ulysses Found*, written by a sailor who spent seven years on a small yacht retracing the travel of Ulysses, using clues from *The Odyssey*.

In the *Pride* office in a downtown high-rise, Armin made final decisions about his crew for the Mediterranean and sent out contracts and plane tickets to get the sailors to Spain. He also mailed out a checklist of things to bring, including khaki pants or skirts, and a blue blazer for dress-up affairs. Reading over the list, Armin's mind flashed back to those frantic minutes when Sarah disappeared behind the dark Baltic waves. There was no doubt that the yellow foul-weather gear she wore that morning helped saved her life by giving the lookouts something bright to spot in the water. Armin took a pen and wrote a special note on the employment contracts for the new hires: "Dark colored foul-weather gear *strongly* discouraged."

Armin headed to New England at Christmastime to visit his parents, who lived in a quiet waterfront community called Salters Point near the whaling town of New Bedford, Massachusetts. The site of an old saltworks and later a farm, Salters Point gave way to tasteful development at the end of the nineteenth century. As a child, Armin and his family spent unhurried summers there, surrounded by weather-beaten shingled houses and clumps of overflowing hydrangeas. With Jennifer off sailing, Armin went alone.

The third of five children and the oldest son, Armin Emil Elsaesser III grew up in landlocked Youngstown, Ohio. His grandfather and namesake was a prominent Swiss surgeon who specialized in the removal of goiters and who moved to the United States in 1911. Armin's father, whom he always called Johnny, attended Yale, got a law degree, and worked as an attorney in the steel business. His mother, Martha, grew up in Ohio but had long-standing ties to Salters Point. It was there that Armin learned to sail in the summers as a teenager, picking up fifteen dollars a week crewing on Buzzards Bay with an Episcopal minister. The Elsaessers eventually purchased their own boat and Armin grew competent enough to take friends on long sails to the Elizabeth Islands, which extended in a line northwest of Martha's Vineyard.

Beginning high school in the late 1950s, Armin followed his father to Choate, then an all-boys boarding school in Wallingford, Connecticut. He went on to the University of Pennsylvania, and in his first year there, a pretty freshman from Connecticut named Eliza Ferris spotted him in a lecture hall and decided he was someone she wanted to get to know. He looked, she decided, authentic. Armin made for an attractive catch—tall, dimpled, and blessed with angular good looks. On their first outing back home in Connecticut, Liza watched in dismay as other women flocked around her date. But the relationship survived four years of college, and they graduated in 1966, Armin pulling down far more C's than A's. They were married seven months later.

With the Vietnam War growing bloodier, Armin joined the U.S. Naval Reserve in 1967 and won a spot in flight school. But the training sessions in Navy jets unnerved him and he dropped out unexpectedly. The Navy responded by shipping the young lieutenant to a remote naval facility in the tiny Persian Gulf nation of Bahrain to oversee a refueling operation. It was tedious work, but more appealing than serving as a junior officer on a patrol boat in Vietnam, the fate handed some other officers who bailed out on flight school.

After his discharge in 1969, Armin and Liza returned to the United States and moved into the Elsaesser home on Salters Point. The next year they bought their own house, a bungalow overlooking Buzzards Bay up the road in the small town of Mattapoisett. A bit of a Bohemian despite his upbringing in a straitlaced midwestern family, Armin began tooling around in a 1965 Mustang, got a lobsterman's license, and plopped seventy-five lobster pots out in the bay. For a while, he ran the ferry out to Cuttyhunk Island but soon found work building wooden leisure boats, eventually launching a business with a friend. During those years, Armin gained sailing experience delivering yachts up and down the East Coast. He also took a stab at teaching shipbuilding and seamanship, but was stung when some of his students said he was cold and aloof. Liza, meanwhile, took jobs in a bank, the library, and, finally, delivering mail.

All the while, Armin and Liza dreamed of going to sea together. In 1975, after a long search, they found a six thousand dollar John Alden design that Armin considered "sound but forlorn." The thirty-six-year-old sailboat had a good-sized keel and Armin deemed it safe enough to take to sea. He had it hauled up to their front lawn and spent months rebuilding it. Finally, they renamed it the *Eliza H.* in honor of Liza, who had given up her middle name, Hitchcock, when they married.

The following summer, Armin and Liza began their life on the water with a trip up the coast to Maine. When the weather turned cold, they took the boat down the East Coast and out to the Caribbean. Both of their families were unnerved by their sailing adventure and, coincidentally, both Liza's mother and Armin's father sent them a copy of the same book, *How to Survive at Sea.*

But the couple survived nicely, sailing to Haiti, the Dominican Republic, the Bahamas, and everywhere in between. Armin liked to do things on a certain schedule but there was also plenty of time to hang loose. He took up scuba diving and would go deep in the clear Caribbean, sometimes for fun, sometimes to spearfish. Often, he resurfaced slightly stunned, not sure where the sailboat was, and the dives eventually gave him severe earaches.

Coming back to the United States, the couple was greeted by a customs agent in Florida who inspected the boat and asked, "Well, did you get it out of your system?" The answer was no. Instead of returning to New England, they docked the boat in the moss-covered town of Beaufort, South Carolina, which boasted a large natural port and rich maritime and boat-building traditions.

Liza went to work in a local school; Armin got another ferry job, this time taking passengers back and forth to Daufuskie Island, just south of Hilton Head. He was determined to make a living on the water, but a motorized ferry wasn't what he had in mind and he looked for other opportunities. In the winter of 1978, at the age of thirty-four, Armin secured his first big-time sailing job, as mate on the *Westward*, the educational sailing ship based on Cape Cod, not far from Salters Point. Eager to sail, Armin left Liza alone on the *Eliza H.* in South Carolina and spent much of the next year on *Westward*, helping sail the boat around the East Coast and teaching college students during their semester at sea.

After years of sailing yachts, the *Westward*, a 125-foot, steel-hulled schooner, gave Armin his first taste of tall ships. He was hooked and began working toward the hours at sea needed to secure a Coast Guard master of sail license. (It would take years, but when he passed the exams to earn the license, Armin wrote a short but joyful note home: "It's over at last!" and noted he had scored an average of 95.4 on the test.)

In the winter of 1979, Armin and Liza were reunited after nearly a year apart but made the mistake of signing up to work as captain and crew on the *Charlotte Ann*, a sailboat doing charter business in the Caribbean. The tropical climate was appealing, as were the tax-free tips earned taking groups of six well-to-do passengers on sailing vacations, but working together on the boat strained the marriage. It collapsed the following spring, when Armin shipped out once again—for his first stint as captain of the *Pride of Baltimore*, then in its fourth year of sailing. Armin was gone for a year. Four months after he returned, Liza filed for divorce.

The divorce was relatively uncomplicated. Armin, who came from a financially comfortable family, was tight with money, but had never shown much interest in most material possessions. That didn't change when it came time to hash out the divorce. Liza figured it would make sense for her to keep the house and for Armin to keep the *Eliza H*. But Armin wanted neither. He walked off to a career at sea—leaving behind a house on the water, a lovingly restored sailboat, and nearly fifteen years of marriage. Liza later sold the boat.

In the fall of 1982, Armin returned to the *Pride* for a second big trip—the schooner's first voyage to the West Coast after five years of cruising the East Coast and Caribbean. While working in the office only ten days before the boat was scheduled to sail, a petite woman with a mop of dark auburn hair and a wide smile came in.

Jennifer Lamb, a recent graduate from the University of Maine who had just turned twenty-three, was looking for a job. Armin glanced over her résumé. Her professional sailing credentials weren't impressive, but she had grown up around boats. The daughter of a Navy officer, Jennifer had spent a year and a half with her family on a boat in the Caribbean—taking her senior year of high school by correspondence course. Intent on sailing for a year after college, Jennifer had looked around the docks of Annapolis, Maryland, for several days but received only one job offer—to crew for a blind captain heading to the Caribbean during hurricane season. She passed. On a whim, she stopped by the *Pride* office; her timing couldn't have been better. A deckhand from Baltimore had quit after a tedious week on the ship spent scraping and painting, and Armin handed Jennifer the last spot in the crew.

Despite their fifteen-year age difference, Armin and Jennifer took a liking to each other on the voyage to California. Armin had his hands full with problems that tested the old-style schooner's sailing capabilities—a sail ripped to shreds by stiff wind, for one—but there were many special moments, including a passage through the Panama Canal and Christmas in Acapulco. By the time they left the boat in San Francisco the next year, their relationship was secure. But Armin and Jennifer struggled to keep it flourishing while building careers. They worked together for a while with a sailing outfit in San Francisco before heading back East. Jennifer crewed on the *Clearwater,* a Hudson River–based sloop involved in environmental education, and later Armin's old ship, the *Westward.* Armin, meanwhile, taught and served as the first captain on the *Spirit of Massachusetts,* a ninety-foot schooner that was inspired in part by the *Pride* and constructed in Boston. It was a plum assignment to sail such a high-profile ship in what amounted to his home state, but the job ended amid squabbles with others in the organization. While idled that fall, Armin signed on to captain the *Appledore,* a sixty-five-foot sailboat jammed with two dozen hard-partying college students, as well as crew and instructors, spending a semester in the Caribbean. Nearly two decades older than the students, Armin was miserable, despite having Jennifer along as a crew member.

A year later, in the fall of 1985, the *Pride* trip through Northern Europe again brought the two together. While the Baltic had been a disaster, the next stop, in Communist Poland, had been wonderful. Some six thousand people turned out in cold, wet weather in Gdynia for a rare Cold War glimpse of America. As the *Pride* pulled away from the dock after a week, an admirer threw a bouquet of roses on board and a deckhand answered with a boom from one of the ship's cannons. Everyone agreed it was one of the *Pride*'s best visits anywhere. A couple of weeks later, the *Pride* reached Hamburg, Germany. In a driving rain, Armin and Jennifer packed their duffels and left the *Pride*.

This time, the three months sailing with Armin convinced Jennifer that she didn't like leading a double life—girlfriend and crew member. "Couples that sail together fail together," was an old saw, but she knew it often proved accurate. Plus, she had gotten tired of working especially hard to prove she, the *Pride*'s first female officer, was worthy of the job and not the beneficiary of a boyfriend's favor. She was aware she had a chip on her shoulder, but couldn't relax enough to let it fall and enjoy the time sailing with Armin. By the time they reached Hamburg, Jennifer was more than ready to leave the boat. She had also decided she would not sail with Armin through the Mediterranean in the spring of 1986 as planned.

Beyond that, Jennifer was anxious to return to a more traditional lifestyle. Her plan to spend "a year" sailing after college was now in its fourth year, and she explored graduate school options that would put her back on land. She was also interested in marriage and children; Armin seemed indifferent to both. They had gone through countless conversations about the future and Armin could vacillate wildly, longing for both the security of a committed life together and the independence of sailing and adventure. "The self-centered saga continues," he announced in early 1985 when he purchased an airplane ticket to make an around-the-world trip alone. At other times, he described himself not inaccurately as "another expensively educated young man searching for contradictions in his life."

A few weeks away from turning forty-two, an age at which many men have long-since burrowed into lives anchored by children and homes, Armin had neither. Knowing little else but sailing, Armin was unsure how to fashion a life that would mesh with Jennifer's. He looked into a one-year program in which he could take the science prerequisites needed to enter medical school, but that seemed unworkable. He had also talked to *Pride* officials about moving into the job running the operation, but that had limited appeal. So eager a decade earlier to make a career at sea, Armin felt trapped in the sailing life.

He was by no means the first sailboat captain to struggle for a graceful way to get off the water. Indeed it was a recurring topic for veteran sailors. Working as a sea captain carried wonderful benefits—travel, adventure, and intensely lived relationships with shipmates. But there was a substantial downside; children and spouses, to be sure, were problematic. The pay was low and sailing jobs often lacked even basic perks such as a pension. Even with the *Pride,* which was considered one of the most prestigious schooners in the country, it had only been in the previous year that the organization had agreed to put its captains on a full-time salary; before, they had been sailing gypsies, scrambling to find other jobs when they weren't on the *Pride.*

Armin and Jeff Bolster, a good friend from the *Westward,* used to joke about the uncertainty of the sailing life. In their darker moments, the two kidded each other about their likely future: sitting together on a Naugahyde couch in front of the Old Seamen's Home on Staten Island, drinking coffee, smoking unfiltered Camels, and talking about the good old days on *Westward.* It was a joke, but both men knew that it was easier to start a career on the sea than to leave one.

With a new year approaching and a return to the *Pride* imminent, Armin wrote to Jennifer to try once again to clarify his thoughts about the future and the prospect of another long separation. The anguished letter was a monument to indecision. On the one hand, he announced, he was ready to buy property, settle down, and make a life with her. But on the other, he offered, maybe they were wasting each other's time. "I am old (well, older) and jaded and my role in life is changing," Armin wrote in rushed cursive. "I want some more security in my life. . . . I envision a continuing routine of separation. Where will I be 100 letters from now? . . . I want to be able to take care of you, but have no firm prospect of employment in a year."

The letter, cathartic when written, spurred doubts the minute Armin slipped it in the mailbox. The next day he wrote a second one, apologizing and saying maybe the outpouring was caused by plain old loneliness, as well as anxiety about returning to the *Pride*. "Here I am reluctantly returning to the ship after a difficult summer—and you won't be there."

CHAPTER 3

December 1985
Baltimore

On December 29, a few days after sending his mournful letter, Armin settled into a coach seat on a World Airways flight to London. Air travelers in Europe were still on edge because of the brazen acts of terrorism two days earlier. At Leonardo da Vinci Airport in Rome, four Arab terrorists fired Soviet-made AK-47 assault rifles and lobbed grenades into a check-in area crowded with holiday travelers. Five hundred miles to the north at Schwechat Airport in Vienna, three men launched a similar assault a few minutes later. After gun battles in both airports, twenty-two people were dead, including four terrorists and five Americans; more than one hundred others were wounded.

The post-Christmas attacks came at the end of a horrific year of terrorism in Europe. In June, two hijackers took over a TWA flight shortly after it left Athens and killed Navy diver Robert Stethem. October brought the hijacking of the *Achille Lauro*, an Italian cruise ship off Egypt, and the slaying of a disabled tourist, sixty-nine-year-old Leon Klinghoffer, thrown overboard in his wheelchair. Just after Thanksgiving, hijackers took over another airliner out of Athens and diverted it to Malta. Egyptian commandos stormed the plane on the tarmac and fifty-eight people died.

By the time of the December airport attacks, many American travelers had seen enough and had canceled vacations in Greece and other European countries. The headlines from Europe also troubled officials with Pride of Baltimore Inc., the non-profit organization that operated the boat for the city. After spending most of 1985 in Europe, the *Pride* was scheduled to make stops at ports around the Mediterranean in 1986 before heading back home in the fall. The itinerary was set—eight European countries, from Malta to Belgium. After the November hijacking, the *Pride* board of directors reconsidered a planned stop in Greece, which seemed to have the worst problems with terrorists. By Christmas, though, the Greece stops were back on—to Armin's relief.

Armin traveled light, prepared for four months of living in the cramped captain's cabin on the *Pride*—yellow foul-weather gear, dark sea boots, and comfortable clothes for sailing. There were also some khaki pants, maroon *Pride* pullovers, a blue-striped, button-down shirt, a *Pride* tie, and the blue blazer he would wear to the planned round of "grip-and-grin" functions, which inevitably involved keys to the city or proclamations saluting the ship.

Then there were his gadgets, chosen with more care than his clothes. The brass Plath sextant he used for celestial navigation was stowed in a mahogany case and was worth well over one thousand dollars. He packed a second, smaller sextant, a handsome pair of binoculars, a handheld compass, and a Nikon 35-mm camera. On his wrist, Armin wore an expensive Rolex watch—the same brand he had been sporting since he joined the Navy twenty years before.

For reading material, he threw in copies of the *New Yorker* that had recently started coming in the mail, thanks to a subscription from Jennifer. He also brought along yellow legal pads with the pieces of a novel he was working on—a historical romance tentatively called "Slaver," about a slave trader who falls in love with one of his captives.

Armin was due in Spain by New Year's to take command of the *Pride* from one of the ship's other two captains, Jan Miles, who had brought the ship south from Germany. Miles's two-month voyage to Spain had gone smoothly and ended exuberantly. On a beautiful November night, the *Pride* entered the Strait of Gibraltar under a full moon, with the crew dancing on deck to Van Morrison tunes. It was the *Pride*'s first trip into the Mediterranean and the first time a Baltimore clipper had sailed past the big rock in at least a century.

The *Pride* had received a typically lavish ceremonial welcome in the port city of Malaga, Spain, with tugboats rushing out to serve as escorts. At the dock, the city's mayor gave a welcoming speech and a loud folk band, complete with guitars, drums, and tambourines, serenaded the crew. During the coming weeks the fanfare subsided, and Miles's crew fell into an increasingly tedious routine of repairs and painting. The crew also began to depart the ship one by one as their contracts expired.

Armin reached Malaga late on the night of December 30 after a stop in London. A taxi brought him to the *Pride*, which was sandwiched between container ships at the western end of the harbor. Armin surveyed the boat on which he had spent so much of the last five and half years.

The sails, of course, were stowed for the winter lay-up, and the enormous head rig, which supported the jib and other foresails, had been dismantled for maintenance. Still, there was no mistaking the *Pride*, with her raked masts and distinctive black hull. The sight of the *Pride* reminded Armin that no matter how many times he had done it before, serving as captain was an awesome job.

"The reality of stepping aboard a boat to take command is striking indeed. It can't be imagined," he wrote Jennifer, who was sailing off the Florida coast. "All preconceptions fall away at the sight of those sticks; suddenly the responsibility is real, not imagined. She's your boat now, skip. You deal with her and her crew."

The ship was quiet and, as usual, the *Pride*'s two cats, Tuck and Bill, had the run of the place. Down below, the winter layover crew had put a fresh coat of white paint on many of the cabin spaces, giving them a warm glow. Armin found reminders of Jennifer everywhere, including stickers and notes in log books. He looked at the bunk she had used the previous year and kept expecting her to peek out over the blue privacy curtain.

Miles's crew from the fall was gone and the replacement crew that would work under Armin had begun to trickle in. Among them were two old *Pride* friends. Sugar Flanagan, a soon-to-be twenty-seven-year-old, barrel-chested New Englander with a bird's-nest beard and hair that wound into tight brown spirals at sea, had sailed on the *Pride* numerous times—to the West Coast, across the Caribbean, and through the Great Lakes, and had re-upped to serve as first mate through the Mediterranean. His twenty-nine-year-old girlfriend from California, Leslie McNish, would serve as bosun. Like Armin and Jennifer, Sugar and Leslie had fallen in love on the *Pride*'s trip out west in 1982. Although he made an exception for himself and Jennifer, Armin didn't like the idea of hiring a couple to work on the boat, as things could go wrong if the couple started fighting. But Sugar's and Leslie's relationship was as sure as any couple's, and their easygoing confidence and long sailing experience gave Armin an immediate sense of security. On board, he shook hands for the first time with James Chesney, a twenty-four-year-old, big-shouldered carpenter with wire-framed glasses and a mustache who had landed the job as cook and had flown in a few days earlier.

After recovering from jet lag, Armin compared notes with Jan, who was six years younger than he. The two captains were both confident and experienced, but their relationship was professional at best. A few years back, Armin, who had seniority in the organization, had played a role in getting Jan removed from the job of directing an overhaul of the *Pride*'s rigging. Jan, who spoke his mind freely on any issue, angrily confronted Armin about the move. The two had managed to continue working for the *Pride*, but they were not buddies.

Sailors who worked under both men saw clear differences in their styles. Armin, with his Ivy League polish, was easier on his crew, more approachable; Jan, who began sailing professionally as a teenager, tended to bark orders. Armin was cerebral and cautious; Jan was instinctive and daring, a schooner cowboy who loved to push the *Pride*. He was far more likely than Armin to bring her to the dock with sails up, a more challenging approach than motoring. Jan sailed from the gut; with Armin, you could always see the wheels turning.

The night after his arrival, Armin and Jan sat down for a New Year's Eve celebration with the three others: Sugar, Leslie, and the cook, whom everybody called Chez. The five sat on sea chests around the small table in the *Pride*'s cramped, dimly lit main cabin, which had only about five feet of headroom under the deck beams. The red Spanish wine flowed and the group swapped stories. Many came from Sugar and Leslie, who had arrived in Malaga a few days before Armin after months at sea. They brought their usual sailing gear: knives, spikes, hand-held radio, binoculars, chisels, and Sugar's Freiberger sextant, as well as a new camera they picked up in Europe. This adventure, their biggest yet, had begun the previous summer in Darwin, Australia, where the couple posted a sign advertising two Coast Guard–licensed captains looking for sailboat work. A yacht owner and his pregnant wife, who wanted to take their forty-foot sloop to Europe, saw the sign and contacted them. They liked Sugar and Leslie so much they hired them on the spot and handed over the boat. Sugar and Leslie prepared the sloop for an ocean crossing and bought provisions, including enough steaks to meet the owners' request for a good cut of meat every other night. They took the sloop across the Indian Ocean, through the Red Sea, and into the Mediterranean via the Suez Canal before getting off in Cyprus. From there, the couple rode ferries and trains through Greece and Italy, eventually ending up in Malaga.

As the night wore on, Sugar fashioned a cannon charge by pouring gunpowder from the ship's cache into a piece of aluminum foil he molded into a cup shape using a beer can. He shoved the powder ball into one of the ship's cannons, and poured fast-burning powder into the touchhole. At midnight, Sugar struck a match and lit the powder leading into the firing chamber and the blast reverberated across the Malaga harbor. After champagne toasts, the group called it a night.

During the first week of January, Jan Miles headed back to the United States and the *Pride*'s new crew swelled to six, with the arrival of the fourth and final officer, second mate Joe McGeady from Baltimore, and engineer Vinny Lazzaro, a commercial fisherman from Maine who had decided to give sailing a try.

McGeady, a twenty-seven-year-old with a model's good looks, had sailed as a deckhand with the *Pride* off and on since graduating from Virginia Polytechnic Institute three and a half years earlier. Armin had finally offered him an officer's job, which might have come sooner if Joe hadn't broken his wrist the previous summer when he fell out of a tree in Denmark during a night of carousing.

The dark-haired Lazzaro arrived wearing a blue ball cap bearing the name Saco Bay Fishermans Supply, but without his bags, which were lost somewhere between New York and Malaga. After years of fishing in all conditions in the North Atlantic, he was amply prepared to maintain the *Pride*'s small engine room. Big and quiet, Vinny looked solid to the *Pride* veterans.

On January 7, the day the two new crewmen reached the *Pride*, President Ronald Reagan issued an order for all Americans to leave Libya, a reaction to the recent round of terrorist attacks in Europe. The drumbeat of a military attack on the Middle Eastern pariah nation was unmistakable. That same day in Baltimore, thirty-five miles up I-95 from Washington, the *Pride* organization's board of directors assembled in a downtown high-rise to talk about terrorism, too. The airport attacks eleven days earlier had spooked the board, which included a handful of Baltimore's most prominent businessmen, and now Reagan was laying the groundwork for military action. If terrorists were willing to take over a cruise ship or shoot up holiday travelers in the Rome airport, why wouldn't they hijack a sailboat? The *Pride*, with its American flag and publicity-oriented mission, might make an attractive target to terrorists.

Gail Shawe, the *Pride*'s longtime executive director who had spent countless hours planning the European trip, disagreed. Although she knew next to nothing about sailing when she took over the job, Shawe had kept the *Pride* organization running for years and didn't mind being referred to as the "mother of the *Pride*." During the board meeting, she argued that the *Pride* was not well-known overseas and would surely be disregarded by terrorists. One *Pride* official pegged the chance that terrorists could attack the ship as remote, perhaps one in ten thousand. While board members accepted the more obvious, everyday risks of sailing, they opted not to take even that small a chance on terrorists and voted to cancel the second leg of the European mission.

More than a year of planning was out the window, and Shawe reached Armin late that night in Spain to deliver the bad news. The board, she told him, had decided that the Mediterranean was too dangerous and they should just bring the boat home.

For Armin, it was a huge disappointment, particularly the cancellation of the intriguing sail through Greece. As he pieced together the implications, Armin realized the change of schedule was doubly distressing. Originally, he was scheduled to take a break from the boat in April to spend time with Jennifer back in the United States. Now, Armin would have to stay on the *Pride* until summer, extending his separation from Jennifer to nearly six months. On the financial side, the change of plans meant he wouldn't be getting a paycheck once the *Pride* returned to the United States in the summer, months earlier than he had anticipated.

Armin wrote Jennifer to break the news. "I'll see you sometime in June if you should be in Baltimore," he wrote glumly. "The absurdity of this relationship grows daily. . . . Love, Armin"

On the positive side, the timing of the decision meant the *Pride* would be able to sail on favorable trade winds heading west across the Atlantic Ocean.

It would be, Armin noted, "a dream trip home at the safest time of year."

CHAPTER 4

Vinny Lazzaro had barely reached Malaga when the news came
that the *Pride* organization had canceled the excursion through the
Mediterranean. A sailing adventure through Europe had intrigued
him. His mother's family was from northern Italy and his paternal
grandfather and namesake, Vincent Lazzaro, was a mariner who
became captain of a commercial sailing ship—a three-masted bar-
que—at the age of twenty-five. The planned trip had appealing
symmetry; Vinny was also a captain at twenty-five and the *Pride*
had been scheduled to spend eight days in his grandfather's home
port of Genoa in May.

Years of deep-sea fishing gave Vinny plenty of experience with
sudden changes of plan. While the Italian stops were appealing, he
had signed on to the *Pride* mainly to do some real sailing; it didn't
really matter where. "When we leave here sometime late in March
we'll be going west instead of east . . . and across the Atlantic,"
Vinny wrote home, displaying no hint of disappointment. In any
case, he added, "we should have some good sailing going across the
Atlantic."

Chez the cook decided the unexpected ocean crossing would be
exciting, and Leslie McNish, the world-traveling bosun, was also

quietly pleased with the cancellation. Terrorism didn't seem like a huge threat, but the *Pride* crew had received some anti-American taunting from drunken Spaniards who would drive up on the dock and bellow, "We hate fucking Americans." Maybe it wasn't such a bad idea to get out of Europe.

Unlike the others assigned to the *Pride*, Leslie had done plenty of sailing in the Mediterranean. And during her one stint on the *Pride*, the lengthy sail from Baltimore to California, she had never much enjoyed the *Pride*'s public relations events, which required her to dress up, put on her "smiling face," and make nice with guests who came on board eating canapés and sipping wine. Such things had to be tolerated until the interlopers left the deck and the crew could have the ship to themselves again.

With Europe canceled, the *Pride* would be sailing home with no formal schedule—and, therefore, no receptions. The way Leslie saw it, the *Pride* organization had handed her and the rest of the crew a gift: a three-month interlude of pure sailing on a beautiful schooner. What could be better?

It was understandable caution that prompted the *Pride* organization to conclude that the boat might make an attractive target for terrorists, but many people back home doubted that any self-respecting terrorist would bother with a goodwill ship from, of all places, Baltimore. The difference of opinion reflected a self-doubt that infected the Baltimore civic psyche at the time. By 1986, the city was well on its way to second-class status. Crime and drug use were spiraling to new heights, and middle-class residents were leaving the city as fast as they could hire a moving van and stick a For Sale sign in the front yard. Even the beloved Colts had fled town for Indianapolis during a February snowfall two years before.

It was a time of despair for a city with a long, vibrant history, a history that was largely dependent on Baltimore's most important asset: the water. The city's waterfront was far from majestic—nothing like the Hudson River or Puget Sound—but it was enough. Baltimore grew up on the upper edge of a tidal basin known as the Northwest Branch of the Patapsco River—Patapsco being an

Algonquin Indian word generally translated as "backwater." This rather homely branch proved to be an enormously strong economic engine, propelling Baltimore into the ranks of the nation's largest cities for most of the nineteenth century. Tobacco harvested in the rich sandy fields of southern Maryland and oysters pulled from the Chesapeake moved through its port. Sailboats from Peru brought tons of guano to be turned into fertilizer, and European immigrants flooded the city to take jobs in canning factories along the waterfront.

In Sparrows Point, a few miles to the east, Bethlehem Steel built an enormous steel mill on the water and the city's shipyards employed thousands. Blessed with a port that lay well inland, and an almost unrivaled railroad system that had spokes leading in all directions, Baltimore remained a vibrant economic hub through World War II. In the inner basin, steamships called regularly during the first half of the twentieth century and tourists eager to escape the city boarded excursion boats that cruised regularly to an amusement park across the bay and elsewhere.

While it wasn't noticeable at the time, the city's population and prestige peaked in the 1950s. White flight began; it was made easier by new highways leading into downtown for commuters. And many neighborhoods—block after block of brick homes squeezed together amid acres of concrete and asphalt—deteriorated badly.

Downtown didn't fare much better. By 1960, two million square feet of office and warehouse space stood empty and urban renewal became the new buzzword. In the first burst of activity, planners created a new office core on the western edge of Charles Street, the city's most prominent north-south thoroughfare. With safe underground garages and modern high-rise construction, including a signature twenty-four-story tower by Mies van der Rohe, Charles Center restored some confidence in downtown as a place to do business.

But the Inner Harbor—the city's longtime commercial and maritime hub—remained an eyesore. By the late 1950s, virtually all cargo commerce in the Inner Harbor came to a halt. The harbor's last passenger excursion boat called it quits in 1962, as vacationers opted to drive instead of steam out of the city. The harbor itself was disgusting. In the mid-1960s, "the river was a bubbling, foamy cesspool . . . It resembled an open sewer more than it did a natural

resource," wrote author Paul Travers. Around the harbor, busi-
nesses closed and left behind rotting piers, abandoned warehouses,
sea gulls and rats—a scene of decay mitigated only slightly by the in-
congruous aroma of cinnamon and other spices wafting out of
McCormick Spice, one of the few downtown factories still operating.

City officials called in some of the country's best urban planners
to take a look at the mess. The planners, it turned out, saw a potential Eden. While some cities had deliberately walled themselves
off from their waterfronts with highways, warehouses, or factories,
the planners urged Baltimore to embrace its harbor and incorporate
it into the fabric of downtown life. People would come back to the
water if given a reason, they predicted, and ideas for the waterfront
flourished: fireworks and barrel organs, picnic grounds, and roving
photographers.

As for the water, the problem remained one of geography. Since
the harbor had only one entrance and exit, you had to do something
to "create activity in the water," recalled Martin L. Millspaugh,
who was in charge of the redevelopment effort. "This was a backwater, not like London. Here, there was nothing going on; nothing
happening." City planners came up with a long list of watercraft
that could call on the harbor, from police boats and hydrofoils to
floating restaurants and a new generation of excursion boats. As
early as the mid-1960s, another item began appearing on the planners' wish lists: the notion of mooring a "restored clipper ship" in
the harbor as a tourist attraction.

The clipper idea was just one of many and was left unexplored
for years as officials moved forward with their ambitious redevelopment of the harbor, buying up hundreds of properties and building
a promenade.

There were other efforts to create "excitement" on the water.
The *USS Constellation*, a decaying but historic nineteenth-century
frigate that sat at an unattractive pier away from the center of harbor activity, was moved to a more prominent location and proved to
be a huge draw. Any doubt about the public's affection for big sailboats was erased by the enormous crowds that visited during the
brief 1972 visit of the *Tovarisch*, a Russian naval-training sailboat.

Around that time, Millspaugh visited San Francisco's Fisherman's Wharf, where beautiful old sailboats added charm and excitement to the waterfront. He and other city officials decided the clipper's time had finally come. None of the planners involved with the Inner Harbor were maritime historians, but all had at least heard of Baltimore clippers and it seemed a replica of one would make for an inviting floating attraction in the harbor. The clippers were pretty and tall and had, to be sure, the right name.

The original Baltimore clippers had little to do with goodwill, and much to do with smuggling, war, and slavery. In the late eighteenth century, this new kind of sailboat began emerging from the shipyards of Baltimore and elsewhere. Early on, they were known as "Virginia-built" or "Virginia models" and resembled the two-masted pilot boats used to ferry captains out to large cargo ships calling on ports in Virginia or up the Chesapeake Bay.

These new boats sat low in the water and had two masts raked aft as well as a raked stem and stern, which made them sleek looking. While it was debatable how much the raking of the masts improved the ships' sailing, it surely contributed to their distinctive profiles. The hull rose at a sharp angle from the keel; rounded bottoms would allow for more cargo, but would also slow the vessel. The deck was a single, flush platform, which made it easier for the crew to maneuver both during sail handling and in combat. They were working boats, with plain black hulls and no fanciful carvings on the bowsprit. The clippers were not enormous—roughly one hundred feet long on deck—but they sometimes carried crews of one hundred. With that many men, intricate maneuvers could be accomplished quickly and captains could sail aggressively.

The Baltimore clipper, as it came to be known, evolved during a time of fierce naval warfare. A ship was needed that could scoot past belligerent vessels and deliver cargo. The Baltimore clipper moved quickly and could sail at angles close to the wind, a key advantage. It could tack into the wind because of its fore-and-aft sail plan; most of its sails were angled astern and off to either port or starboard to catch the wind. Bigger British man-of-wars cruised with huge expanses of rectangular sails that pivoted off of masts.

Such sails, while powerful, limited the big ships to downwind sailing, which, of course, limited their maneuverability.

When war between the United States and Great Britain broke out in 1812, the American navy was far too small to take on the powerful British fleet, forcing President James Madison to turn to the nation's private vessels. Many Baltimore clipper captains received letters of marque, empowering them to act as privateers—essentially legal pirates—and disrupt British trade. The demand for the speedy Baltimore clippers grew and shipyards up and down the coast cranked out the sailboats. A crew near Boston finished two, with each one taking eighteen days to complete, according to historian Howard Irving Chapelle's authoritative study of the Baltimore clipper.

With such feisty names as *Lynx, Musquidobit, Dolphin,* and *Racer,* these heavily armed boats launched a seagoing guerilla war on British merchant vessels up and down the coast, through the Caribbean, and sometimes across the Atlantic. The Baltimore clipper privateers preyed on British ship convoys, even those protected by warships. Thanks to its ability to sail close to the wind, the clipper could usually outmaneuver and, if necessary, outrun the bigger British vessels.

The most famous of the privateers was Thomas Boyle, a Massachusetts native who went to sea at the age of ten with his father. He was a master by sixteen, moved to Baltimore three years later, and became a wealthy and sought-after captain by the time the war broke out. Early on, he captained the *Comet,* a Baltimore schooner built for wartime. *Comet,* ninety feet on deck, captured several British vessels and in one memorable encounter, used its ability to sail into the wind to neutralize a Portugese fighting brig that was escorting two cargo ships. Both vessels were captured.

In 1814, Boyle took command of another, much bigger schooner, the *Chasseur,* a fighting machine equipped with 16 cannons and measuring 116 feet in length. The aggressive Boyle opted to take *Chasseur* across the ocean to harass British ships near their own coast. Ever confident, Boyle audaciously had a proclamation posted in London declaring that Britain was in "a state of strict and rigorous blockade." While the blockade was far from absolute, *Chasseur* and other ships did make life miserable for the British merchant fleet, and word of Boyle's exploits reached Baltimore.

The Baltimore clippers were such a nuisance that the British attempted to destroy shipyards up and down the Chesapeake during their assault on Baltimore in 1814. However, the British were turned back by American forces at Fort McHenry, in Baltimore, in an intense artillery battle, inspiring Francis Scott Key to write the poem that became "The Star Spangled Banner."

Boyle was a fanatic about practicing and he drilled his crew in sail handling and artillery. The practice paid off in early 1815 when the *Chasseur* was tricked into a fierce side-to-side battle with the *St. Lawrence*, a British gunship, itself a former privateering vessel. The *Chasseur* prevailed in the bloody battle, but Boyle allowed the British crew to go free, although the *St. Lawrence*'s cannons were tossed overboard.

Not long after, the *Chasseur* returned to Baltimore, sailing past Fort McHenry, and up into the harbor. A writer with the Niles' Register, an early-nineteenth-century newspaper, gave the ship a new nickname, "the Pride of Baltimore," and hailed it as "perhaps the most beautiful vessel that ever floated on the ocean."

"Those who have not seen our schooners have but little idea of her appearance. As you look at her, you may easily figure yourself the idea that she is about to rise out of the water and fly in the air, seeming so light to sit upon it."

By 1830, well after the war, the Baltimore–style schooners were being referred to as "Baltimore clippers," a clipper being any kind of sharp-bowed sailboat built for speed. Life aboard these ships was difficult. The crew was not paid but shared in the cargo plundered. Sailors were crammed in by the dozens, sleeping on deck, always wondering when the next engagement might come. (A good number of the sailors on board were black, some of whom were no doubt attempting to escape slavery.) It wasn't unusual for sailors to be washed overboard and swallowed by the sea, and the rope rigging used at the time was known to give way in the worst storms, sending heavy masts and spars raining down.

It's not known how many of the Baltimore clippers sank, but records indicate that many did, usually vanishing without a trace.

Howard Chapelle made clear the risk: "Over sparring was always common and the clipper schooners and brigs built for the privateering and naval services had this fault, almost without exception. But they were safe if in the hands of an officer who was acquainted with their handling; in the hands of an unskilled commander, however, their antics, as described by eyewitnesses, were hair-raising to say the least. These long-sparred vessels, in spite of this, do not seem to have suffered capsizing as often as one would have expected."

Whatever their liabilities, the Baltimore clippers represented a high point in American maritime development, and America's much more powerful naval rivals across the sea looked on them with envy. George Coggeshall, a nineteenth-century American privateer who also authored a history of the era, wrote that a British naval officer once confided that his countrymen were intimidated by the Baltimore clippers and their crews.

"In England, we cannot build such vessels as your Baltimore clippers," the British sailor told Coggeshall. "We have no such models, and even if we had them, they would be of no service to us, for we never would sail them as you do. We are afraid of their long masts and heavy spars, and soon would cut down and reduce them to our standard. We [would] strengthen them, put up bulkheads, after which they would lose their sailing qualities, and are of no further service as cruising vessels . . . These schooners are built expressly for fast sailing, but require very skillful management and constant watchfulness; otherwise they are very dangerous."

After the War of 1812, with privateering a thing of the past, Baltimore clippers were pressed into new use. Some headed to South America for wars of independence. Others plied cargo routes in the tropics, helped in the opium trade in Asia, or served as slave transports. Shipbuilders tinkered with the design to add more room below and larger sails above to allow the slave ships to sail effectively in the sometimes light trade winds crossing from Africa. Despite their relatively small size, the Baltimore clippers still managed to carry a considerable human cargo. One account from the time tells of a clipper that carried an almost unimaginable load of 250 men and 100 children from Africa to Havana in a single trip.

By mid-century, the Baltimore clipper had fallen out of favor. Its speed-favoring design precluded it from carrying the increasingly larger loads preferred by shippers; the slave trade had finally come to a halt as well. Meanwhile, the new standard was the three-masted clipper ship exemplified by the *Cutty Sark*, which could both haul enormous loads and make good time crossing the ocean.

The last Baltimore clipper of the era was probably built around 1830.

Officials at the quasi-public agency redeveloping downtown Baltimore in the early 1970s assigned the job of finding a Baltimore clipper to Jay Scattergood, a lanky, recently discharged Navy jet pilot from Philadelphia. Scattergood, who had sailed on the Chesapeake for years, researched Baltimore clippers and consulted with naval architects. Scattergood, twenty-seven, quickly determined that all of the clippers were long gone—either torn apart, rotted to pieces, or under water. There was one offer worth checking out—a guy in San Diego offering to sell the city the *Golden Dragon*, a "replica" clipper he had built. It turned out that the *Golden Dragon* was only two-thirds the size of the old-time Baltimore clippers and had been built partially with laminated plywood and fiberglass—not the most authentic of materials.

City officials passed on the *Golden Dragon* and concluded they would have to build their own sailboat. During his research, Scattergood found a description of a nineteenth-century schooner that would make a suitable model—the *Experiment*, which was built in 1812 and survived until it was broken up in 1859, but not before her lines were recorded in Sweden. The nineteenth-century drawings of her hull would give an architect a model to work from and several men expressed interest in designing the project. The city officials also had a marketing brainstorm: the sailboat would be built right in the harbor to give tourists something to watch.

In looking for an architect, Baltimore officials made it clear that they wanted the boat to be certified by the Coast Guard as a passenger-carrying vessel or as a sailing-school operation. For such sailboats, Coast Guard regulations set minimum standards for stability and other sailing characteristics to ensure a certain safety level. Other boats—so-called un-inspected vessels—did not have to meet such safety requirements but were prohibited from carrying passengers or students. Naval architects consulted by the city had mixed opinions about the feasibility of building a historic boat to Coast Guard standards. One Massachusetts architect took a look at the city's idea and concluded it would be "unlikely" that a Baltimore clipper replica, with its inherently racy design, could receive Coast Guard approval.

James A. McCurdy, a prominent Long Island architect, agreed, but said there was an alternative. He said his firm could design a historic boat with just enough compromises to accommodate the Coast Guard's safety requirements. The firm had designed two other historic wooden vessels, the *Harvey Gamage* and the *Bill of Rights*, both of which were certified by the Coast Guard to carry passengers.

"Our past experience indicates that an exact replica of an old sailing vessel is unlikely to meet Coast Guard requirements," McCurdy wrote to city officials in the summer of 1974. "However, we can see no reason why changes in hull and rig proportions necessary to meet Coast Guard standards could not be accomplished without destroying the flavor and appearance of the vessel."

McCurdy's track record and attention to Coast Guard safety requirements appealed to Scattergood and others at the redevelopment agency, and they attempted to hire his firm. But the process bogged down in early 1975. There were problems getting approval for McCurdy's contract from a municipal bureaucracy that had more experience with asphalt paving companies than with schooner designers. There were concerns about spending more than $300,000 on a boat, a large sum for a financially strapped city in the early 1970s. And there was the nagging question of what the city would do with its boat once it was launched: sail it, dock it, or both.

The project sat in limbo for several months, until an Annapolis artist-sailor named Melbourne Smith stepped forward in July 1975. The forty-five-year-old Smith had sailed professionally, built boats, and published hundreds of detailed paintings of ships. He had also dreamed for years about actually building one of the historic sailboats he painted. Already aware of the city's interest in building its own schooner, Smith took the initiative and presented an impressive, unsolicited proposal. He would construct the ship with a team that included a local naval architect and experienced boat builders. A bit of a showman, Smith also readily accepted the idea of building the clipper not in a faraway boat yard but right on the Baltimore waterfront. Once the boat was finished, Smith said, it would sail for a while and then be set up as a public exhibit—literally inside a glass pavilion on the edge of the Bay.

Smith was born in the steel-producing city of Hamilton, Ontario, and sailed for four years as a teenager in the Royal Canadian Sea Cadet Corps; this included time on a 112-foot ketch in the Great Lakes. Smith skipped college but earned a living as a musician in Hamilton, playing drums and trumpet well enough to perform at both Polish weddings and in the backup bands for Nat King Cole and Sophie Tucker.

He also worked as a merchant marine and by the time he reached his mid-twenties, he was living in New York on the *Wooden Shoe*, a forty-five-foot Dutch fishing vessel known as a "botter." He made some extra money taking *Wooden Shoe* around the harbor to tape-record the sounds of various ships' horns; these were then sold to NBC for use on the radio and television. Smith graduated from the botter to a Brixham trawler, a larger, two-masted vessel named *Sans Pareil*, which he bought in England and planned to take to the West Indies for use in the charter business. Instead, the boat got hit by a gale off Cherbourg, France, and was lost, along with a half-dozen other vessels. Smith moved on to Gibraltar and found *Annyah*, a three-masted schooner, which he did use to get to the West Indies in the early 1960s (but only after a stint sailing around Spain, during which he made good money smuggling cases of Scotch to a British foreign-service officer in Cadiz.) After several months doing charter sailing around the islands, Smith ended up in Guatemala, where his boat attracted the attention of what passed for the Guatemalan navy. The navy at the time had about one hundred men and its fleet amounted to a few patrol boats with non-working bow-mounted machine guns and a single frigate that wasn't seaworthy. After negotiation, Smith chartered his boat to the navy and, as part of the deal, was given a commission as a lieutenant commander. For the next year, Smith lived on the schooner in a depressed port town on the Gulf of Honduras and turned the cabin into a classroom for teaching celestial navigation to Guatemalan naval cadets. But without any auxiliary engine power, *Annyah* was unable to take the cadets out sailing to test their navigation skills.

Smith's time in Guatemala ended stormily, when a 1963 coup unseated the country's president, a general named Ydígoras Fuentes, whom Smith had come to know over lunches in Guatemala City. Smith bought a car and fled to Mexico, leaving *Annyah* behind. (He later was able to sneak the boat out of Guatemala, after giving thousands of dollars in bribes.)

He then went to Belize, where he hooked up with a local carpenter to begin a boat-building business. Smith had visions of getting rich constructing yachts with Central American hardwoods, but he failed to drum up much business. He and his partner, Simeon Young, built three sixty-five-foot wooden tugs used to haul sugar-laden barges, and a thirty-three-foot, single-masted sailboat known as a cutter. After a while, though, Smith gave up on shipbuilding and moved to Annapolis, where he took jobs as an illustrator for books and magazines. Smith also got into the boat-delivery business and crewed in ocean sail races.

By the late 1960s, Smith was determined to find a way to build a historic sailboat. He lost out on an effort to construct one for a Canadian trading company, but he came closer with a Maryland maritime preservation group that was considering recreating the *Peggy Stewart*, a boat that was burned in Annapolis in 1774 as part of the ongoing dispute over the British tea tax. That project, though, was also put on hold.

A few years later, the perfect opportunity presented itself when Smith got wind of the city of Baltimore's intention to build its own clipper. Headstrong and charming, with a noticeable trace of Canada in his voice, Smith presented a proposal that dripped with romantic references to the 1812-era clippers and made clear his love for old-time sailing. "The Baltimore clipper type of sailing craft is a delicate creation not unlike a fine violin or a thoroughbred racehorse with the ultimate purpose for its existence being only one thing—performance," Smith wrote.

He added that the boat he wanted to build, unlike those conceived by others, would stand no chance of being certified by the Coast Guard, given the inherent risk of its design. "The vessel must be considered extremely dangerous if allowed to be sailed with incompetent crew. The very nature of the design would not meet with Coast Guard approval for commercial use and passengers would not be permitted while under way."

Smith added, "It is, of course, these features that make the type exciting."

The proposal itself generated excitement at the redevelopment agency's office. Baltimore circa 1975 was starting to fall apart, but the city still had one hell of a history, and Smith's proposal tapped into it nicely. City officials tried to assure themselves that Smith was not a kook or an impractical visionary, although checking out some of his credentials (Guatemalan navy, Scotch-smuggling, to name two) was not easy. His background in construction was slim, but he had sailed widely and had a good knowledge of maritime history. It didn't hurt when he pointed out to one of the city officials considering his proposal that he, Smith, had painted the framed print of a Baltimore clipper hanging in the redevelopment office.

Sold on Smith's vision, Scattergood and his bosses set the wheels in motion to hire him. If they moved expeditiously, the project could begin in the winter of 1975 and be in full swing as a tourist attraction by the time of the American Bicentennial celebration the next summer. Meanwhile, any lingering thought about building the boat to Coast Guard specifications evaporated, given Smith's firm insistence that such regulations were inappropriate for this kind of historically accurate vessel.

By the time Smith's proposal surfaced, the powers-that-be in Baltimore had established a streamlined system of governance that gave the mayor and a handful of men he appointed almost unchecked power to reshape the look of downtown. Running City Hall at the time was Mayor William Donald Schaefer, a bald, bowlegged Democrat with a dour lady friend named Hilda Mae Snoops and a guiding philosophy of "Do it Now!" He was a softy for big gestures and quick action, and he wasted no time approving Smith's proposal for an authentic clipper.

In October 1975, a city finance board approved a $365,000 budget for the project. In a nifty bit of financing, about a quarter of the money came from federal urban renewal funds, which were raining down on the city at the time. Some black members of the City Council complained that the city of Baltimore, with a majority black population, was building a replica of a ship used prominently in the slave trade. But the Council had no role in approving the contract.

The clipper project was one of dozens of projects the city's redevelopment team would tackle during the rejuvenation of the Inner Harbor. For the planners in charge, the ship was an intriguing diversion because of its uniqueness, but it was far from a priority, given the much larger projects going on.

City officials approved the sailboat without public debate and with no firm long-range strategy. With construction about to begin, plans for the clipper could be summed up in a couple of sentences: It would be docked in the harbor. With a small crew, it would take an occasional pleasure sail out into Chesapeake Bay. All other questions, if they occurred to anybody, went unanswered.

With approval in hand, Melbourne Smith was ecstatic about finally landing a job to build a historic ship. The night he signed his contract with the city, Smith went to celebrate at a favorite saloon in his hometown of Annapolis. On his way out after a night of toasting, Smith tripped on a curb and broke his arm.

CHAPTER 5

Armin and his winter lay-up crew of five fell in love with Malaga, with its cheap wine, temperate weather, and charming streets lined with orange trees and old buildings. Founded by Phoenicians in ancient times, Malaga had been controlled variously by Greeks, Romans (who left a substantial theater), and Moors (who built a fortress and castle). Its most famous son, Pablo Picasso, was born in a second-floor apartment near the Plaza de la Merced in 1881. A century later, the busy port city in the heart of the Costa del Sol was home to a half-million people.

The *Pride* was tied up among huge cargo ships and cranes in Malaga's port at a quay equipped with power lines and fresh water. While protected by a seawall, the harbor was still subject to occasional wave surges, which rocked the *Pride* so much that working in the rigging was all but impossible when they occurred. Ships carrying grain, oranges, and olives came and went on a regular basis and the bumpy Sierra Nevada rose in the distance north of the city.

With the *Pride* not scheduled to leave until mid-March, Armin and Sugar drew up an extensive list of maintenance and repair projects. The weather was close to perfect: January days in the sixties, with dry air and only brief patches of rain. At night, the temperature dropped into the forties, making for chilly but comfortable sleeping conditions aboard ship.

In mid-January, a second American tall ship tied up in the harbor, a 156-foot gaff-rigged schooner named *Te Vega*. The boat was operated by a Massachusetts high school and took students with learning disabilities out for months at a time. In the small world of tall ships, some crew members on any two boats were bound to know each other. This time, Armin had two longtime friends on *Te Vega*—the captain Steve Wedlock and his wife and sailing partner, Kim Pedersen.

The couple had good news: Jennifer had agreed to take the second mate's job on *Te Vega* for the spring. She would meet the ship in Italy and sail back to Massachusetts. The best news was for Armin: Jennifer's schedule would allow her to stop in Spain to visit on the way to the boat.

Near the end of *Te Vega*'s stay, Armin joined his friends for dinner at a waterfront café. With the wine flowing, the conversation turned to the incident in the Baltic and Armin described in cool detail how he'd almost lost Sarah Fox. He had a sympathetic audience. Wedlock and Pedersen told about a night on *Te Vega* when a lookout spotted something glowing and drifting away from the ship, possibly a light attached to one of the ship's life preservers. Someone called "man overboard" and the crew scrambled into action. For a terrifying few minutes, the thought took hold that someone had been lost—possibly a student. When the crew finally located the bobbing light, it turned out to be only a battery-powered safety light, not a crew member.

Over dinner, Armin talked a lot about his ship. After years at the helm, culminating with the problem in the Baltic, Armin said he wasn't sure just how much stability the *Pride* had. This was not an academic concern as a captain could not afford to *guess* how much his boat could take before going over. A sailing veteran, Wedlock fully understood that the *Pride* was an extreme vessel, but Armin clearly thought it was more extreme than others did. Even so, Wedlock detected no sense of fear. Whatever questions Armin had about the *Pride*, he was sure he could handle the boat.

Armin told the couple this was going to be his last big trip on the

Pride as he was determined to establish a lifestyle with some security and room for Jennifer, although he wasn't sure how he would make it work. Armin's talk of the future was so inconclusive that Wedlock found the dinner unsettling. He could tell that Armin was out of sorts.

A couple of days later, on January 31, *Te Vega* left Malaga, after Wedlock had sent a misbehaving student home by plane to the United States. Unlike the *Pride* organization, the Landmark School, which operated *Te Vega*, had decided to keep to its sailing schedule, despite the rash of terrorism. While the *Pride* was preparing to sail west across the ocean, the *Te Vega* headed east toward Italy.

Friday January 31 was also Armin's forty-second birthday, and he marked it by setting off on a weekend trip across the Strait of Gibraltar to Morocco. Chez, Vinny, and Joe tagged along, taking a two-and-a-half-hour ferry ride to Tangier. In the bustling bazaar, Armin purchased small rugs for his parents back at Salters Point, and Joe and Vinny picked up hand-woven blankets. Chez was thrilled with his purchase, a brown, hooded robe known as a jalaba that looked like something out of a Star Wars movie. After a night of drinking, they crashed in a small pensione.

The next morning, the group was awakened by a crowing rooster and the Muslim call to prayer. Some of the group walked around Tangier in the rain and finally found the apartment of Ann Hess, Armin's admiring niece, whom he had seen back home in Massachusetts at Christmas. The group warmed up in Hess's apartment and recounted their adventures navigating the mazelike streets of Tangier.

The only hitch in the trip came when the group met up for the ride back across the Strait. The usually competent Joe somehow got disoriented and climbed aboard a ship he thought was the ferry. It turned out to be a freighter from, of all places, Libya, which by then had become America's primary enemy. An armed guard angrily accosted the young American and demanded his passport. After much miscommunication, Joe convinced the guard he had made a mistake and the Libyans let him go.

Joe's mistake could be chalked up to a kind of *Pride* insularity. Outsiders and news of the world were scarce, leaving the crew to develop its own culture, rules, and language. With that came an intense confidence built on the knowledge that at sea there were only twelve of them, and as a group they had to handle whatever came their way. "That was a challenge and a joy, everybody depending on each other," remembered Chris Rowsom, who sailed as first mate the previous year.

No *Pride* sailor enjoyed the sailing more than Joe, who had been on board off and on since 1982 and loved scampering up the rig to handle sail. In the right conditions, he would get back to deck by sliding down a thick rigging cable, landing with an exaggerated pirate's hop, and maybe throwing in an "Aaarghh," for good measure. This wasn't pretending to be a nineteenth-century schooner sailor; it was pure exuberance.

On land, the attitude sometimes turned into a swagger. Joe felt comfortable claiming a space in whichever port bar he and his *Pride* drinking buddies picked for the night, their knives and spikes strapped to their belts like pistol-packing cowboys in a Dodge City saloon. "You get to be very independent and confident," Joe once explained. "You're going into strange places, but you know how to find your way around and trust people, and have a good time."

The common sentiment among *Pride* sailors was that they were leading a life of awesome privilege. Not in the accommodations or pay, both of which were minimal, nor in the work, which could be tedious, but in the adventurousness of what they were doing. Generally in their twenties and college graduates, *Pride* crew members deliberately turned their backs on a traditional lifestyle. Some, including Armin, Sugar, Leslie, and Joe, came from comfortable families but had no homes of their own and next to no belongings after years of living out of duffel bags. Mundane things were for other people, the ones too afraid to chuck everything and go sailing for a while.

"We were so cool, so worldly," one veteran *Pride* sailor recalled years later. "We were above the masses."

Sometimes sparks flew when inhabitants of the *Pride* tried to re-enter the real world, as Sugar was reminded one day when he left the ship at lunchtime. Looking to purchase a new flannel night-gown for Leslie, he navigated Malaga and found a clothing store. Inside, he asked a clerk for help locating ladies' nightgowns. "Follow me," the clerk said pleasantly enough, escorting Sugar through the store and to a door. The door led to a rear exit. "Here," the man said.

Astonished, Sugar was ready to object but looked down at him-self and realized why he had been ejected from the store. As usual when working on the *Pride*, he was wearing beat-up clothes that were stained and painted; his hands and face were smeared with black tar he had used to recoat parts of the ship that morning.

No wonder, Sugar thought to himself as he headed back to the *Pride* empty-handed. *I'm a mess.*

Growing up in the small town of Niantic, Connecticut on the Long Island Sound, Sugar, or John as his family knew him, had been around boats his whole life. His father, a physician, did cancer re-search; his mother was a social worker. As the youngest of five chil-dren, John went sailing with his family as an infant and learned the basics early on.

John enjoyed being on the water, which allowed him to escape a sometimes turbulent household, one he fled for good as soon as he finished high school. He found his own apartment, secured a good-paying job with a printing company, bought a van and a motorcycle, and figured he had pretty much made it. But when his bosses began pushing him to take more responsibility, John decided work-ing in a noisy print shop wasn't his life's plan and he quit.

Fortuitously, John's father and his famous uncle, future U.S. Surgeon General C. Everett Koop, were getting ready to sail the family's yacht to the Caribbean and they invited him to tag along. The sail south was wonderful. It got even better in the Caribbean when they ran into another Niantic resident, a family friend who was sailing a sixty-five-foot, gaff-rigged schooner, the *Voyager*. Looking for crew, he offered John a job. *They're going to pay me to go sailing in the Caribbean?* the nineteen-year-old thought to himself. *That's a neat idea.*

John became a deckhand on *Voyager*, helping with the sailing and taking care of the sometimes demanding passengers. One, an aging Southern belle who sported a diamond embedded in one of her fingernails, managed to give him a new nickname. The woman drank Coca-Cola for breakfast and got in the habit of asking the curly-haired deckhand to fetch her sodas. Bad with names, she'd coo, "Sugar, I forgot my Coca-Cola. Would you mind getting me one, Sugar?" The rest of the crew chortled and John was Sugar from there on out.

He spent the next year sailing and eventually landed a job on the *Pride* (helped in part by encounters with Jan Miles in waterfront bars in the Caribbean). By the time he reached the *Pride*, crew members had heard through the sailing grapevine about a kid named John working on the *Voyager*. When he came on board the *Pride*, one of the crew heard his name and said: "You're Sugar!"

During his first stint on the *Pride*, in 1981, the twenty-one-year-old Sugar got a taste of the *Pride*'s unforgiving relationship with the water. Sailing in Lake Erie, he was near the bow watching the jib boom bang through the waves and feeling pretty much invincible. Suddenly, a wave crashed over the deck, knocked him off his feet, and washed him back to the *Pride*'s main shrouds, a good fifty-foot ride down the ship's leeward deck. It was a spooky moment; Sugar loved it.

Over the years, he became legendary for his fearlessness climbing the *Pride* rigging, using both hands to work aloft on sails, even in heavy blows. He also made history one day sailing toward Key West, where the *Pride* was due to make a semi-official stop later in the day.

"What's the dress?" someone asked Jan Miles, who was in charge that trip.

"*Pride* shirts only," the captain responded. There was no need to put on khaki pants or shorts since this would not be a fancy event.

Hearing that, Sugar exchanged a knowing look with a fellow deckhand named Gary Surosky, a bearded free spirit everyone called Leroy. A little while later, the two deckhands emerged from the cabin and proceeded to climb the rigging to handle a sail, wearing *Pride* shirts and absolutely nothing else.

* * *

Sugar, Armin, and the other four members of the *Pride*'s winter lay-up crew handled most repairs and maintenance themselves. One task they couldn't manage was the re-inspection of the ship's life rafts. The *Pride* sailed with two black rafts covered by an inflated orange canopy. In the case of an emergency, a CO_2 cartridge would inflate the rafts, each of which was designed to hold six people.

On deck, the rafts were kept in a hard-plastic canister under the tiller, secured with a hydrostatic release that would free the rafts when submerged in water. Before the *Pride* left Baltimore nearly a year before, the crew had taken the rafts to a Baltimore company that inspected them for damage and inflated them to make sure they would hold their air. The inspection, though, was good for a year, meaning the rafts had to be inspected again in Spain.

In Malaga, the crew removed the rafts, each of which weighed a good seventy-five pounds, and loaded them on a truck owned by the provisioning company helping the *Pride* in Spain. The truck took the rafts ninety-five miles west to a raft-servicing firm named Servimar-Sur in the port town of Algeciras, a little west of Gibraltar. The company, which had been owned for a dozen years by a former merchant ship captain in his fifties named Ernesto Ibanez, operated in a small shop in a waterfront warehouse. Servimar-Sur serviced rafts for a wide range of ships, including the ferries operating out of Algeciras.

Ibanez had two part-time helpers but did most of the work himself. For the *Pride* job, Ibanez was to inflate the rafts, check that the CO_2 canisters worked properly, and ensure that the rafts would hold their pressure. When done, he was to deflate the rafts, vacuum out the residual air, and reseat the plugs that filled the air openings. The plugs had to be hammered carefully into the air holes in the raft lest they pop free should the rafts be inflated. Finally, the rafts would be repacked—along with certain food, water, and safety supplies—and returned to the *Pride*.

On February 13, Ibanez signed an invoice for inspecting the rafts, at a cost of 57,075 pesetas, including tax, or about $425. Included in the cost were several new provisions, among them a supply of concentrated food bars, seven boxes of anti-seasickness tablets, three hand-held flares, and one distress signal attached to a parachute. Soon, the provisioning company brought the two rafts back to Malaga and the crew replaced them on the aft deck. Assured that the most important safety equipment the *Pride* carried was in good shape, Sugar and Armin checked another thing off their to-do lists.

CHAPTER 6

February 1986
Malaga, Spain

In mid-February, the *Pride* was hoisted out of the water and into a Malaga dry dock for a full inspection. It had been a year since anyone had gotten a look at the ship's hull and eight months since the *Pride* had run aground on a pinnacle rock in Norway, an embarrassing mishap for Armin several weeks before the problem in the Baltic.

Armin walked around the hull to take a look. There were the usual barnacles, but the hull was holding up well. As for the grounding, the damage was minor and Armin took photographs for the office back home. One mid-ship section of the worm shoe, a six-inch-thick part made from tropical hardwood and attached as a protective layer on the bottom of the keel, had been crushed and splintered; a second piece was damaged on one edge. But he saw no other problems to the keel itself or to the planks that formed the hull's outer layer.

A local carpenter replaced the damaged worm-shoe pieces with Armin, the former boat-builder, watching. Workers also reconditioned the ship's propeller, which was showing signs of wear. The leisurely pace of the Spaniards' work infuriated Armin, a stickler for schedules. Despite a rule against it, Armin had his own crew do some of the dry-dock work themselves. With the Spanish workers gone, the crew re-caulked some of the hull, and Armin and Vinny refastened seven seacocks, or drains, with new brass bolts to replace pieces that were badly corroded. The ship's underside got two coats of dark green paint, and the upper section got two coats of black.

While Armin could perform almost any task on the *Pride*, his preference was to handle the paperwork and the plans, leaving the messy stuff to others. His first mate was in heaven with all the work. One day Sugar needed to pick up some shackles from the provisioning agent's enormous warehouse in Malaga and stared in awe at the amazing array of maritime *stuff* lining the shelves.

As the weeks progressed, Sugar supervised the crew as it brought down the forward topmast to recondition all of the shrouds and stays. The crew gave all forty of the ship's blocks a new coat of warm ivory paint, making them positively glow in the Spanish moonlight. Some of the rigging received new leather covers, the main bolt rope and the head rig got a coat of black tar, and most of the ship's interior was repainted. What wasn't painted was re-varnished, including the booms, topmasts, tiller, cap rail, and dining table. Even *Irie*, the fifteen-foot sailing skiff Armin had built for the *Pride*, got a new coat of white paint and some repairs. The name *Irie* came from a Jamaican word that could mean both, "Good day," or "all right," as in, everything's cool, mon.

After weeks of work in ideal conditions, things were quite all right with the *Pride*. "The ship is now looking as good or better than I've ever seen her look," Armin told the office back home.

The *Pride* was born, in a sense, in the tropical forests of Belize in Central America. That's where Melbourne Smith headed in the winter of 1975, with a cast on his arm from the fall outside the Annapolis saloon, to hunt for wood. While the new clipper was supposed to be grounded in historical authenticity, Smith opted, from the very beginning, to bend the notion—at least when it came to building materials. Instead of using the type of North American wood that would have been available to Baltimore boat builders of the early nineteenth century, Smith set out to find some of the best wood in the world.

Smith had built a few boats in Central America years earlier and appreciated the region's hardwoods. To construct this grandest of sailboats, he recruited his shipbuilding partner Simeon, a local carpenter, and headed into the woods. After days of hunting, the men found a tall, straight lignumvitae tree, a tropical evergreen that produces some of the densest hardwood on the planet, three times as hard as English oak. Thanks to its high resin content, the wood was often used for submerged pieces on ships and Smith wanted the tree for the ship's keel, at the base of the hull. His crew cut down the tree, and after measuring and placing it at the side of the road to be picked up later, the men retired to the nearest bar. The next day, they returned and discovered that another crew making railroad ties had happened upon the tree and thought it was meant for them. The beautiful piece of wood had been cut into four very old and very durable railroad ties. Smith regrouped and found another tree to use.

Smith and his crew also harvested long-grain yellow pine for the decking and hull planks, Santa Maria wood for the massive interior framing pieces, and bullet wood for other structural parts. They also secured mahogany, rosewood, and cedar, and Smith ordered Douglas fir from Oregon for the larger spars.

While Smith had come up with the conceptual drawings of the clipper, he turned to an old friend to do the actual design. Thomas C. Gillmer, sixty-four, had retired earlier in the year from the U.S. Naval Academy, where he taught engineering and naval architecture for more than three decades. A former naval officer himself, Gillmer had written two books on stability and naval architecture that were used at the Academy and other colleges, and had designed dozens of yachts and sailboats. Smith had the vision, but Gillmer had the credentials to do the actual design.

Several paintings and sketches from the early nineteenth century gave a good sense of a Baltimore clipper's sail plan and rigging. There were also drawings of some of the old clippers' structural layouts, which Gillmer used for guidance in designing a hull. He produced the blueprints of a ghost—an authentic schooner that could have emerged from the shipyards of Baltimore more than 150 years earlier.

The ship would be a topsail schooner, with a distinctive rectangular topsail hung between wooden yards, or booms, more than fifty feet above the deck. The two masts would rake backward—the eighteen-inch-thick foremast at an angle of thirteen and a half degrees, the slightly narrower mainmast tilting an additional three degrees aft. There would be cannons but no engine. A wood-burning brick oven would suffice for cooking meals, and barrels on deck would hold drinking water. While modern sailboats have wheels for steering, this schooner would have an old-fashioned tiller to move the rudder.

By the spring of 1976, with the design finished and the Central American wood on hand, Smith set up a shipyard on a grass lot in the Inner Harbor and began work. Simeon Young came up from Belize, along with four carpenters from Belize and the Caribbean, and there were several builders from Maryland. Smith erected a small reviewing stand at the side of the boat yard and crowds gathered each day to watch the old-time sailboat take shape. Smith's workmen used adzes and some old-fashioned construction techniques, although electric tools were also employed. A Baltimore man with a bushy white beard and blacksmith skills set up a shop on the site to forge nearly all of the ship's metal pieces. Sails were made of all-natural materials—cotton duck, flax, or Egyptian cotton. The keel was cut and hewn to size and laid in place. Smith's crew measured, cut, and attached the ship's structural ribs to the keel, followed by the hull planking and the deck structure.

While Smith had hoped the foreign carpenters could provide expertise in old-style wooden boat building, it didn't take long to realize they weren't working out. They drank too much and spent too much time in the city's strip bars. One cut off a finger and another disappeared for a week, only to report later that he had been kidnapped. With one exception, they all went home after a few weeks on the job.

*   *   *

As construction proceeded, the city's development team worked to flesh out plans for its clipper. From the beginning, the goal had been to build what amounted to a museum that would sit elegantly at an Inner Harbor dock, or perhaps even on land, just down from the *Constellation*. People would come aboard, admire her clean lines, and get a quick lesson in maritime history. At most, the thinking was, the ship would take occasional goodwill voyages down the Chesapeake.

But with the determinedly romantic Smith involved, plans for the schooner became more ambitious. Even before construction began, Smith lobbied to take the clipper to sea for a four-month winter sea trial to document for the first time how a Baltimore clipper handled. The trip could be filmed by a documentary crew to provide publicity for the new boat (and, to be sure, for Smith as well). With construction underway, he amended his idea to suggest that the boat should become a "working ambassador" for the city and its port. Smith even proposed taking the boat across the ocean, assuring city officials that it would be quite capable of sailing to foreign ports, as long as the trips were made at the right time of year. "I would like to see her going around the world," Smith told a reporter in the summer of 1976.

This new, more ambitious proposal came as Baltimore, like much of the rest of the nation, was falling into the grip of Bicentennial fever. As the clipper took shape on the shoreline that summer, a dozen tall sailing vessels arrived in town for a maritime festival, the city's first. The ships were a sensation and people drove in from hours away to see them.

Many visitors stuck around to take a look at Baltimore's tourist sites, such as they were. This was unheard of. Unless you lived there, Baltimore was a place you rushed through to go somewhere else; it was not a destination. Overshadowed by Washington, D.C., an hour to the south, Baltimore had plenty of quirky charm but not much to attract tourists. Those that came were hard-pressed to spend more than a day, plenty of time to visit the *Constellation* and Fort McHenry, and grab a crab cake somewhere along the way. (Other visitors, of course, headed directly to The Block, the city's neon-tinged red-light district with its prostitutes and strippers.)

Martin Millspaugh, the head of the harbor redevelopment, watched in amazement as the crowds poured into town to stare at sailboats. *My God, maybe we can attract tourists here,* he thought to himself.

Other Baltimore officials also marveled at the popularity of the tall ships. Suddenly, like Smith, they could envision a much bigger role for the clipper that sat half-finished on the water's edge. If it could be a tourist magnet in the harbor, why couldn't it also travel around to different cities like the other big sailboats? The idea had wide appeal within the city's government, and by Labor Day, the question wasn't whether the boat should go to sea, it was a matter of when and where. The new sailboat was going to be more than a floating museum after all.

Such a radical change of mission for the boat required changes in its design. If the boat was expected to reach destinations on a certain schedule, it couldn't rely solely on unpredictable wind power. Tom Gillmer, the designer, came up with a plan to wedge in an engine and the construction crew muscled holes through some of the thick structural sections at the aft end of the boat for the propeller shaft. They also sliced out a crescent-shaped piece of the rudder to make room for the propeller. Instead of Spanish cedar, the builders used stronger pieces of fir and spruce for all of the masts and spars. Other equipment was added, including an auxiliary generator, a device to record the ship's speed and distance, and a radio. A three-burner kerosene stove was added to supplement the brick fireplace. All of these were anachronisms, but even so, the clipper would still have fit in just fine in nineteenth-century Baltimore.

The revisions did not include watertight compartments. For decades, modern ships had been built with compartments designed to stem below-deck flooding by holding seawater behind waterproof bulkheads and doors. Without such compartments, a capsized ship would quickly sink once water poured below deck. While some ships with watertight bulkheads—most memorably the *Titantic*—sank anyway, their chances of staying afloat were far better.

Some people involved in the project questioned the omission. "You couldn't help but talk about [the lack of bulkheads]. Anybody who knew anything about sailing vessels would notice that," said

Steve Bunker, a student of maritime history who was hired to dress in period costume and talk about the construction process.

One insurance company said it would not write a policy for the vessel unless one watertight bulkhead was installed near the bow, in case the boat crashed into something and opened up a hole. Gillmer added the required bulkhead to his working drawings, but other insurers weren't so demanding and the bulkhead idea was dropped.

The debate over bulkheads illustrated the sort of vexing choice faced by builders trying to balance historic authenticity with safety on an old-fashioned boat. Smith argued against watertight bulkheads even though the ship would be far more vulnerable to a disaster at sea without them. The city's planners were sympathetic to the argument. "We couldn't find a real [Baltimore clipper] so we decided to make one as authentic as possible," said Millspaugh, the planner who oversaw the Inner Harbor redevelopment. "Everything else in the Inner Harbor was real. We felt we had to have something that was absolutely authentic."

The question of bulkheads was settled. The purists won.

Smith made it clear from the start of the project that the sailboat he wanted to build was all about historical accuracy, not safety. Such a vessel, he predicted confidently, would never win Coast Guard certification to carry passengers or conduct sailing classes. Without such certification, the *Pride* would be left to sail from place to place with a paid crew—and an occasional non-paying guest. Everyone else would have to watch.

There was one other important matter to resolve—a name. With the contract in hand to build the boat, the puckish Smith proposed a series of names, including the *Johnny Unitas* or the *Blaze Starr*, in honor of the city's most famous football player and stripper, respectively. His first choice, though, was simple: *Pride.*

Some thought the name *Pride* was a reference to the famed *Chasseur*, which had been nicknamed "the Pride of Baltimore" for its heroic sailing in the War of 1812. But Smith said that was not the case. The name reflected the goodwill he was sure the sailboat would create among the citizens. The powers-that-be in Baltimore loved it.

Using traditional boat-naming techniques, the name of the boat would have been carved on the ship's stern:

Pride

Baltimore, Maryland

That way, Smith figured, people would refer to her as Pride of Baltimore. But when the official naming documents were being prepared, a secretary typed in "Pride of Baltimore," Smith recalled. It rankled Smith but that became the official name, so he dutifully carved it in the stern. With plenty of room above the name, Smith carved in the name of the home port, too, so the stern read:

Baltimore, Maryland

Pride of Baltimore

In the end, Baltimore got its name on its schooner not once but twice.

Adding the engine and strengthening some of the rig's wooden parts on the newly named *Pride* postponed the planned launch by eight months. Mayor Schaefer, the political father of the sailboat, had to be talked into the idea of taking the boat out of Baltimore as a goodwill venture, but he finally endorsed the idea. A natural showman who once donned an old-fashioned swimming suit and plunged into the National Aquarium seal pond as a publicity stunt, the mayor had a couple of ideas about how to promote the *Pride*. Six weeks before the boat was to be launched, he scrawled an action memo.

"When (and if) the *Pride of Baltimore* leaves the Inner Harbor for a voyage, I want a bell or whistle announcing its leaving & its return: (an event in other words)," he wrote. Officials scurried around and successfully secured a loud ship's whistle. The *Pride* was commissioned on May 1, 1977, in a ceremony at the Inner Harbor attended by thousands. The boat was an immediate hit in a city desperate for things to treasure. By then, the city had agreed to let Smith take the boat on a shakedown cruise to Bermuda and then up to historic Mystic, Connecticut, and other spots on the East

Coast. During the ceremony, Smith spoke twice: as the builder and as the ship's first captain. Mayor Schaefer got to speak three times. After the speeches and a blast from the mayor's new whistle, the *Pride* set off down the backwater known as the Northwest Branch of the Patapsco River and into the Chesapeake Bay, on its way to Bermuda. Wearing a dark blue suit and waving his captain's cap at the crowds, Melbourne Smith was in heaven.

The *Pride* went only as far as St. Michael's, a short trip across the Chesapeake. Smith had already realized that the ship's rigging, which kept the masts upright, was stretching dramatically. He had no choice but to re-rig the entire ship, replacing the natural-fiber rope with much stronger steel cable clad in synthetic rope. The new rigging was another anachronism but an essential one if the masts were going to stay up. With the boat re-rigged, Smith set off for Bermuda.

On May 8, the ship's first full day on the water out of St. Michael's, a deckhand named Patrick Smyth was speared in the face by a piece of wood that splintered as he used it to tighten some of the forward rigging. The shard left a deep gash near Smyth's left eye and sent the young sailor into shock. Melbourne Smith offered to sew up the wound or suggested the sailor just keep it tightly bandaged until the *Pride* reached Bermuda. Smyth, though, wanted off the boat and Melbourne Smith called in the Coast Guard, which sent a helicopter to airlift the injured sailor off the *Pride*. It was a dramatic evacuation, occurring as a thunderstorm hit. The problems continued early the next morning, when a nasty squall hit the new schooner, snapping a key line and forcing the boat to barrel along without sails for nine hair-raising hours. Later, water on the deck nearly washed one of the mates off the boat through a cannon door.

With only a low-power radio, the *Pride* was unable to let anybody know about the problems it was having, and the schooner limped into Bermuda three days late—to the relief of Gail Shawe, the *Pride*'s executive director, who had flown down and was waiting anxiously with a reporter from Baltimore. The trip reminded Smith that the historic design of the *Pride* could cause serious problems at sea and he wrote to city officials back home asking for extra time to make changes.

"Much of the rigging gear is authentic for the period (1812) . . . However, it is extremely dangerous to handle under storm conditions. (Men were expendable in 1812. Today, more safety precautions are required.) I can alter the gear without it being noticeable or affecting the authenticity of the clipper schooner."

The purists may have won, but reality was forcing many concessions. As for Smith, the man with the original vision, his time with the *Pride* would end less than a year later amid a dispute about money and the operation of the ship.

CHAPTER 7

Jennifer arrived in Spain while the *Pride* was still suspended in the Malaga dry dock. The grueling trip began when she rushed straight from an interview at the University of Maryland graduate school in Baltimore to the airport. Her luggage was lost and her trip had taken thirty-six hours, but she was thrilled to see Armin. He had rented an efficiency apartment a short walk from the harbor, and the two spent a couple of weeks together. With the exception of Chez, she knew the others on board from sailing on the *Pride,* or in Vinny's case, from an Outward Bound camp in Maine where they both worked. Armin showed her around Malaga and they made a trip to Grenada, buying some decorative tiles that Armin stowed under his bunk.

Armin and Jennifer also tried to map out a future. The trans-Atlantic trip with the high school kids on *Te Vega* would likely be Jennifer's last big sailing adventure. If she was accepted in the graduate program in physical therapy in Maryland, she would enroll for the summer semester.

Armin, too, figured this stint on the *Pride* would be his first and last ocean crossing. Sailing jobs, he told Jennifer, could always be found, but how much more time could he spend at what was essentially a young man's game? As always, though, the alternatives, including the chance to move into the executive director's job in the *Pride* office, remained less than enticing. But with six months left to serve on the ship, Armin delayed making any definitive decision, as he had before.

Before Jennifer left for Italy, the two set up a schedule for radioing each other in the coming months. Above his bunk, Armin taped a photograph he thought captured both Jennifer's happiness and her "wired" attitude about life. Jennifer bought a fancy pen for Armin and headed off on the train. After a depressing separation of more than two months, their unexpected reunion in Spain had been nothing short of miraculous. Armin figured the time together had salvaged the relationship, even if the future remained murky.

Back in Baltimore, Nina Schack spent the late winter intensively training to sail on the *Pride*. A hair less than four feet ten inches tall, the twenty-two-year-old college student was deceptively strong. As a teenager, she passed lifesaving tests and learned enough jujitsu to flip an opponent. By February, she was in the best shape of her life, thanks to a regular routine of swimming, lifting weights, and jogging through the leafy neighborhoods of North Baltimore.

No one hired to sail on the *Pride* over the years had dreamed about such an adventure as much as Nina Schack. A decade earlier, during the summer and fall of 1976, the thirteen-year-old with long brown hair faithfully trekked downtown to observe Melbourne Smith's crew at work on the historic boat. There was something thrilling about watching the unusual project take shape behind a huge painted sign: Baltimore Clipper. The *Pride* was launched on Nina's fourteenth birthday, May 1, 1977; naturally she and her mother were part of the crowd. Five years later, when she was finishing her senior year at Baltimore's Bryn Mawr School for girls, Nina won a spot as an unpaid trainee on the *Pride*. By no means an experienced hand, she had at least learned the basics of sailing in Hawaii during frequent outings on her uncle's boat. Her first day as a *Pride* trainee, a mate told her to climb the rigging to grease the main mast; Nina scampered up the rope ladder without hesitation. She spent six days sailing around the Chesapeake Bay and up the Potomac River with the paid crew. She took her turn at the tiller and worked the overnight watches. And like the others, she put on khakis and a blue blazer for a shipboard reception in Alexandria, Virginia. During downtime on the ship, Nina took a sheet of notebook paper and made an ink drawing of the *Pride*, carefully labeling all of the rigging. By the time she got home, her love affair with the boat was cemented.

Two years later, in the summer before Nina's junior year at Cornell, her mother, Roma Schack, saw in the newspaper that the *Pride* was accepting applications for crew for the ship's European tour. Roma relayed the news to her daughter in Ithaca, New York. Nina, who had plastered her apartment with photographs of the *Pride*, jumped at the chance and wrote to Gail Shawe to apply. She wrote again a month later stressing how much she wanted to be part of the European trip; she volunteered to take a semester off from school if necessary. It was a long shot but she had two things going for her. She was a woman—a plus on a ship determined to have a co-ed crew—and she was a Baltimorean, a plus since the *Pride* organization felt compelled to hire at least some locals to work on the boat, which was, after all, owned by the city. Finally, Nina's enthusiasm and competence in 1982 left a good impression and Armin approved her as a deckhand for the first segment of the Mediterranean tour. She would work twenty weeks and be paid four hundred dollars a month. Just before Thanksgiving 1985, Armin mailed out the final schedule. She would meet the boat in Malaga in early March. They would sail through the Mediterranean, and Nina would leave the boat in Portsmouth, England, in July.

Nina and her mother were captivated by the itinerary. For Nina, it was a chance to do some real sailing—and to see Europe. Roma was thrilled that her daughter would be stopping in Italy, Roma's ancestral homeland, and she quickly made plans to take her mother, who lived in New Jersey, to Italy to meet the *Pride* during its stop in Livorno in April.

For Nina and her mother, the excitement about an Italian adventure ended abruptly in early 1986. They were in Hawaii for a family wedding when a friend called after New Year's Day with

word that the *Pride*'s European trip was canceled. It was a huge
blow. Roma's maternal instincts kicked in, and she called Shawe
in Baltimore to find out what the cancellation meant for Nina's future.

"What are you going to offer the people who were going to sail
in Europe?" she asked. Shawe told her that crew members could, if
they wanted, help sail the *Pride* across the Atlantic instead of through
the Mediterranean. There was, Shawe added, an appealing conso-
lation prize at the end of the trip. The *Pride* organization was already making plans to have the boat take part in New York City's
July Fourth parade of tall ships celebrating the one-hundredth anniversary of the Statue of Liberty.

Roma rejected the idea completely, in part because of her own
experience. She had once crossed the Atlantic on a boat—on the
Andrea Doria in the 1950s, only a couple of years before the great
Italian ocean liner collided in the fog with a Swedish liner and sank
near Nantucket, with fifty-two lives lost. More importantly, she figured her daughter was not experienced enough for ocean sailing.
Nor, she suspected, was Nina physically strong enough. A coastal
passage in the relatively protected waters of the Mediterranean was
one thing; crossing the ocean on a sailboat was another.

Nina was unsure as well. For more than a year she had counted
on sailing the Mediterranean. What if she couldn't cut it as an
ocean sailor? She began to pack to return to Cornell for the spring
semester. But before heading back to Ithaca, Nina spent an afternoon helping out at the *Pride* office downtown. Pictures of the
schooner lined the walls and she talked to the staff about the trip
she was giving up. By the end of the day, she had made up her
mind. "Mom, that's it, I'm going across the Atlantic." Roma Schack
gave in. Nina was twenty-two; an adult, after all.

As the winter raced by, Nina practiced tying knots and reviewed
the *Pride*'s complicated rigging. For entertainment, she made
copies of entries from the family's encyclopedia about the ports
where the *Pride* would be stopping. Nina consulted with other
sailors about the kind of clothes and gear she would need. No de-

tail was too insignificant. "Velcro flap over fly," she wrote to herself in a note about the right kind of pants to buy.

Finding foul-weather gear that would fit proved difficult. Nina called suppliers around the country, finally locating a yellow jacket and pants, size XX-S, in Annapolis, thirty-five miles away. Another pair of pants she bought was too long in the legs and had to be shortened. She picked up a flashlight, sea boots, three pairs of sailing gloves, and a safety strap to hold her glasses on. Finally, she found the right knife, a simple but sturdy Case whaler, with a solid handle made of dark brown wood and a single two-inch-long blade.

Growing up in Baltimore, Nina had done her share of partying, bopping around reggae shows with a bandanna on her head, and had attracted a string of boyfriends. But her size and bubbly enthusiasm made her seem young, innocent even. One night, Nina attended a party with several other people associated with the *Pride*, including Sue Burton, one of the deckhands aboard the *Pride* during the Baltic scare the previous summer. Nina talked excitedly about the trip ahead but needed Sue's advice.

"How many pairs of underwear should I bring?" she asked.

Sue, a *Pride* veteran, couldn't begin to explain just how unimportant clean underwear was. She took a look at the enthusiastic young woman and thought to herself: *She just doesn't get it.*

On March 2, after weeks of exercising, knot-tying, and list-making, it was time to go. That morning, a blustery Sunday, Nina and Roma Schack went to mass at a Catholic church not far from their house. Later, as she finished packing, Nina realized her duffel bag had gotten so heavy she would have difficulty carrying it alone. She and Roma made an emergency trip to a nearby mall to buy a small luggage cart. That afternoon, she got dressed for the trip, putting on a pair of tight jeans, a red turtleneck, a pair of dangly silver earrings and a *Pride of Baltimore* sweater, which was navy blue with red buttons on the shoulder. After packing her gear in the back of Roma's small Honda, Nina said good-byes to some neighbors. Before leaving, she and Roma sat for a moment in the car, under the sycamore trees in front of their comfortable house.

"Are you scared?" Roma asked her.

"Yeah."

"It's normal. I'm scared right now, too," Roma said. "When you get to be with other people, it will be okay."

At the Baltimore airport, Nina met up with four other deckhands she would be sailing with for the next few months: three men and a young woman she already knew from Baltimore, Susie Huesman. Like Nina, Susie had sailed on the *Pride* as a trainee. A recent graduate from Bucknell, she had been ecstatic to land a real job on the *Pride* and was taking a break from a job with an engineering firm to go sailing. The two young women made a fetching pair: Nina with her thick dark hair cut short and a gorgeous wide smile; Susie, a little taller at five feet two inches, her round face crowned by blond curls.

Another Baltimore native, Scott Jeffrey, had finished a master's program at Louisiana State University a year before and had fallen in love with tall-ship sailing during a stint on the *Westward*. It was a reunion for the other two men, Danny Krachuk and Barry Duckworth, who had met while working on a historic boat in Philadelphia. Duckworth, the oldest of the group at twenty-nine, was laid-back and wiry. He had gone nearly bald but sported a neatly trimmed red beard. At twenty-one, the curly-headed Krachuk was the youngest, but had been trying to land a job on the *Pride* for two years. Only three months earlier, Armin had rejected his application again, only to reverse course and hire him in January when another deckhand canceled.

Of the five deckhands, two had graduated from college and one was attending an Ivy League school. The three, all from Baltimore, had little professional sailing experience. The other two—Duckworth and Krachuk—had skipped college; their trip on the *Pride* was an important step in their careers at sea.

Under the fluorescent lights at the World Airways gate, the five crew members looked like teammates in their matching blue *Pride* sweaters. They made nervous efforts at small talk, while their families did the same. Roma Schack chatted with Susan Huesman's father, a Baltimore attorney. The conversation naturally turned to the sailing adventure awaiting their children. "We must be crazy to let our girls do this," Roma told Joe Huesman.

About twenty people were clustered at the gate for a brief fare-well ceremony, including some members of the *Pride* board, and Jan Miles, who was back in the United States. A Baltimore television crew even made the thirty-minute trip out to the airport on a Sunday night to roll some tape of the five deckhands. Baltimore, it seemed, never grew tired of stories about the city's schooner—even a mundane one about a crew changeover. Scott Jeffrey tried to explain to a reporter the lure of ocean sailing: "When you are out at sea you are alone . . . There is a different kind of noise. No airplanes, no traffic, just the noise of the boat."

Jan passed around glasses and popped open a bottle of champagne. "A little bit for everybody," he said soothingly as he poured a drink for the five departing sailors, who toasted to a safe trip home. When it came time to board the seven p.m. flight, Nina and Roma hugged good-bye and the five crew mates disappeared down the ramp toward the jet. Roma, on an impulse, bolted down the ramp and called Nina's name. The young woman reappeared and they embraced again, enough time for Roma to deliver four words: "Nina, I love you."

In London, the five groggy deckhands were greeted in the morning at Heathrow Airport by the unsettling sight of machine-gun-toting British soldiers patrolling the halls. The post-Christmas terror that had diverted the *Pride* back home had also prompted a major change in airport security in Europe.

With time to kill until their flight to Malaga, the five took a whirlwind trip through the city, downing bangers and mash and pints of ale. Later they headed back to the airport and reached Malaga that night. Sugar Flanagan and Joe McGeady, the first and second mates, met them at the airport and the seven headed back to the wharf in two taxis as a light rain fell. Joe, who didn't speak Spanish, knew enough to say "El Barco Negro," the black boat. "Ah, si, si," the driver responded. After four months, the *Pride* had become a familiar presence along the Malaga water-front.

At the dock, the five newcomers piled out into the rain to take a look. While Nina and Susan had sailed on the *Pride*, none of the three men had. Scott Jeffrey, despite growing up in the Baltimore suburbs and hearing about the *Pride* for years, had never even laid eyes on the boat. Now here he was gazing at the city's goodwill vessel on a moonless March night thousands of miles from the Inner Harbor.

Soon, the newcomers headed down below, through the *Pride*'s main cabin hatch. Barry, who would serve as the ship's carpenter, stowed a white canvas bag holding his carpentry tools; Scott had brought his guitar. At the bottom of the ladder, Scott, who stood only five feet four inches tall, received a bracing introduction to the cramped conditions when he smacked headfirst into one of the boat's low deck beams; a huge bolt left an impression in the middle of his forehead.

Nina lugged her heavy duffel on board. As a trainee on the *Pride* almost four years earlier, she had already met Armin, Sugar, and Joe. Vinny Lazzaro, though, was a new face. As for Vinny, he took a look at Nina and then a second look, doing nothing to disguise his interest. The sixth deckhand, Robert Foster, a quiet blond sailor from Virginia who had recently graduated from the merchant marine academy, had flown in a couple of days before and he, too, was introduced to the newcomers.

With the five arrivals from Baltimore, the *Pride* had all twelve sailors. Four veterans were in charge: Armin as the master; Sugar Flanagan, Joe McGeady, and Leslie McNish as the watch officers. All four had sailed for years on the *Pride* or other boats, and all had Coast Guard licenses—a remarkably experienced group. Vinny would take care of the ship's engines and Chez would cook.

Armin was thirteen years older than the next oldest crew member, Leslie. Nobody was sailing for the money. The crew pay ranged from $400 a month for four of the deckhands to $900 a month for Sugar. The job paid Armin an annual salary of $22,500.

Joe, who had more than paid his dues as a deckhand before being rewarded with the second mate's post, took a look at the new deckhands and wondered to himself what was up with this group. There wasn't a big guy in the bunch; no one who could really be counted on for muscle. The two women had done some time on the *Pride*, but nothing serious. The men all had some sailing experience, but none on the *Pride*, with its old-fashioned rigging and quirky handling requirements.

This crew had been assembled to sail the *Pride* through the Mediterranean, not across the ocean; it showed. *Who*, Joe wondered to himself, *are the good deckhands? The guys like me?*

CHAPTER 8

March 1986
Malaga, Spain

The next day, the twelve crew members gathered in the main cabin for an orientation meeting. For Nina and Susie, this was a refresher course, but new material for the other four deckhands.

The *Pride*'s snug main cabin was about twenty feet across and served as kitchen, dining room, parlor, and dormitory all in one. A large, varnished table took up part of the central area adjacent to the galley. The low-ceilinged space was flanked on either side by bunks for ten—three sets of double-decker berths to starboard; two sets on the port. Each berth was nothing more than a thin cotton mattress on a wooden board crammed into an enveloping space with a couple of feet of headroom. A wooden storage shelf ran along the outer wall of each bunk, next to the mattress. A blue curtain, hung from a string, gave the suggestion of privacy, but anyone in a bunk could hear every last slurp from those who were eating at the table a few feet away, and anyone at the table could hear every last snore, fart, or yawn from the bunks.

As bare as the living accommodations were, they were an improvement. When the *Pride* was launched in 1977, the crew slept in hammocks slung from beams in the cabin, just as nineteenth-century sailors did. The bunks were added later at Armin's insistence, and Jan had a reading lamp installed in each berth, a small item but essential for crew sanity. For their belongings, each sailor was assigned a sea chest, some made of varnished wood, others painted white. One chest sat below each set of bunks, meaning the crew members in those bunks climbed on and over a chest to get out of bed. The other chests were lashed together and placed around the dining table and used as seats. It was an inelegant but functional combination of storage and seating.

The twelve crew members shared two toilets, or heads, one forward and one aft. The aft head was connected to the aft cabin by a half door that was about three feet tall. That head also held the single-sideband radio and the fax machine for receiving weather reports—equipment, added to the *Pride* over the years, that just wouldn't fit in the aft cabin with the rest of the navigation and communication equipment.

The boat had a single cold-water shower, located forward in the main cabin, but it was rarely used on long passages, given the need to preserve fresh water. Underway, the crew would use a hose on deck to shower with saltwater. Crew often brushed their teeth on deck, using a small amount of fresh water in a cup, to free up the head for others. At sea, it was no big deal to brush and spit at the rail, but when the ship was in port, a crew member could often have an audience. "Look! She's brushing her teeth," the dockside passerby would say, forgetting for a moment that this was a human being, not an animal in the zoo.

Only Armin, as captain, and Sugar, as the first mate, got their own berths, slightly more private bunks in the rear cabin. Their mattresses sat on platforms a couple of feet off the ground, on either side of the cabin, and were shielded by brown curtains. The cabin floor was wide, dark-stained boards. The officers' saloon felt somewhat more spacious than the main cabin, as its ceiling extended a couple of feet above the deck. A small mirror hung on one wall near a brass kerosene lamp. A wooden chair sat at a wooden writing table used for navigation; above it, a small shelf held books, charts, and maps. Two doors led forward, one to the head, the other into the engine room. Getting through the doors required a deeply crouched maneuver or a quick crawl on hands and knees.

Those were the living quarters. Around them were the cramped engine room, storage areas for anchor chains, paint, and varnish; old ropes and sails; and essentials such as diesel fuel, water, and food.

Chez, who was already in his third month on the boat, showed the deckhands around the *Pride*'s galley, a cozy space with a single sink, a tiny bit of counter space, and a fussy diesel stove, which had replaced the even fussier brick oven and the kerosene stove. Pots and pans hung on one wall, and knives and spatulas were shoved into a nearby wall rack. A big bag of garlic that Chez purchased in a Malaga market hung by the stove. Each crew member picked out a mug to use for the trip; they were hung from hooks near the table. Chez did most of the cooking but everyone had to clean up his dishes and take turns tidying up after each evening meal.

Vinny took them in groups of three to learn about the ship's cramped engine room—a sweltering space housing the noisy engine and generator. Each crew member was expected to know how to do the basics: turn the engine on, use the generator to pump the bilges, and record engine temperature and oil pressure.

By early March, Vinny was beginning to wonder what he had gotten himself into. He had enjoyed exploring Malaga's winding streets and bodegas, with their sixty-cent bottles of wine. And then there were the beautiful Spanish girls. "Long dark hair and [dark] eyes and, best of all, they all want me—they just don't know it yet," he wrote a friend back in Maine. "It's hard being a stud when all you can say is 'hello,' 'good-bye,' and 'one more beer please.' "

But after two months of *Pride* work, Vinny had grown weary of what he derided as the arts and crafts of old-fashioned sailing: the sail repairs, the leather-working, and the tarring and varnishing. To use a word coined by an old fishing friend, the work was "tiddlier" than the no-nonsense stuff he was used to on steel fishing boats. Although, he added wryly, "I'm learning how to use all kinds of different tools besides hammers and crowbars."

At the age of twenty-six, Vinny was making a major shift by going to sea on a sailboat, not the first unexpected turn his life had taken. By all indications, he had been destined to be some kind of artist. His father, Victor, was an architect and talented visual artist; his mother, Maria, did weavings and was also an artist. Vincent, as his family called him, grew up in Connecticut with a brother and sister in a wood-frame house his father had designed on a secluded five-acre site near a pond. The house had high ceilings and plenty of windows looking out on the surrounding woods. There was no television and the children were encouraged to draw, read, and play musical instruments. As a twelve-year-old, Vinny produced an impressive twelve-page newspaper devoted to the world of chess, complete with drawings, interviews with chess pieces, references to Chaucer, and ads showing what the well-dressed king and queen should be wearing.

After graduating from high school, Vincent was rewarded by his parents with a sailing course at the Hurricane Island Outward Bound School in Maine. The experience could have been a disaster, as it rained twenty-three out of twenty-six days; it was one of the worst stretches of bad weather the instructors had encountered. But Vincent loved it—sleeping on small pulling boats, and learning to survive on water and land. Once he got home, the usually quiet Vincent couldn't stop talking about his adventure on the rocky Maine islands.

Vincent enrolled at the University of Rhode Island and began working toward a degree in anthropology, but he ended up on a dormitory floor with a bunch of hard-living guys enrolled in the college's two-year commercial fisheries program. They called him Vinny and lured him into the fishing program, too. His parents, the soft-spoken artists, were appalled, but they chalked up his decision to a young man's natural rebellion and love of adventure. He worked on fishing boats during summer break and finished up an associate's degree in fishing in 1981.

That summer, Craig Pendleton, a college buddy who had completed the fisheries program a year earlier and returned to his home in Maine, helped land Vinny a job on an enormous, 108-foot scalloping boat out of Portland. Vinny figured life on such a big ship would be a piece of cake, but the day trips on small boats out of Rhode Island had done little to prepare him for big-time fishing. His first time out with Craig, the ship was heading to the fertile fishing areas on Georges Bank when it ran into a tropical depression. The ship jogged in place for three days, rolling and pitching but doing no fishing. Vinny had never been so seasick. When Craig came to look in on him at one point, all Vinny could muster was a heartfelt, "Fuck you!"

Craig and Vinny, along with a cousin of Craig's, soon went to work as the entire crew on a ninety-foot steel boat called the *Virginia Dare*, which was owned by a large Maine fishing company. The three, all in their early twenties, went to sea for ten-day stretches, raking in a hold full of pollock, haddock, flounder, and monkfish that would be turned into fish sticks or Filet-O-Fish sandwiches at McDonald's. Setting the enormous nets and handling tons of fish was grueling, dangerous work. In 1984, Craig bought his own ship; a seventy-five-footer called the *Coastal I*, an Eastern-rigged, wooden fishing boat with a house aft. Again, he brought Vinny with him, along with a third fisherman, Ron Peterson. Being at sea brought grinding, treacherous work, but the money was good. Vinny became a capable fisherman and mariner, able to do or figure out just about anything connected to the boat. He also shared with Craig a strong respect for the sea. Fishing, they knew, wasn't worth the risk in the worst conditions.

Sometimes, though, the risks were not so apparent. On March 1, 1985, Vinny, Craig and Ron were about one hundred miles off the coast of Gloucester, Massachusetts, on *Coastal I*, fishing near Cashes Ledge, when the weather turned rough—thirty-knot winds and ten-foot seas. With the forecast looking just as bad, they decided to pull in the net and head home. That morning, after the fish had been dropped in the hold, Vinny and Ron went to sleep, leaving Craig alone in the captain's house. At about nine, an alarm began sounding to indicate there was water in the engine room. Craig went down to pump it out and then ran back to the captain's house to check on the boat, which was slogging home through the waves on autopilot. But the alarm continued to sound and Craig couldn't handle the two chores alone. Soaking wet from all the water in the engine room, Craig found Vinny asleep in the galley. "Jesus Christ, Vinny, we're sinking," he said.

Sure enough, *Coastal I* was taking on water and her pumps weren't working fast enough. The men fiddled with the pumps for hours, with no improvement. Finally, Craig used the VHF radio to reach the Coast Guard, which promised to deliver portable pumps by helicopter. With nothing to do but wait, Vinny decided to eat, heating up some turkey pot pie that Ron's mom had prepared. As the boat slowly filled with water, Vinny ate while Ron, too nervous to eat, finished off a pack of cigarettes. Finally, the helicopter reached the sinking boat and lowered three pumps to the deck. The men got them running, but the pumps kept getting swamped as the boat continued to roll in the ocean waves. It was a losing proposition: the water was flooding the boat faster than they could pump it out. Craig radioed the Coast Guard and said they had no choice but to abandon ship. The helicopter lowered a rescue basket and the three men were lifted one by one to the chopper. Thirty minutes later, as the men flew back to the Coast Guard station on Cape Cod, word came over the radio that *Coastal I* had disappeared into the Atlantic.

In a letter to his Aunt Josie that spring, Vinny described the sinking in unemotional detail, but used one of Melville's famous concluding lines from *Moby-Dick* to express his appreciation for a sea that had so easily swallowed up *Coastal I:*

"Now small fowls flew screaming over the yet yawning gulf . . . and the great shroud of the sea rolled on as it rolled five thousand years ago."

After the March 1985 sinking of the *Coastal I*, Vinny worked for a while on another fishing boat but began looking for a change. In the summer, for the second year in a row, he worked at the Hurricane Island Outward Bound School, the place that had made such an impression on him as a kid fresh out of high school. The previous summer, his first as a staff member, he had run students around in thirty-foot boats and had done some teaching. He had also made friends that summer with Jennifer Lamb, who was working as an instructor. She, in turn, introduced Vinny to Armin when he visited and Vinny became intrigued with the idea of sailing on the *Pride* some day.

In the fall of 1985, back from the European trip on *Pride*, Jennifer stopped by Hurricane Island and ran into Vinny. She passed along word from Armin that the *Pride* needed an engineer for the European trip. Vinny wasted no time sending in a formal application. He reminded Armin that he was a veteran of long trips to sea. When something on the boat broke during one of those trips, he said, they either found a way to fix it or lost good money by coming in early.

Armin offered him a six-month stint as engineer, but warned him, "the living conditions are close and Spartan. Pay is admittedly low; six hundred a month." Vinny was intrigued with the prospect. Back home for a visit, he talked excitedly to his parents about the *Pride* and showed them a picture of the schooner.

"What do you think?" he asked his father.

Victor Lazzaro stared at the photograph of the ship and all of its sails, then looked up at his son. "Be careful, Vincent. It looks awfully top-heavy."

During the first couple of days of orientation, Sugar gave an overview of the ship's sails, which were controlled by about a hundred separate lines—halyards, sheets, downhauls, brails, and so on—each with a specific function. Each had to be coiled in a certain way and hung in a certain way, not for tradition's sake, but to ensure they would not tangle or cause other problems during the quickly paced moments of sail setting and striking.

The crew got an explanation of the ship's safety equipment, including the two life rafts and the three small boats on deck—the wooden sailing skiff *Irie*, the inflatable known as *Rhino*, and a small rowboat attached to davits above the *Pride*'s stern. Joe had worked on the rowboat, but it had taken such a beating during bad weather that the crew wasn't even sure about its integrity and never used it.

There was also a demonstration of how to activate the ship's two EPIRBs (emergency position indicating radio beacons), hand-held

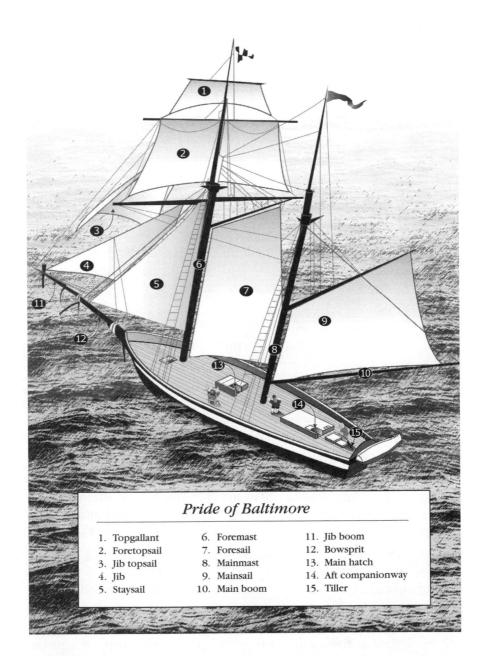

Pride of Baltimore

1. Topgallant
2. Foretopsail
3. Jib topsail
4. Jib
5. Staysail
6. Foremast
7. Foresail
8. Mainmast
9. Mainsail
10. Main boom
11. Jib boom
12. Bowsprit
13. Main hatch
14. Aft companionway
15. Tiller

transmitters that would send a distress signal when turned on. Each EPIRB beamed out a special signal that identified it as coming from the *Pride of Baltimore*. The signal would be picked up by satellites, which would send the information about the distress call to authorities on land.

On the *Pride*, the EPIRBs were kept out of sight since they were too modern for the historic look of the vessel's deck. One was clamped just inside the companionway leading from the aft cabin to the deck. The second was in an open box in the main cabin, near the ladder heading up to the deck. Both were close enough to an exit that someone could easily grab them in case of an emergency and send out a distress signal with the flip of a switch. While some boats had water-activated EPIRBs that would automatically send a distress signal when covered with water, the *Pride* did not. The captains worried that with the wet conditions on the *Pride*, the EPIRBs would be activated accidentally and cause unnecessary problems on shore. The EPIRBs had been on board the *Pride* for years and had never been used.

Each crew member was given several pieces of safety equipment: a harness, which could be clipped to something solid on the boat to keep the wearer from falling off the deck or out of the rigging; a life jacket; a smaller life vest; and a survival suit, a buoyant and bulkier version of a wet suit that zipped over a person's clothes. The crew practiced slipping on the "Gumby suits," tested the whistles that were attached, and waxed the zippers to make sure they were working smoothly. The suits would keep a person's head out of the water, and his body protected against hypothermia for days. If it ever came time to abandon ship, each crew member was responsible for getting to a life vest or survival suit. Neither was kept on deck. Instead each crew member was instructed to store them within easy reach in their bunks.

Finally, each member of the crew was assigned a task to perform during different emergencies: fire, man overboard, or abandon ship. The crew paid close attention. Danny Krachuk had experienced what it was like to go through two serious storms in the middle of the ocean on sailboats, including one hurricane. And, of course, Vinny didn't mind recounting the loss of the good ship *Coastal I* in the North Atlantic.

After hearing the story, Chez told Vinny he didn't like the sound of working on a fishing boat—the long hours, the dangerous equipment, and the threat of storms. Vinny was nonchalant in his response: "It's no more dangerous than sailing across the Atlantic in a canoe." The canoe was the *Pride of Baltimore*.

CHAPTER 9

March 1986
Malaga, Spain

As the March 12 departure date approached, Armin began to doubt the ship would leave on schedule. The *Pride* had contracted with a sail-maker in Maine to sew a new jib and to mend some rips in the foresail. The work in Maine was complete, but a Spanish dock-workers' strike had crippled the waterfront and the sails were lost in transit.

While he figured the sails would arrive eventually, Armin was less certain about the issue that had been on his mind since well before the Baltic incident. Just how safe was his boat? Armin had no formal training in naval architecture but had built, inspected, and sailed many boats, and instinctively understood the rudiments of stability. He also knew the *Pride* as well as anybody did.

In sailing jargon, the *Pride* was an "extreme" boat that sat low in the water and sailed with a towering rig—a top-heavy assemblage of wood, wire, rope, and sailcloth. On its bottom, the *Pride* was built old-style with no extra weight below the keel, the sturdy piece of wood that ran the length of the hull. Instead, the boat relied on nineteenth-century-style internal ballast—pieces of lead, iron, and stone—to keep from rolling over. Internal ballast was historically appropriate but had drawbacks. For one, it could shift when a boat heeled sharply. If ballast did shift to one side of the boat during a heavy wind, the vessel would have little chance of re-righting itself. Secondly, having the ballast inside the hull instead of under it raised the ship's center of gravity, the most crucial component of a vessel's stability.

Complicating matters, the *Pride* was never outfitted with the amount of ballast specified by its architect. In his initial design, Tom Gillmer called for the boat to have twenty-five tons of iron as ballast. That figure climbed to thirty tons after the city agreed to take the *Pride* to sea. At the same time, Gillmer and the builders decided it would be prudent to use lead instead of iron. Lead was far more dense, which meant that it would sit lower in the boat, therefore bringing down the ship's center of gravity. Similarly, the same amount of lead would fill less of the space in the ship's hold, a plus from a design point of view. But lead was also two and a half times as expensive as iron. Working under a tight budget that had already grown by nearly a third when the ballast question surfaced, the builders and city officials who were footing the bill compromised and used half lead and half iron.

As construction proceeded, Gillmer determined that the ship needed even more weight, and increased the necessary ballasting from thirty to fifty tons, but the *Pride* never got its fifty tons. In early 1977, the building crew painstakingly loaded the ballast into a central, twenty-foot section of the ship's hold, beginning with fifteen tons of lead in pieces weighing fifty pounds. Next came fifty-pound pieces of iron encased in epoxy to stave off rust—another fifteen tons. Finally, Melbourne Smith secured extra ballast at no cost—about ten tons of bulky Belgian paving stones donated by the city—for a total of about forty tons.

With the bulky but free paving stones taking up more space than lead or iron, there simply wasn't room for the remaining ten tons. Part of the reason was that some of the hold area originally designated for ballast was instead given over to house diesel fuel tanks, which was a necessity given the change of mission and the addition of an engine to the design. The fuel and tanks were by no means as heavy as the originally planned ballast, meaning the *Pride* was launched with as much as ten tons less ballast than planned. As the boat was being launched, Gillmer figured the extra weight would be added eventually. In the meantime, he said, the missing ballast was an important consideration for the ship's captains, as its absence increased the ship's center of gravity, essentially making it more top-heavy.

"The balance (to ultimately be added) is not considered vital to the sailing characteristics but *must* be considered when sail-carrying and heavy weather is encountered," Gillmer wrote in a 1977 scholarly paper about the *Pride*. There is no record that any of the remaining ten tons of ballast was added.

Such details were not widely known. But in the East Coast sailing world, experts both real and self-appointed had their opinions about the *Pride*'s seaworthiness. And it wasn't hard to find a critic.

She is a nice bit of history, they might say. *But, hey, don't ask me to take her out to sea.*

Of course, any discussion of the matter evolved into a question of relativity. If a detractor called the *Pride* "dangerous," the answer would come back, "Not if you know what you're doing." That was true enough and close to Armin's view. There were certain things the *Pride* could do extremely well; for example, sail on a broad reach. Other kinds of sailing, though, were difficult—particularly beating to wind. This sometimes caused the head rig to go under the waves and sent water pouring into the bilges through holes and seams.

But *Pride* sailors were confident the boat could handle such things with the right sails up and skillful hands on the tiller and lines. Indeed, the undisputed fact that the *Pride* was an extreme boat was exactly why some of her crew returned again and again to sail her. On the *Pride*, the sailing highs—the giddy speed and the sheer beauty of the sails working in tandem with the wind—were so high. The lows? Well, they would just have to be endured, and the dangerous moments avoided. In any case, they'd point out, nothing is entirely safe, especially sailing. There was no right or wrong opinion in the debate.

Al Nejmeh had experienced the Baltic scare and wasn't about to get back on the *Pride* for a second ocean crossing, although he went on to spend another decade as a sailboat captain. But others on board that morning in August 1985 would have jumped at the chance to sail her back to the United States. At the same time, veteran sailors never disregarded the risk of sailing on the *Pride*. When the ship was preparing to go to Europe in the spring of 1985, *Pride* veterans Joe McGeady and Jennifer Lamb conferred before choosing a bunk for the long passage, the ship's first ocean crossing.

"Which bunk do you want?" Joe asked.

"The one closest to the hatch," Jennifer answered quickly, the implication quite clear to her shipmate.

"Well I'll take the next closest one."

Were the two sailors kidding each other about their concerns? Only partially.

"After the first three or four months, I never trusted the boat," Jennifer said later. "You understood it was a very dangerous boat." For her, though, the anxiety about sailing on the *Pride* was always worse on land. Concerns melted away as soon as she was back on the boat sailing. "We joked about the *Pride* being the Flexible Flyer," she added. "But it wasn't going to sink on us."

From her first days, some people who understood such things wondered about the *Pride*'s stability given the extreme design of the Baltimore clippers. But those concerns grew in 1984 for a couple of reasons. In early June, news came of the sinking of the *Marques*, a British educational vessel. Built in 1917, the eighty-seven-foot-long *Marques* was overwhelmed and lost during a squall off Bermuda; there were nineteen deaths. Questions soon arose about the seaworthiness and stability of the *Marques*, whose rig and sail plan had been added on to several times to allow the boat to appear in movies. Even before the official inquiry into the sinking began, the accident was a sobering reminder of the stakes of ocean sailing.

At the same time, the *Pride* organization completed plans for the ship's first ocean crossing—a significantly more rigorous trip, involving longer passages across open seas than the ship had yet attempted.

There were doubters. Baltimore's Mayor Schaefer didn't like the idea, but not because he knew anything about the risks of sailing; he was just a natural worrier. Peter Boudreau, a veteran ocean sailor who helped build the *Pride* and was considered the most conservative of its three captains, passed on the chance to go to Europe. He wasn't interested in such a long trip on a boat that was both uncomfortable and demanding.

Andy Davis, who also helped build the *Pride,* was startled by the news that the boat was going to Europe and shared his concerns with Armin in 1984 when they worked together to launch the *Spirit of Massachusetts;* Davis was its builder and Armin its first captain. "Europe? That's across the Atlantic Ocean, isn't it?" Davis said to Armin, only half-kidding, when he heard about the plans. "Armin, I know the party line is that the *Pride* is a wonderful, seaworthy vessel. But it's a piece of shit. It's going to sink." Armin was not amused by the pointed critique of his vessel. (When the *Pride* reached Europe in 1985, Armin made sure that word reached Davis.)

The trip also caused consternation for the *Pride*'s insurance carrier. In 1984, a year in which it sailed only in North America, the *Pride* had little trouble obtaining a $750,000 policy for loss or damage to the ship, but the company that wrote the policy, Lexington Insurance Co. of Boston, balked at continuing coverage for the European voyage. Lexington eventually renewed the policy, but added $10,000 to the premium cost to cover the first part of the European trip and tacked on a whopping $30,000 deductible. Most importantly, Lexington reduced the total coverage amount to $475,000—about what it had cost to build the boat nine years earlier but far less than what it would cost to replace it.

The insurance problems continued in 1985, when *Pride* officials found few takers to secure coverage for the next year, a time when the boat would be sailing solely in Europe. Of six firms contacted, only one—Lexington—even bid to insure the *Pride.* This time, Lexington nearly doubled its premium. The insurance situation was complicated again by the Norwegian grounding mishap in late June. While the grounding caused minor damage to the hull, the accident was apparently more than enough for Lexington Insurance. In September, the firm canceled the *Pride*'s policy as of the end of 1985. *Pride* officials scrambled and secured a new policy on the boat, but again for only $475,000.

The concern about the *Pride*'s stability mounted in July 1984, after a marine architect in Maine, Roger Long, visited the *Pride*, which was docked on the Kennebec River at the Maine Maritime Museum in Bath during its summer-long trip up the East Coast. As other guests admired the ship and sipped drinks during an evening cocktail party, the naval architect proceeded to measure the *Pride*'s freeboard—the area of the hull above the waterline—jotting down numbers as he went. With his measuring done, Long headed home.

Long made the somewhat furtive visit to the *Pride*'s deck as part of a major study of sailboat stability he had undertaken with his partner, Parker E. Marean III, the first such study in two decades. The analysis had been commissioned by an association of sail-training schools and would compare stability information for a number of American sailboats. Among the numbers being compiled were each boat's center of gravity, how far each could each lean before going all the way over, and at what angle of heel seawater would begin to flood the cabin.

After determining the various boats' stability characteristics, the architects would plot them on a graph to look for patterns. Along with the actively sailing vessels, the study looked at a few boats that had been lost at sea, including the *Marques* and the *Albatross*, a ninety-two-foot sail-training vessel that sank in the Gulf of Mexico in 1961. The architects would use the findings to recommend minimum safety standards for sail-training vessels, which would eventually lead to regulations to be approved by the Coast Guard.

In preparing the study, Long obtained a set of stability calculations for the *Pride*. According to Gillmer's calculations, the *Pride* could right itself from an angle of more than ninety degrees—at least theoretically. Long sensed that the numbers were too good to be true, prompting the visit to the *Pride*'s deck.

After crunching the numbers, Long decided the stability calculations provided by Gillmer were indeed inaccurate. The calculations, which were actually made by a computer-mapping firm using

Gillmer's blueprints, had mistakenly added two feet to the height of the deck, placing it at the top of the ship's rail. That extra height, multiplied by the length and width of the *Pride*'s deck area, increased the supposed buoyancy significantly. That, in turn, led to artificially inflated stability figures.

Using the more accurate measurement, Long estimated that the *Pride*'s range of stability extended to an angle perhaps as low as seventy-six degrees, not the ninety-plus degrees estimated by Gillmer. This was a significant difference. When Long plotted what he figured were the *Pride*'s actual stability characteristics on a grid with those of other ships, the findings were worrisome. On one side of the grid were most of the other ships that had been analyzed. On the other side—the *wrong* side of the stability chart—were the *Marques* and the *Albatross*, two ships that had already been lost. The *Pride*'s stability numbers weren't as poor as those of the two lost ships, which were considered disasters waiting to happen, but they did fall squarely into what longtime naval architect Parker Marean called a "fringe" region.

Long and Marean considered the findings troubling enough that they decided to contact Gillmer. "We all were concerned that the vessel was being operated with a false sense of security based on the incorrect righting arm," Marean wrote later, referring to the figure depicting the ship's ability to right itself from a steep angle. Long called and wrote Gillmer in Annapolis to inform him of the discrepancy.

Long also met Armin at a meeting of sailboat captains and talked with him about the findings, both face-to-face and later by phone. Long explained the numbers and made it clear that they depicted a boat with less ability to right itself than Gillmer's figures suggested. Armin told Long he was grateful for the information.

Gillmer's response, however, startled the Maine architects. Gillmer wrote that he had "always been fully aware" that the calculations done on the *Pride* had been inaccurate. But he added, "It is my feeling that righting moments beyond the angles approaching maximum arms are pretty academic for ship-safety prognostication." In other words, the stability figures may have been inaccurate, but it didn't matter, since the numbers were theoretical and couldn't predict real-world behavior. For further information, Gill-mer, the former professor, referred his Maine colleagues to two "fairly reliable" textbooks on the subject of stability; both were au-thored by Thomas C. Gillmer.

Gillmer had bristled at the outside critique, but four weeks after re-ceiving the letter he took a new look at the *Pride*'s stability, his first re-examination since its launch in 1977. The *Pride* organization was under no requirement to have the ship's stability tested, given her status with the Coast Guard as an un-inspected vessel, but the doubts raised by the Maine architects all but obligated Gillmer to re-examine the *Pride*. With the boat back in the Inner Harbor in August, Gillmer oversaw a labor-intensive study known as an in-clining test. Under his direction, the crew moved the *Pride*'s four cannons, each weighing 640 pounds, between four pre-selected spots on the deck, going from port to starboard. The farther the cannons were from the ship's center line, the more the boat tilted. With each shift of weight, Gillmer used a long plumb line hung below deck to note the degree to which the boat heeled. Using those measurements to make a series of calculations, it was possi-ble to determine the ship's center of gravity—the most important measure of a ship's stability.

The August 1984 test basically confirmed Long's analysis. Gill-mer concluded that the *Pride*'s center of gravity had risen more than seven inches since 1977, going from 9.14 to 9.75 feet above the keel, a significant increase for a boat the *Pride*'s size. (Without more information, Long's firm could not pinpoint the *Pride*'s center of gravity, but estimated that it was at least 9.7 feet above the keel and possibly higher.) A ship's center of gravity can rise and fall as weight is added or removed. Over the years, the *Pride* had accumu-lated all sorts of extra cargo—heavy things like old sails and a re-frigerator, as well as lighter objects such as half-empty cans of paint and books left behind by departing crew members.

Working with the numbers, Gillmer determined that a second related measure of stability for the *Pride* had also fallen signifi-cantly—the distance between the center of gravity and the boat's center of buoyancy. Gillmer estimated that the distance between those two calculated points had decreased to 5.55 feet.

The inclining results were of concern to the designer—particularly given the plans to send the boat to Europe—and he took the unusual step of drafting a pointed memo to the *Pride* office suggesting changes in the boat's operation. He pointed out that while the *Pride* organization had paid significant attention to the structural integrity of the boat, "very little" attention had been paid to "the equally important subject of stability."

Moving forward, he said, the boat must take on little additional weight—no more than 3.2 tons—and it must be stored low enough to help bring down the ship's center of gravity at least three-tenths of a foot.

He made specific suggestions as well. "No fuel drums or full water casks should be stowed on deck," Gillmer wrote. This was not the first time he had made such a recommendation for a ship that routinely sailed with heavy containers of fuel and water on deck. In 1983, when Jan Miles brought the *Pride* back from its first trip to the West Coast, lashed securely on deck were several containers of diesel fuel. *That shouldn't be done*, the former professor instructed the captain. But captains of the *Pride* were left with little choice. Without adequate fuel storage in the hold, the deck was the only place to store the fuel they believed they needed.

Gillmer also suggested an important change for the trans-Atlantic crossing—sailing without the two topmasts, and the yards and sails that extended above the masts. The high-flying top rig reduced the ship's stability considerably.

"Basically, for cruising at sea and transatlantic, the reduction of weight aloft—including top masts, topsail yards, and associated rigging and sails—will contribute significantly [to improved stability]," Gillmer wrote. While the architect didn't explicitly recommend sailing without the top masts, the memo made clear he thought it wise.

It wasn't such a radical idea. The original Baltimore clippers sailed with crews of one hundred or more men in order to respond quickly to new weather conditions. Such crews could quickly strike a ship's topmasts in stormy seas, and just as quickly put them back up when needed. Peter Boudreau, while serving as the *Pride*'s captain, generally took the topmasts down for open-ocean crossings to Bermuda or the Caribbean, both for stability reasons and because the top rig had design problems that made it more trouble than it was worth, in his estimation. Similarly, Armin kept the topmasts on deck while taking the boat to the Caribbean on the way to the West Coast in the fall of 1982, rather than risk running into a fall storm that could overwhelm the boat.

Gillmer concluded the memo by saying it was "urgently" recommended that another inclining be performed before the boat headed for Europe.

Over the winter, crew members getting the boat ready for Europe did remove some unnecessary items and shifted some things lower in the boat. Boudreau supervised much of the preparation work and claimed that the effort to stow weight as low as possible was based on common-sense sea knowledge, not advice from Gillmer.

In March 1985, a few weeks before the *Pride* left for Europe, Gillmer again inclined the ship. After adjusting the calculations to account for gear not yet brought on board, Gillmer concluded that one key measurement—the distance between the center of gravity and the center of buoyancy—had improved slightly, from the 5.55 feet he had calculated the year before to 5.78 feet. The summer before, Gillmer had said the target should be 5.9 feet; the figure of 5.78 was an improvement, but not what he had hoped for.

On the bottom of a stability report he drew up just before the *Pride* left for Europe he typed, "DON'T RETURN TO *5.55* FEET."

Gillmer may have been the ship's designer and unofficial stability adviser, but on decisions about sailing the *Pride*, he deferred to captains. Although Gillmer requested a meeting to discuss his concerns with the three *Pride* captains—Elsaesser, Miles, and Boudreau—there's no record of or recollection about it taking place. In any case, the *Pride* captains did not follow two of his most specific proposals. With Jan Miles in command, the *Pride* sailed to Europe with two fifty-five-gallon containers of diesel fuel and three slightly smaller water casks on deck. While these were considered crucial necessities in case the ship ran into delays crossing the Atlantic, the full stores of water and fuel added more than seventeen hundred pounds on deck. The boat also sailed with its entire top rig up, as it was considered necessary for efficient ocean sailing.

As the *Pride* headed off to Europe, Armin talked again with Long and asked about the possibility of having him do a thorough stability analysis, one that was more in-depth than the brief summaries Gillmer had produced. Such a study, of course, would have to wait until late 1986, when the boat returned from Europe. The message was clear: Armin wasn't sure about Gillmer's calculations. Later, Armin wrote Long to thank him for the insights. "I've already learned a lot from our short conversations. . . . You can see how ignorant some of us are about the specifics of stability."

Ten months later, as the ship prepared to sail from Malaga, the *Pride*'s stability remained even more of a question mark for Armin, given the boat's lackluster performance in the Baltic, and he discussed it with both Gail Shawe, the *Pride*'s executive director, and Sugar Flanagan. If he had his way, Armin told his first mate, he would remove the cobblestone and iron ballast and replace it with denser lead. It would lower the ship's center of gravity and take up less room.

Looking to the future, Armin wondered how long the *Pride* could continue sailing as a promotional and goodwill vessel. Such a mission generated little revenue, which meant the organization had to raise money constantly. Before coming to Spain, Armin had met with the key leaders of the *Pride* organization and discussed the feasibility of getting the ship involved in educational activities or linking up with an environmental group. It would be a long shot for the *Pride* to meet the Coast Guard safety standards required for carrying passengers, but adding denser ballast and improving its center of gravity would be a start.

As for the return trip across the Atlantic, Armin made some changes to reduce the weight on the boat. With the European tour canceled, the ship's cache of promotional materials was unnecessary, as was the big wooden Pride of Baltimore sign the crew would have set up during official stops. Armin also deemed a laser disc player extraneous. Similarly, since there would be no occasion to fire the ceremonial guns on this trip, Sugar, Joe, Vinny, and Leslie hauled their heavy carriages off the *Pride* and dragged them up the concrete pier, a curious bit of nineteenth-century-style weaponry amid the modern cranes and ships of Malaga harbor. In all, the crew got rid of some two thousand pounds of excess stuff, which the ship's provisioning agent arranged to have sent back to Baltimore on a cargo ship. The ship's four cannons, which weighed a ton and a half all together, were taken off the deck and stowed below, lashed tightly to the ship under the bunks.

Despite taking those steps, Armin had lingering misgivings. On March 8, four days before the scheduled departure date, he sat down and wrote Shawe. He still wasn't sure how the *Pride* stacked up, and he wanted someone other than Gillmer to figure it out.

"I'm still very concerned about *Pride*'s stability," Armin wrote. "Our visit to Bath would be an ideal time to have Roger Long measure the ship." However strong those concerns were, Armin opted to sail with the *Pride*'s entire rig up as well as seventeen hundred pounds of fuel and water lashed on deck.

That same weekend, Armin wrote Jennifer. "I must admit I'm a bit anxious about heading to sea, the events of last summer are lodged so deeply in my subconscious mind. However I must not dwell on them. Let's get on with it! I know that all the fear and doubt dissolve once you get underway. The ship is certainly ready."

He closed with a familiar admonition for Jennifer, who would also be crossing the Atlantic: "Sail safe, sail smart."

CHAPTER 10

March 1986
Malaga, Spain

White tablecloths and dozens of bottles of wine awaited the twelve members of the *Pride* crew as they gathered for a farewell dinner a couple of days before leaving. The meal, at a seaside restaurant, was a thank-you from the ship's provisioning agent; Chez, in particular, was pleased to eat someone else's cooking—marinated octopus, paella, fresh pike, and roasted pig meat. The wine and beer flowed "in torrents," Armin noted approvingly, and the new sailors got their first taste of the hospitality that earlier *Pride* crews had routinely received over the years.

Over the next two days, Chez finished his provisioning. Concerned about running out of food at sea, he bought huge amounts and ended up stuffing supplies anywhere they would fit; kilograms of cheap beef and chicken in the freezer, canned goods and flour in the shower, crackers and drink mix in other corners of the head.

As for his own things, Chez found room for bottles of extra-virgin Spanish olive oil he had bought for his mother, and he made special preparations for his most prized purchase, tying the Moroccan jalaba to the survival suit stored in his bunk. If the *Pride* went down, he figured, he'd put on the survival suit and make it home with at least one souvenir.

For the veterans, there was the familiar excitement about getting back on the water. The newcomers to *Pride* were feeling jittery after doing chores on the boat for a week. "The night before departure. We are all anxious and apprehensive . . . ," Scott Jeffrey wrote in the crew log. "None of us . . . deckhands that is . . . have ever worked together. I'm sure the same thoughts are passing through all of our minds . . . What will it be like out there? How will the ship fare? How will I fare? In the end, I'm sure, all will be fine. And we as a crew will make a toast, at journey's end, to each other's friendship and seamanship."

Barry Duckworth, who had tried so long to land a spot on the boat, also wondered about the crew, writing: "For years I have been hearing about *Pride*. Well let's see *Pride* do its thing and see if we are up to it."

Around 10:15 P.M. on March 11, a month late, a truck delivered the last essential items: a new, sparkling white jib and the patched-up foresail. The next afternoon, Chez loaded fresh produce on board and the *Pride* was finally ready to leave. All twelve crew members assembled on deck in bright warm weather, while the ship's cats, Bill and Tuck, snuggled in Barry's bunk. Under Sugar's supervision, the crew cast off the ship's dock lines, which had grown stiff from being tied in place since the *Pride* came out of dry dock a month earlier.

Armin ordered the engine turned on and he slowly eased the schooner through the Malaga harbor and out into the Alboran Sea toward Morocco. The faint wind provided ideal, low-stress conditions for Sugar and the other veterans to instruct (or at least remind) the six new deckhands, the cook, and engineer on schooner sail handling.

For veterans and newcomers, there was a moment of pure joy as the mainsail rose above the boom, caught the wind, and billowed full. Behind the boat, the Malaga harbor's cranes and ships slowly disappeared from view. The crew set three more sails in succession and tacked the boat south and west. The sailing was splendid and Armin admired the Spanish mountains off to the right, standing, he decided, in "grand, hazy profile." When it was time for Chez to take the helm, Armin kept it simple: "Just keep the wind in the sails." When Scott took his first turn handling the great schooner, he had one thought: *This is pretty cool.*

By dinner time, the breeze filled in from the west, something the local forecaster had not foreseen and a development that quickly complicated Armin's plans. Before long, the west wind picked up to a healthy thirty knots; the newcomers to the crew discovered just how rough it could be fighting through the weather on the *Pride.*

The ride grew more exciting after the sun set at about 6:30. A tiny sliver of moon provided little light and disappeared not long after sunset. In the pitch darkness, the crew could hear the *Pride*'s bow crashing into waves and the water washing down the deck. It was thrilling, even a bit unsettling, and utterly unproductive. After hours of beating into the weather, the *Pride* was no closer to Gibraltar.

What did we do to deserve this? Pounding to weather already? Armin asked himself. He had the option of doing more tacking to make progress upwind, but with boats clogging the Strait, tacking in the dark with a new crew would be foolhardy. Armin opted instead to park the ship's nose directly into the wind and wait out the conditions. Coming square on the bow, the wind and waves shoved the boat up and down relentlessly. Chez got seasick; others weren't doing much better. When a squall line hit before dawn the next morning, conditions on board grew miserable and Armin gave up. The crew turned the ship around and the *Pride* limped back to the Malaga harbor it had left seventeen hours before.

After a day spent checking both the boat and the weather forecasts, Armin ordered the *Pride* to set out the following morning, chalking up the first day's fiasco to practice. This time, the wind died down and the boat motored across a flat sea heading once again for Gibraltar. An easterly breeze, perfect for leaving the Mediterranean, picked up and Armin set sails and maneuvered the boat into a fast-flowing current. A fleet of ships, both large and small, made their way through the passageway between Europe and Africa. Pushed by sea and wind, the *Pride* shot out through the Strait and into the Atlantic, a canopy of stars overhead.

*   *   *

Malaga sits only about four degrees south of Baltimore in latitude; the most direct course home would send the *Pride* almost due west. But such a heading would also take the sailboat straight into the prevailing eastbound winds that sweep north along the coast of North America and east across the ocean to France and Spain.

Instead, Armin made the obvious call, choosing a southerly route that would take the ship past Gibraltar and down the African coast to the Portuguese islands of Madeira, almost due west of Casablanca. From there, the *Pride* would head even farther south and west, almost directly toward Caracas, Venezuela. On that heading, the ship would next make landfall 2,800 nautical miles away on the island of Barbados, about 275 miles off the South American coast. The *Pride* would then make her way through the U.S. Virgin Islands before the northwest run up to the Chesapeake Bay, a passage the ship had made many times before. The route to Barbados promised a comfortable sail in trade winds blowing reliably westward. Columbus made a similar crossing five hundred years earlier and explorers, cargo haulers, and slavers had followed the route ever since. Heading south added hundreds of miles to the trip, but was far safer and easier than attempting a westbound trek across the North Atlantic.

Because of the last-minute change of plans, the *Pride*, for the first time in years, had no fixed schedule. There would be no official functions and no big hurry to get anywhere until June, when the ship was to take part in ceremonies in Virginia. The key goal was to get to Baltimore in time for Welcome Home festivities and then on to New York by July Fourth.

The first night out from Malaga, Armin left standing orders for the watch officer to consult him whenever a ship came within two miles. In charge of the early-morning watch, Leslie found herself bothering Armin almost constantly, given the amount of boat traffic around Gibraltar.

"Armin, you're going to be up all night," Leslie told him.

"It doesn't matter," he said. He wanted to know anything that was going on with his ship.

The mid-March weather off Africa was still nippy and the heavy ocean swells made for slow going toward Madeira. With each roll, the *Pride*'s mainsail and foretopsail fell slack. At best, the ship managed to make four knots—an uncomfortable four knots because of the constant rolling.

Taking care of one early chore, the crew rigged safety lines a foot or so above the cap rail around the deck. After the Baltic, Armin was determined that his crew would wear their safety harnesses more often on deck. The weblike harnesses fit around a sailor's torso. From the chest, a five-foot tether led to a clip, which could be attached to something secure, usually one of the safety lines. It would be almost impossible for a crew member to be washed off the boat while clipped in.

At the dock, the crew had worked mainly during the day, with plenty of time at night to explore Malaga. At sea, of course, a few people had to be working at all times. Before leaving, Armin and Sugar decided to use a system of three watches for sailing the boat. Armin was excused, although he was on call around the clock; Chez, with plenty to do in the galley, was also left out of the watch rotation.

Trying to balance strength and experience, Sugar was assigned Danny Krachuk and Scott Jeffrey. Joe, the second mate, was assigned Nina Schack, Susan Huesman, and Robert Foster. And Leslie, the bosun, oversaw Vinny and Barry. But after Vinny strained his back lifting something in Malaga, Nina was moved to Leslie's watch to compensate for his reduced physical strength.

In the old days, a Baltimore clipper would have carried dozens of sailors—more than enough to handle quick sail changes. The huge crews were also ready if and when the clipper seized a cargo ship. Once the ship was seized, the clipper would leave some of its crew on board to sail the prize home. On the *Pride,* with only twelve sailors—ten if you didn't count the captain and cook—keeping things running was a logistical challenge. Armin used a rotating schedule of two six-hour shifts during the day, one starting at six a.m. local time, the other at noon, and three four-hour shifts through the night beginning at six p.m., ten p.m., and two a.m. Having three watches move through five shifts in a twenty-four-hour period meant each watch got a twelve-hour break every third day.

The most trying aspect of the schedule, of course, was lack of sleep. The crew learned to doze off in short snatches, often at odd times. Complicating the problem, sleep patterns changed constantly as the three watches rotated through the twenty-four-hour schedule; for example, a watch would work one night from ten p.m. until two a.m. But the next night, it would work from two a.m. to six a.m. and so on. It took getting used to, but Scott decided he liked the rotating shifts. Over any three-day period, each sailor had the chance to sail the boat at all times of the day or night, experiencing sunrises, sunsets, and everything in between.

The members of the on-duty watch took turns at the helm and relied on a large compass in front of the tiller to keep the boat on a course Armin had set using the charts in the aft cabin. While the officer in charge of the watch usually took at least one turn at the helm, the others handled most of the steering. When not at the tiller, watch members took care of chores, pumped water from the bilges, and made an hourly check around the boat, noting the condition of the engines, checking for fires in the galley or other major problems, and observing the level of water in the bilges. Every hour, a crew member was supposed to record a variety of information in the ship's log in the aft cabin—wind, sea, air pressure, and cloud cover—as well as the speed and heading of the boat and the distance covered since the previous notation. To chart the wind conditions, the crew used the Beaufort scale, developed in the early 1800s by Sir Francis Beaufort, a British admiral. Under the scale, winds ranged from Force 1, or dead calm, to Force 12, a hurricane.

One day early on, Robert was ordered up into the rigging to help with the topsail as the *Pride* motored along. He climbed steadily up the black rope ladder leading to the top of the foremast but stopped once he was some fifty feet up into the rigging. Looking down, he watched in amazement as the *Pride*'s deck rolled back and forth in a pendulum motion, buffeted by wind and waves. The mast itself swayed out over the water dramatically each time the ship pivoted.

The sight was overwhelming and Robert froze. He considered climbing right back down to the deck, but thought better of it and held on for a while longer. Chez, who had also climbed up, noticed that Robert was not moving.

"Hey, you're going to be cooking if you don't watch out," he shouted gleefully. Moments later, Robert shook off the willies and got back to work.

The twenty-three-year-old had been sailing since he was a little kid. Growing up in the Virginia suburbs of Washington, D.C., Robert spent eight summers at a sailing camp on the Chesapeake Bay, learning how to handle everything from a Sunfish to a twenty-four-foot sloop. It was a relatively safe place to learn to sail, although storms had blown his boats around the bay enough for him to appreciate the ocean's power.

Motorboating on the Chesapeake one day, Robert witnessed the splendid sight of the *Pride of Baltimore* sailing, the first time he had seen her. A member of the crew asked to come aboard his small boat for a while to take pictures of the *Pride* from afar, and the encounter with the schooner stuck with him for years.

As a teenager, Robert saved money to buy not a car but a small catamaran, and later an International 505, a speedy racing dinghy sailed by a two-person crew. When college approached, Robert was determined to have a career at sea but couldn't figure out how to do that on sailboats. So he did the next best thing and enrolled at the U.S. Merchant Marine Academy in Kings Point, New York. Much of his four years of college were spent on the water, including an around-the-world trip on a cargo ship his junior year.

At graduation, Robert secured a job on a Mobil tanker working on the West Coast. Before heading out, he looked into sailing with the *Pride* at some point. He interviewed with Armin, who was noncommittal, and Robert spent the second half of 1985 on the tanker. As the end of the year—and the end of his tanker job—approached, Foster sent regular updates to Armin, and finally got a call in December offering him a spot for the European tour.

It hadn't taken long to figure out that sailing a topsail schooner was nothing like lumbering along on an oil tanker. There were no crusty old sea salts on the *Pride*; the crew, except for Armin, was thirty or under. There was, however, plenty of old-fashioned sail handling, which meant tugging repeatedly on stiff, thick lines that would rub un-calloused hands raw in no time. Robert took a good bit of ribbing because he alone had broken out leather sailing gloves, but he was glad he did.

On board, there was group camaraderie, a schedule of activities, and plenty of projects to be done. It was, Robert decided, much like summer camp.

The camp director, of course, was Armin, who was in charge of everything and kept an eye on all of it. Working with Sugar and the other mates, Armin watched weather reports and the ship's course, and directed the sail handling. He also assigned himself the some-times exasperating chore of communicating with people on shore. On the way to Madeira, he tried to check in with the *Pride* office in Baltimore every day. To call, Armin had to use the *Pride*'s single sideband radio, which was installed above the toilet in the aft head, to reach a maritime operator on the East Coast. The operator would then patch the call through via telephone line, at least in theory. Depending on the volume of maritime radio traffic and the atmos-pheric conditions, placing such a call could be a tedious process.

Pride captains had been radioing home for years and had devel-oped certain tricks to avoid running up huge bills for maritime calls. In one favorite dodge, the captain would reach a maritime op-erator and ask to place a person-to-person call to a fictitious person in the *Pride* office, a "John Smith," for example. When the operator patched it through to the office, the person answering the phone would not accept the call, but would understand the pre-arranged message: the *Pride* was safe.

In the name of publicity, Armin was also obligated to check in occasionally with the Voice of America and a Baltimore radio sta-tion tracking the *Pride*'s homeward journey. Finally, Armin tried every day to raise Jennifer on *Te Vega*, which was still in port in Sardinia. That, too, was frustrating. Sometimes there was no con-tact at all; other days, Armin could hear Jennifer but she couldn't make out his words.

* * *

By the third day at sea, the winds picked up and the *Pride* began to average eight knots of speed—a healthy, mast-groaning clip. The newcomers to *Pride* reveled in the sailing, which was sweet relief after many more hours of grinding rolls through the waves.

Whatever the conditions, water often sloshed around on deck, so much so that a slippery green growth appeared near mid-ship. The wet conditions often forced the crew to batten down some of the passageways leading below deck, making the cabins even danker. In sum, the *Pride* was a cramped, wet boat.

It was also a high-maintenance wooden structure, the first of its kind launched in a century and a half, meaning there were plenty of flaws. Blocks snapped, spars cracked, and all its parts demanded attention. "We gaze about constantly wondering 'what will break next,' " Armin wrote.

Some of the ship's flaws—the "Flexible Flyer" effect, for example—were more troubling than others. As first constructed, the ship's deck boards were laid so that two sets of pine boards met end-to-end partway up the deck. The arrangement of the boards was a disaster. With the boat working in the waves, the ends of the boards ground and pushed against each other. In steep waves, the boards moved in opposite directions, creating a disconcerting hinge effect that the crew could see and feel through their feet. Eventually, the deck boards were re-laid to remove the joint.

Melbourne Smith had made many substantive changes to his original creation and many more were made in later years to strengthen the ship's structural integrity. Most notably, several hanging "knees," L-shaped steel braces, were added under the deck. They weren't authentic, but they surely made the boat stronger.

Over the years, though, leaks were hard to plug and remained one of the most annoying problems. Early on in the *Pride*'s life, leaks were so commonplace that the crew slept with plastic sheets taped in place over their bunks. By the time the boat headed toward Madeira, the plastic wasn't necessary; the leaks continued, however, including a particularly annoying one in the captain's bunk. "We've stopped the torrents by caulking here and there. But the leaks persist," Armin noted.

While Melville marveled at how quietly a ship's sails do their work, the *Pride* could be a very noisy vessel. As the ship made its way down along the African coast, Barry Duckworth pulled out a brass oil can and worked relentlessly to lubricate a spot where the ship's enormous main mast was noisily rubbing against a wooden beam. One day, after squirting and squirting, Barry looked up and smiled, waiting for Chez to finally notice that the annoying squeak had ceased.

One night, Scott lay awake in the dark listening to all her creaks and groans, trying to count the different sounds. First, of course, he could hear the distinct burbling noise made by the *Pride*'s hull as it pushed through the water. Then, with the *Pride* doing a brisk nine knots, the ocean was regularly breaking over the rail and crashing down onto the deck, a steady refrain just a few feet above his head. The enormous masts strained in the wind, and he heard them grinding against the ship.

In the cabin, the frames of the ten bunks rubbed and groaned against each other with each wave. The ship's food, wedged in every cubby and corner, slid into bulkheads, while pots and pans hanging on the galley wall clanged against each other in nautical rhythm. That said nothing about the engine, the "iron topsail," which filled the cabin with a dull roar when it ran. "Whoever said life at sea was quiet must have sailed rubber ducks in the bathtub," Scott scribbled one night.

Aside from the noise, the *Pride* was also cramped, and the tight sleeping quarters discombobulated more than a few of its crew. Joe woke up once sure that he'd been buried alive; the same thing happened with Robert.

Oh my God! Am I in a coffin? he asked himself after waking in a panic. Hardest hit was Dan Krachuk, the youngest crew member, who twice awakened the rest of the ship with his shrieking nightmares. Leslie gave her slightly roomier bunk to Danny, which seemed to help.

Short and muscular, the twenty-two-year-old Danny had glasses and a head full of curly hair. Some of the crew found him to be insecure, a lost puppy, but Armin considered him eager to learn, and Sugar liked working with a kid so intent on establishing a career as a sailor.

Danny grew up in the Philadelphia suburb of Springfield, Pennsylvania, and studied mechanical drafting in high school. Within days of graduating, he was working on the *Young America*, a nineteenth-century brigantine based in Atlantic City, New Jersey, which took tourists sick of losing money in the casinos out on two-and-a-half-hour sails. In a sign of his devotion to the maritime life, he later worked as a "ship's visitor" for a seaman's church, helping inbound sailors take care of needs, both material and spiritual. He went on to work on the restoration of the *Gazela Primiero*, a nineteenth-century three-masted barkentine that sat at the dock in Philadelphia.

He got a taste of real sailing during eight months on the *Romance*, a ninety-foot brigantine constructed in the 1930s that had been used in the movie *Hawaii*. Danny was part of the crew as the boat went from the Caribbean up to Quebec. On the way back to Martinique in the fall of 1984 *Romance* got pounded by Hurricane Klaus southeast of Bermuda. Danny and the rest of the crew hunkered down for some seventy-two gut-wrenching hours as the ship turned into the approaching winds and rode out the storm. Some on board the *Pride* figured that brush with disaster may have had something to do with Danny's nightmares.

Sunday March 16 dawned hazy and damp. The *Pride*'s deck and cabin floor were covered in dew. Later in the day, Armin suspended the rule against drinking on board and ordered up a rum "swizzle" to mark the *Pride*'s crossing into a new time zone and picking up an extra hour. Drugs and drinking on the boat were generally forbidden; on shore, *Pride* sailors drank with abandon and some managed to smoke dope or ingest stronger drugs. Even the ban on drinking while sailing was not always obeyed. In 1983, when Armin guided the boat under the Golden Gate Bridge with seven sails flying, the crew, led by the bearded *Pride* veteran Leroy Surosky, surprised him by popping open celebratory cans of National Bohemian beer, cases of which had been donated to the ship by a Baltimore brewery. Armin just grinned and sailed on.

Heading to Madeira, the crew feasted on rum punch and popcorn, and placed one dollar bets predicting the date and time the *Pride* would arrive. Armin didn't wager since he could, in theory, rig the outcome with his orders. That night, the *Pride* made one hundred miles in just twelve hours—a healthy pace.

In the quiet times, the crew slowly got to know each other. Sugar and Leslie, of course, were a couple. Joe grew friendly with some of the guys and had nice chats with Armin, whom he had known for years. But he mostly kept to himself, still smarting from the breakup with a woman back home. He was also disappointed that there wasn't another sailing rogue like himself on board—someone who had worked his way up the *Pride* ladder, through the "hawse pipe," in sailing lingo.

Besides Leslie, the other two women on board, Nina and Susie, latched onto each other and became confidantes. It also began to dawn on the others that Nina was gravitating toward Vinny, who had been so impressed with the dark-haired beauties of Malaga. With her dark brown hair and bright eyes, Nina had caught his attention the minute she came on board. Likewise, she was drawn to Vinny, who was handsome, tall, and broad-shouldered. There was just enough physical similarity that they could have passed for brother and sister. But they were not an obvious match. At twenty-two, Nina was four years younger and more than a foot shorter. She was still in college, while Vinny had been out on his own for years. She was attending an Ivy League school; he had finished a commercial fishing program. While she bubbled over with girlish enthusiasm, he was laconic. She liked to wear pretty clothes; he was rarely without his dark jeans and blue cap pulled down over his dark hair. Unlike the others, who generally favored sneakers or sea boots, Vinny tended to wear tan construction boots, or thigh-high fishing boots, a habit formed during his fishing days.

Being paired on the same watch, thanks to Vinny's bad back, gave them plenty of time to talk as the boat sailed across the ocean. It didn't take long for the two to discover many things they had in common. They each had a parent who spoke Italian, and in the traditional Italian manner, they both called their grandmothers "Nonna." Nina's real name was Jeanette Francesca; Vinny had a cousin named Francesca. And both their fathers were architects.

By the time the boat was under sail, the two were already paying special attention to each other. Armin, a good observer who had witnessed many shipboard romances, was one of the first to notice. "As you predicted, Vinnie and Nina seem to be cooing to each other," Armin wrote Jennifer, who knew both of them. Later, he added, "Sweet, innocent Nina has flipped for . . . you guessed it, Vinnie, and he for her, and that is a little tiresome. The first stages of a romance played out on board—isolation, distraction, the search (futile) for privacy . . . you know. Oh well."

Of course, Armin and Jennifer knew firsthand the difficulties of pursuing a romance on the *Pride*, as they had done just that during their 1982 trip to California. There was so little privacy. In many cases, the best place to get away and talk alone was on deck. For the truly determined, there was also the storage area forward of the main cabin. It was a cluttered compartment filled with sails and other gear, but it didn't get much traffic. The crew called it the Honeymoon Suite.

The crew barely noticed as St. Patrick's Day came and went, the big news being the huge squid that plopped on deck and confounded the ship's cats. Late the next night, as cumulus clouds skittered across a quarter moon, the crew spotted the sparkling lights and six thousand-foot-high peaks of Madeira. A northerly breeze pushed the *Pride* easily over the flat water on the south side of the island for a smooth arrival. By four a.m., the boat was anchored in the harbor at Funchal after five days of sailing.

"When the sailing is good and you arrive at a place like this, what could be better?" Armin asked Joe once they were settled in. After a day cleaning the boat, the crew began exploring the island, the largest in the archipelago belonging to Portugal. Vinny and Nina, along with Robert and Scott, set off to see *Tightrope*, a Clint Eastwood movie, and had beers afterward in one of Madeira's many bars. They found some of Madeira's dramatic cliffs and Robert took a quick plunge into a beautiful but frigid stream. Joe hitchhiked around and met up with a local family, who fed him in their small farmhouse. Armin also explored alone, admiring the terraced gardens and breathtaking views of a place the Romans had reached centuries before and named the Purple Islands.

"What a destination this is! Bright green mountains covered with flowers and a profusion of produce, including, of course, grapes," he wrote to his parents in Massachusetts.

The trip from Malaga was nothing more than a delivery job, so there had been no farewell splash in Spain and no welcoming party in Madeira. Typically, the schooner's arrival was choreographed carefully to ensure maximum fanfare. Small dinghies and cigarette boats cruised alongside and a photograph of the boat was almost sure to grace the front page of the local paper the next day. Once in town, the *Pride* often served as the setting for a string of dockside wine-and-cheese parties. Corporations with ties to Baltimore used the deck to schmooze potential clients, and experience showed that a reception on the *Pride* guaranteed a far bigger turnout than one in a stuffy hotel meeting room. After all, it wasn't every day that executives could come aboard an old-time clipper.

But this time, the *Pride* slipped into Madeira unannounced and this crew, unlike others before it, had yet to get dressed up. The pinstriped shirts and khakis that were to have been put to repeated use during the goodwill tour of the Mediterranean were stowed. Nobody on the crew, particularly Armin, missed the on-board functions. *How many sausages can you eat?* he once groused to a reporter in California when asked about all the shipboard receptions.

The *Pride* almost always won rave reviews everywhere it visited, but generating goodwill for its beleaguered home port was a different matter. In May 1979, for instance, the *Pride* docked in Brooklyn for a party put on by Baltimore's Mechanic Theater to generate interest in bringing touring shows from New York. "The Shuberts don't have a boat. The Nederlanders don't have a boat. We have a boat. So we thought, why not use it?" the Mechanic Theater director told a reporter. Actors Lynn Redgrave and Eli Wallach were recruited to attend the glitzy event and a big sign out front read, "Baltimore wants you." One gray-haired woman, however, took a look at the sign as she walked onto the boat and sniffed, "But who wants Baltimore?"

Indeed, there was a chasm between the romantic image the boat projected and the reality of life in Baltimore, which was setting ugly records for drug addiction and homicides. The *Pride* epitomized the city's zest for affluent escapism; it wasn't lost on some of Baltimore's black leaders that this goodwill ship, representing a city with a majority black population, routinely sailed with an all-white crew, most of whom hailed from out of town.

There was only one quasi-official obligation in Madeira, a dinner appearance by Armin with the American consular representative and his unnerving wife. She was, in Armin's words, "a socially aggressive Dame somewhat past her prime," whose heavy British accent sounded affected and who was, no doubt, taken with the polished American captain sitting next to her. Adding to the discomfort was the fat, drunken Portuguese businessman sitting across from Armin, who reminded everybody, "I am an important person" and occasionally broke into Beatles songs.

The food, at least, was good.

CHAPTER 11

March 1986
On the Atlantic

After a week in Madeira, the *Pride* began its Atlantic crossing on March 27; a twenty-eight-hundred-mile passage that would take at least two weeks and be the ship's longest ever, easily surpassing the previous year's trip from Bermuda to the Azores. The skies were overcast and Armin imagined the sea surges were due to horrendous storms wracking Great Britain and northern Europe.

"And so, without the usual fanfare, we slipped out of the harbor—twelve brave souls in a small but well-found ship—heading out into the vast lonely wastes of the sea," Armin wrote, bundled up against the March chill in a wool cap and several layers of clothes. Before leaving, Armin called Gail Shawe in Baltimore to discuss the difficulty he was having trying to reach her every day on the radio. The two agreed that he would give up the daily attempts and check in every three days.

As the ship pushed farther south in search of the trade winds, the weather continued to be gray and cool. After a time, the sun began to peek through the overcast sky more often, and one day, dolphins appeared for a morning frolic off the bow, a good omen. Finally, on April Fools' Day, the *Pride* seemed to cross an invisible barrier. While the air was still cool, the clouds changed from a depressing gray to pure white cotton, and the water suddenly turned translucent blue. Flying fish landed on the deck so often that the crew rarely had to feed Tuck and Bill, who waited patiently for the next serving to appear. The ship cruised effortlessly in the trade winds and Armin couldn't remember better sailing on the *Pride*—ever.

"The jib boom points skyward and our ship rushes ahead throwing spray and foam then settles back into the deep with a thunderous roar. The Power! The Energy! The giddy feeling of soaring through liquid blue space . . . ," Armin wrote one evening.

For long stretches, the big ship handled like a big wooden surfboard, gliding down wave after wave. In sailing talk, the trip toward Barbados was all downhill and Armin almost had to invent reasons to worry. Every so often, he had the crew jibe the boat—turn to a new tack with the wind at the stern. But, he complained at one point: *We haven't tacked in days.* How would the crew get any practice tacking before joining in July's tall ship parade in New York? While the consistent east wind made tacking unnecessary, Armin had the crew set and strike various sails each day—like raising and lowering the blinds, he said. Setting the sails was a methodical process with several crew members assigned to various lines. It took several minutes and almost the entire crew to set the mainsail, for example, and the method was about the same as on the original Baltimore clippers. It worked best if the haulers developed a rhythm, so the crew often fell into a chant of "Two, Six," followed by a yank. "Two-Six-uunhh! Two-Six-uunhh!" The big guys—Sugar and Vinny—could be counted on to muscle a sail taut. When it was fully set, one of the mates barked out, "Make that," and at the end of the line, a crew member quickly hitched the line around a cleat, shouting "all fast," when it was done. Armin or another officer made sure each sail was trimmed appropriately for the wind conditions.

Typically, the ship moved west under no fewer than seven sails: the main, fore, stay, and jib, as well as three topsails. Given the relatively light trade winds coming from the east, Armin was grateful to have the topsails, despite any lingering worries that the extra rigging up top made the boat excessively unstable. In particular, the ship's rectangular sails—the foretopsail and the topgallant—helped power the boat effectively with the wind coming off the stern, since they hung squarely over the middle of the boat. Sailing without them, and only with sails hanging to the side of the two masts, would have required the *Pride* to do more zig-zagging to stay on the wind as it headed west. "An effective downwind rig is crucial, i.e. squaresails," Armin wrote Jennifer.

Some of the topsails required the crew to scamper up into the rigging. The high-flying topgallant and the sixteen-foot-long wooden yard from which it hung had to be hoisted up by rope from the deck and lashed to the foremast nearly seventy-five feet above the deck each time it was used. Before it could be struck, someone went back up, furled the sail, and prepared the yard and sail to be lowered to the deck once again. Mounting the larger foretopsail, which flew just below the topgallant, required at least two sailors to climb fifty feet to the topmast and slide out on the eight-inch-thick yard to release gaskets securing the stowed sail. Sugar and other veterans did it without a second thought, but others had to warm up to the climbs. Scott's first ascent at night to stow one of the sails was nerve-racking as the mast rolled in great arcs while the white-capped Atlantic surged dizzyingly below. It was hard enough in reasonably pleasant conditions, but his mind thought back to the nineteenth-century sailors who made such climbs in bare feet in freezing weather, furling a sail only after shaking the ice free.

"Concentration was absolute," he wrote later. "It went smoothly and I have no fears of going aloft . . . at least not in the conditions I've experienced so far."

Some days, the crew mounted rarely used, smaller sails: a ringtail near the stern and stunsails stretched out from the ship's foretop yard. Once the sails were up in the morning, though, there was often little reason to mess with them as the day progressed.

The billowing expanses of white made for an impressive sight— for the crew at least, since there was rarely any other vessel around. Several people brought cameras aboard and tried to capture the *Pride*'s beauty. Barry volunteered to be the ship's unofficial video cameraman, a job that required him to lug around the heavy camera and a recorder strapped on his back.

Compact and wiry, the twenty-nine-year-old Barry seemed to

have the soul of an old salt transported from the early nineteenth century. With a red beard and bandanna atop a thinning hairline he certainly looked the part. Barry grew up outside Washington, D.C., where his father introduced him to sailing. It was true love. His interest grew even stronger when he was a teenager and moved in with his mother and her new husband, Bob Jewett, who bought Barry a small wooden sailboat. Barry painted it red and yellow and named it *Ishtar*.

After school, Barry would bike four miles to a marina and take *Ishtar* out on the Potomac River, wearing long jeans and ankle-high flight boots; he never wore a life preserver. It was an odd choice for someone who had an aversion to the water and could barely swim. But Barry hated the idea of sailing with a life preserver and refused; his mother reluctantly gave in. During those years, Barry and some friends also designed and built a ten-ton staysail schooner out of cement, a project unusual enough to get written up in the local newspaper.

After high school, Barry found work on a Connecticut-based schooner named *Defiance*, eventually becoming its captain. He crewed on yacht deliveries along the East Coast and went to work on the *Gazela* in Philadelphia, picking up valuable sailing and carpentry experience and getting to know Danny Krachuk. In 1985, after years of trying, he was finally offered the position of deckhand/carpenter on the *Pride*.

In February 1986, with nothing to do before meeting the *Pride* the next month, Barry flew out to Seattle to visit someone he considered a younger brother, or at least a stepbrother—another free spirit who had renamed himself Moss Willow. Moss was the son of the woman whom Bob Jewett married after Barry's mother died. The two had bonded in Jewett's well-blended family. In Seattle, they took a drive west, out to the tiny town of La Push, and explored the rocky beach on a cold, cloudy day. Barry talked about his upcoming voyage on the *Pride* and the sheer enormity of the undertaking.

"Just think," he told Moss, "you're a little speck on this vast plain of water; this immense amount of air above you and this immense amount of water below you on this thin strip of wood."

Like the rest of the family, Moss knew Barry was scared of the water. "What happens if the boat sinks?" Moss asked him. "I'll deal with it," Barry replied in a resigned voice.

After a few days in Seattle, the two took a road trip down the coast to Oakland, California, with a couple of Moss's friends to catch a couple of Grateful Dead concerts. Moss was a hardcore Deadhead; Barry liked the partying as much as the music. After the first concert, the group spent the night in the Volkswagen van they were driving. The next day, Barry set out to get his first tattoo—a must, he figured, for any sailor making a trip across the Atlantic. In the makeshift community set up by the Deadheads in the parking lot of the Kaiser Auditorium, he found a heavyset guy sporting a beard, wearing a tie-dye shirt and leather vest, and doing cheap tattoos. Barry, or "Ducky" as his family often called him, picked a shooting star an inch or two long, inked on the outside of his arm. He was pleased with the final result. That night, the friends took in a second concert, which concluded with a version of Bob Dylan's "It's All Over Now, Baby Blue."

The next day, Barry headed back East to stay with his step-parents at their log cabin home outside the small town of George-town, Delaware. Barry, nearing the age of thirty, was unmarried and far from settled, having lived mainly in communal homes when he wasn't sailing. In the late winter of 1986, though, he was thoroughly excited about his future. His goal was to become a tall-ship captain, and Barry figured the *Pride* gig was a key stepping-stone for his career. "I'm really only happy when I'm sailing," he told Jewett.

But he had no illusions about the *Pride*, and neither did Jewett. Barry had built boats and both he and Jewett had done plenty of sailing. They knew that the *Pride*, with its lack of watertight bulkheads and extreme rig, was vulnerable. "What are you going to do if you have a bad storm?" Jewett asked his stepson one day as they worked together on a wiring project. "Oh, well," Barry responded, his hands held out in a shrug.

While killing time in Delaware, Barry worked on a project he had carefully planned—a meditation hut in a secluded spot in the woods a short walk from the house. Barry designed a small triangular structure suspended above the ground and poured three concrete pilings, using a twenty-gallon drum as a mold. Eventually he

planned to put down a wood floor and use dried bamboo to make
screens to create privacy. By early March, the meditation hut was
barely started, but Barry was due in Spain.

The crew celebrated Easter at sea on March 30. The three women
created a hard-boiled-egg likeness for each of the twelve crew
members. Leslie took extra time making the one for her sweet-
heart, Sugar, using sawdust to create his brown beard and hair.
Barry's egg came with a reddish paper beard and a bandanna. Nina's
came with cats, a testament to her tendency to yank Tuck and Bill
by their tails from her bunk because of her allergies. Chez cooked
up a semi-traditional dinner of ham and sweet potatoes and the
crew wolfed down chocolates and jelly beans.

With the *Pride* cruising effortlessly westward in the trade winds,
the crew fell into an almost hypnotic rhythm. There was no television, radio, or video player on board, but there were plenty of books
and the weather was good for hanging out on deck to read, write
letters, or daydream. In his log Armin noted, approvingly, that the
crew had not fallen into the bad habit of sleeping away downtime.

Small things such as one of Leslie's carrot cakes broke the monotony. When Chez baked his first batch of bread, he was proud
enough to bring the dark brown loaves up on deck to be pho-
tographed. The crew grew more familiar with each other and could
often communicate in shorthand only the twelve of them fully understood. There was plenty of teasing and silliness. Some of the
crew took to using old mustard crocks as their all-purpose drinking
vessels. Admiring them, Scott put his dibs on the next one that got
used up. Chez and others conspired to secretly keep refilling the
open mustard crock. Scott never got his crock and never caught on
to the trick.

Joe gave the men haircuts, and with the weather so warm, the
crew took saltwater showers every few days using the ship's fire
hose. The ocean-water shower left a coating of salt—on top of the
briny buildup that was unavoidable after several days at sea—but at
least they smelled better. In spare moments, crew members were
required to make an old nautical standby called "baggy wrinkle," by

weaving together strands of fiber taken from old ropes. Once enough fibers were braided together, the result was a piece of soft padding that resembled a long mop head; this could be placed on rigging to ease the chafing against the sails, a problem that had plagued the *Pride* since its launching. The chafing was so bad on the trip over to Europe the previous year that the crew had wrapped old pieces of cloth throughout the rigging to stop the rubbing. It looked like hillbillies had taken over the boat and the crew had to climb up and take all the rags down before arriving in Ireland.

Several members of the crew also passed the time learning celestial navigation. There were at least five sextants on board, and on some days, five people would be taking sun shots, using the instrument to determine the sun's angle from the horizon. Armin had taught the quickly disappearing skill and was considered an expert, and Robert knew enough from his years at Kings Point to help others. The *Pride* was equipped with a satellite navigation device to provide accurate latitude and longitude information, but using the sun and stars as a backup seemed like the right thing to do on a historic throwback like the *Pride*.

Armin spent time in his cabin working on his novel or jotting down log entries that meditated on life at sea. The crew learned that he could be prickly when it came to running a ship, a prototypical Yankee stiff. He was, at heart, an elitist who figured he was smarter than most of the people around him, and often let them know it. But in more relaxed moments, he was a patient teacher and an affable leader who stood with a loose-shouldered slouch that made him seem approachable. He pitched in with the dishes once in a while, and enjoyed the silly banter the crew lapsed into.

A keen observer of the people around him, Armin tried to master the native Baltimore accent, a kind of tight-lipped, Philadelphia-meets-Cockney drawl. And under the right circumstances, he would imitate "Bitsy," a downtown streetwalker who often visited the *Pride* when it was docked at the harbor—a riff that usually generated hysterics. One of his earlier crews had felt comfortable enough teasing him that they defaced a Crew Only sign that Armin had carved, adding the warning, Keep Out Assholes. Chez also used an exaggerated nasal inflection to imitate Armin's repeated attempts to reach Jennifer on the radio: *"Pride of Baltimore, Pride of Baltimore, Pride of Baltimore.* Come in *Te Vega, Te Vega, Te Vega."*

All the same, it was clear that Armin was *not* really one of the guys. He was the captain, or as some of the crew called him, "the old man." As for the old man, the easy weather and glorious sailing did wonders for his outlook, which had been contemplative, if not gloomy, in Spain. Discussions about his uncertain future or his concerns about the *Pride's* stability were on hold. "Right now, I wouldn't want to be anyplace else. Period!!," he wrote in early April.

The favorite topic on the trip, by far, was the sea—old stories or legends, or books about the sea. Armin talked about Conrad's novels and several on board were reading sea stories. "Why do these ships captivate us so much?" Armin asked one night, sparking a long back-and-forth about the sailor's life.

Later he quizzed Scott, who had the only master's degree in the bunch, about why the ocean water color had changed from sapphire blue to a deep black-green as the ship came closer to the Caribbean. Scott wasn't sure but made a note to look it up later. At the age of twenty-six, Scott had modest sailing experience but was energetic and eager to prove himself. Like Vinny, he received his first real taste of sailing at the Hurricane Island Outward Bound program in Maine. Both attended the school in the summer of 1977, although they didn't cross paths. Scott went on to earn a degree in geography at a Maryland college and then ventured down South for a master's from Louisiana State University, in geography. His thesis analyzed how storms—including hurricanes—contribute to the rapid loss of coastline in Louisiana. Looking for work after graduate school, Scott contacted the Sea Education Association, which operated the *Westward* out of Woods Hole, Massachusetts. He figured his knowledge of oceanography might be a good fit but nothing came of it. Out of the blue, after weeks of waiting, Scott got a call from Cape Cod.

"Can you be in Miami tomorrow?" An assistant scientist had broken an ankle and had to be replaced immediately.

Scott drove through the night and slept in his car on a Miami dock near the 125-foot schooner. He spent several months on *Westward*, instructing undergraduates in basic oceanography and weather topics, and helping with the sail handling. Scott's time on *Westward* ended that fall, but after two lengthy sailing trips he was hooked, not with the science but with the sailing. He had joined the great schooner sailing network and he applied for a spot on the *Pride*'s European trip. Armin, who had spent many months as a mate on *Westward* years earlier, interviewed Scott and decided that as a Baltimorean with some sailing experience, he was a good fit.

Scott was thrilled. If he was going to get into a real professional sailing career, what better place than the *Pride*? On *Westward*, sailors talked about the *Pride* with a bit of awe. The ship's captains, Armin and Jan Miles, and veteran mates such as Sugar Flanagan were well-known and respected. They were, in Scott's mind, sailing legends.

By April 3, the eighth day out from Madeira, the crew prepared for a second swizzle. Susan and Leslie mixed together mashed bananas, pineapple juice, coconut, and a liter of rum, and put the whole concoction in the freezer overnight. The next day, the sun broke through the clouds just in time for a late-afternoon party as the boat crossed into a new time zone and everyone set their watches back an hour. While the crew drank the punch and munched on ship-made pretzels, Nina read about Barbados from *World Book* encyclopedia entries she had copied at home. Bob Marley's reggae blasted from the boom box.

The good vibrations faded that evening with Danny at the tiller. Sailing *Pride* could be a tricky affair, requiring the helmsman to work with a long rosewood tiller and not a more manageable wheel typical of modern sailboats. In many conditions the *Pride*'s hull design caused the ship to turn into the wind, requiring constant attention at the helm. Early on in the *Pride*'s life it had taken two sailors to handle the tiller in rough conditions, but a block-and-tackle assembly had been added, allowing one person to maintain control. Physical strength was less important than concentration and a perceptive feel for how the seas and wind affected the boat. Nina, the smallest of the *Pride* sailors, was among the best helmsmen, able to keep the *Pride* consistently within five degrees of its course.

That evening at around eight, Danny had the helm as his watch mates, Scott and Sugar, inspected a creaking noise coming out of the main boom several yards forward. Sugar, who had sailed thousands of miles on the *Pride* and was in tune with the slightest change in her handling, suddenly felt the sails collapse, a sign that the boat was turning dramatically. He knew instantly what was happening.

"Watch out for the jibe," Sugar shouted as he tore back to the helm.

As he moved aft, Sugar watched as Danny, in a moment of confusion, move the tiller to starboard, exactly the wrong move. Sugar ran to the tiller and shoved it back to port as far as it would go, but it was too late. The ninety-foot vessel turned sharply onto a new course. The fifty-foot-long boom sped across the deck's center line and picked up the wind once again, completing an unplanned jibe. A preventer pin designed to keep the main boom in place snapped under the pressure of the wind, and the foretopsail collapsed.

The jibe startled Armin awake and he climbed quickly through the aft companionway. He called for a second watch to come up on deck, and the crew brought the ship under control. An unplanned jibe can be disastrous for a sailboat; in the worst case it can lead to the collapse of the heavy top rig. In this case the damage was minor. Even so, it took a good hour to fix the sails and "chafe-proof" the lines. Armin chewed out Danny, calling the jibe unacceptable, and Danny berated himself even further for the mistake.

"You better be mad at yourself," Sugar added later. The three-man watch continued until ten p.m. and was cloaked in tension.

A day or two later Danny was again at the helm when Sugar and Armin, below in the aft cabin, felt the ship's pace slow considerably, a sometimes ominous sign that the helmsman has taken the boat off course. The two officers sprinted up the ladder to the deck. "Danny, what's going on?" they shouted. "I'm not doing anything,"

Danny said defensively and the two officers realized the *Pride* had simply run into a patch of sea with little wind. Sheepishly, they returned below.

In the succeeding days, the crew's patience with sailing and each other grew increasingly thin. The ship seemed smaller, and the lack of privacy became more oppressive. All in all, everyone on board was getting tired of being with the same group for so long. On an early-morning climb up the rigging to retie some lines—a tedious chore made harder by a lack of sleep—Scott and Danny muttered a string of expletives about Sugar and the other watch officers. Robert wished he could just go to his own room and shut the door on his eleven new playmates.

The change of attitude was not unexpected. A trip to sea could often be divided roughly into thirds: The first part was one of anticipation and routine-building; the second, and the most enjoyable, part was one of predictable cruising; the third was the hardest part, as sailing became nothing more than a chore and the crew, like horses racing back to the barn, eagerly awaited the time when they would get off the stinking ship.

But the tension on the *Pride* disappeared in a heartbeat on the afternoon of April 12, when the crew spotted a green dot in the distance: Barbados. Actually, they could smell land—an acrid odor that wafted out over the sea—before they saw it. Everyone was ready for a change. "It will be such a pleasure to stop rolling for the first time in sixteen days," Armin wrote a few hours before making land. About the *Pride*: "She's tired now and needs a rest—so do we."

By nightfall, the *Pride* was anchored in the New World, in Bridgetown harbor, and disco music could be heard wafting out from shore. Armin and his crew had covered the 2,875 miles from Madeira in only sixteen days—an average of 180 miles a day—spotting just three boats along the way. Thanks to the steady trade winds, the *Pride* had used its engine for only eighteen hours. It had been a spectacular crossing.

As eager as each of the twelve had been to sail away from the dock in Madeira thousands of miles ago, each was even happier to be back in port.

Armin was exhilarated—and relieved. "We've made it," he scribbled on a postcard to his parents, which he dropped in a box in Bridgetown. He sent a similar note to Tom Gillmer, the architect of the *Pride*. The hard part, he figured, was over.

When writing Jennifer, he couldn't resist the urge to crow a bit at the naysayers who had scoffed at the notion of sending the *Pride* across an ocean and back.

"Well, we did it," he wrote, the *Pride* safely anchored in Barbados. "What all the skeptics and dockside admirals said couldn't be done. All the smooth-water schooner boys and schooner know-it-alls laughed at *Pride* to Europe and back. Look at that ship with a little reverence next time, boys!"

The *Pride of Baltimore* turned heads wherever it sailed. Here, it moves quickly with the wind in San Francisco Bay in May 1983. (By Greg Pease)

Melbourne Smith, a sailor, boat-builder, and dreamer, had the vision for the *Pride of Baltimore* and oversaw its construction. (Courtesy Melbourne Smith)

The big schooner takes shape in downtown Baltimore in the summer of 1976. (Courtesy Lew Beck)

Woodworker Andy Davis works on the *Pride* in February 1977. He was later sharply critical of the quality of the boat's construction. (By Andrew Keen; courtesy the Hearst Corp.)

Pride designer Thomas Gillmer (*left*) confers at the tiller with Fred Hecklinger, who helped build the boat. (Courtesy the Hearst Corp.)

Melbourne Smith, builder and captain, salutes the crowd as the *Pride* leaves on its maiden voyage, May 1, 1977. The ship had to stop and be re-rigged before it could leave Chesapeake Bay. (Courtesy the Hearst Corp.)

A Coast Guard cutter tows the *Pride* to harbor in April 1979, after the boat almost sank in the Delaware Bay following a harrowing blowout to sea. (By Paul T. Whyte; courtesy the Hearst Corp.)

Sugar Flanagan working high in the rig on the *Pride* in November 1982 in Jamaica. (By Greg Pease)

Armin Elsaesser (*center*) and some of his crew have a meal in the *Pride's* cramped galley in August 1983 in San Francisco.
(By Greg Pease)

Crew members rely on strong backs and arms to raise the *Pride's* anchor in May 1984. Rob Whalen (*with mustache*) was on the boat a year later during near-knockdown in the Baltic Sea.
(By Joseph Kohl; courtesy the Hearst Corp.)

Scott "Scooter" Gifford climbs down the *Pride's* rigging in San Francisco in 1983.
(By Greg Pease)

Jennifer Lamb and Armin Elsaesser in Maine. The couple struggled to cement their future together. (Courtesy Jennifer Lamb Bolster)

The view from the bow of the *Pride*. The "widow strainer" safety net was added after the boat was launched. (Courtesy Jennifer Lamb Bolster)

The *Pride*, shown crossing the Atlantic for Europe, was often a wet boat. (By Jan Miles)

Vinny Lazzaro wanted to give sailing a try after years of commercial fishing.
(Courtesy Victor and Maria Lazzaro)

Nina Schack learned the basics of sailing on her uncle's boat in Hawaii. (Courtesy Roma Foti)

Nina Schack with her cousin, Jim Foti, in January 1986, two months before joining the *Pride* crew.
(Courtesy Roma Foti)

Scott Jeffrey during the *Pride* stop in Madeira in 1986. (Courtesy Scott Jeffrey)

Leslie McNish, Nina Schack, and Robert Foster *(left to right)* in Madeira. (Courtesy Scott Jeffrey)

Nina Schack, Susie Huesman, and Leslie McNish—the three women on the *Pride's* Atlantic crossing in 1986. (Courtesy Scott Jeffrey)

Barry Duckworth tried for years to land a job on the *Pride*. (Courtesy Robert Jewett)

Armin Elsaesser steers the "wild black mare" during the 1986 Atlantic crossing. (Photo by a *Pride* crewmember; courtesy Ford Elsaesser)

Joe McGeady works with some *Pride* lines in the Caribbean in 1986. (Courtesy Scott Jeffrey)

Joe McGeady gives James Chesney a haircut during the *Pride's* Atlantic crossing. (Courtesy Scott Jeffrey)

James Chesney takes a turn at the tiller while wearing the jalaba he purchased in Morocco. (Courtesy Scott Jeffrey)

Vinny Lazzaro, wearing his usual long pants and work boots, handles the tiller during the 1986 Atlantic crossing. (Courtesy Scott Jeffrey)

The *Pride* with all sails flying in the Virgin Islands, May 1986.
(Courtesy Scott Jeffrey)

Sugar Flanagan inches out on the main boom while sailing in the Virgin Islands, May 1986. (Courtesy Scott Jeffrey)

Scott Jeffrey, still wearing a jumpsuit from the Toro Horten, at the welcome home press conference for the eight survivors, May 21, 1986. (By Barbara Haddock; courtesy *Baltimore Sun*)

Dan Krachuk, without his glasses, which were lost at sea, at the press conference. (By Barbara Haddock, courtesy *Baltimore Sun*)

Leslie McNish fell in love with Sugar Flanagan on the *Pride*. (By Barbara Haddock, courtesy *Baltimore Sun*)

From left: A shaken Gail Shawe, executive director of Pride of Baltimore Inc., Sugar Flanagan, and Captain Jan Miles at press conference in Baltimore May 21, 1986. (By Joseph Kohl; courtesy the Hearst Corp.)

The eight *Pride of Baltimore* survivors (*from left:* Chez, Danny, Scott, Susie, Leslie, Sugar, Joe, Robert) at Sugar and Leslie's wedding in Somis, California, August 30, 1986. It was the last time all eight were together. (Courtesy Joe McGeady)

CHAPTER 12

April 1986
Barbados

After sixteen days at sea, the *Pride* crew all but exploded off the ship. Bodies flew into the blue-green water for an afternoon swim and before long several of the crew were downing beers in one of Bridgetown's many bars. That night, most ended up drinking in a brothel, where the beer was cheap and the madam offered a good exchange rate for the dollar. The music was so loud that some of the *Pride* crew broke off cigarette filters and stuffed them in their ears. The men had no problem finding someone to dance with, and Danny, the youngest of the bunch, made everyone laugh when he danced with the elderly madam.

Armin found a phone and called Gail back in Baltimore to let her know they had arrived and he talked with his sailing buddy, Jeff Bolster, who was getting married in Maine later in the summer. Armin teased his old friend about the move—maybe they wouldn't be growing old together at the retired mariners' home on Staten Island after all. From his end, Bolster, who had done plenty of sailing on schooners, could tell from Armin's confident, relaxed manner that the *Pride*'s trip across the Atlantic had been a good one.

Armin found little to like about Barbados. The stores and restaurants charged too much and he thought the black natives scarcely disguised their distaste for the white tourists. But as a student of the American slave trade, Armin saw the interaction between the races in a historical context. "It must take a great deal of forebearance to tolerate a race that has enslaved you and continues to do so in some not so very subtle ways," he wrote in his log.

The *Pride* and its crew were essentially killing time in the Caribbean. They would spend a month there—heading west to the tiny island of Bequia, then up through the U.S. Virgin Islands—before sailing north to Baltimore. The home office had put together a splashy June Fourteenth celebration for the *Pride*'s return to the Inner Harbor to commemorate the successful, if truncated, European voyage. From Baltimore, the *Pride* would go to New York, where she had been given a place of honor as the second boat in the procession, behind only the *Eagle*, the enormous Coast Guard training vessel.

Planning the month in the Caribbean, Armin was determined to use the time to let his crew really learn the schooner. The trip from Madeira had already given the *Pride*'s newcomers a taste of its joys and limitations. On the eve of his twenty-seventh birthday, Vinny called his parents in Connecticut to tell them about the trip across the Atlantic; as for the *Pride*, he said, it was nothing but "a floating museum."

Even as the *Pride* was reaching Barbados, Jennifer and the rest of the crew of *Te Vega*, including first mate Al Nejmeh, the former *Pride* sailor, scrambled to get out of Europe as quickly as possible. Another terrorist flare-up—this time the early-April bombing of the La Belle disco in Berlin—had re-stoked American-Libyan tensions. With a retaliatory military attack looming, the Massachusetts school that operated *Te Vega* decided the Mediterranean was no place for an American sailboat carrying thirty high school kids. A visit to the Spanish island of Menorca was cut short and a stop in the Atlantic port town of Agadir, Morocco, was canceled.

By April 15, the four-hundred-ton, steel-hulled schooner was heading west, only fifteen miles off the coast of Algeria, when the BBC brought news that American warplanes had bombed two Libyan cities, prompting anti-American demonstrations in parts of the Muslim world. The news spooked *Te Vega*'s crew, and Captain Gregg Swanzey put radio use on hold to avoid attracting attention. Swanzey also made a contingency plan to have one of the students on board, a Spanish speaker from Bolivia, handle the radio in case the boat was confronted; this would disguise the fact that the ship was carrying Americans. But *Te Vega* made it through the Strait of Gibraltar without incident and headed south toward the Canary Islands and the trade winds.

"Santa Claus!"

Sugar glanced up at the teenaged boy watching the *Pride* dock in Admiralty Bay, Bequia. With his bushy brown beard and broad shoulders, Sugar was a memorable figure. But this was rather amazing. In December 1981, the *Pride* had called on the same port in Bequia and Sugar had dressed as Santa Claus to hand out gifts from Baltimore as a goodwill gesture; he turned his hair gray with powder, wore sea boots over some red long johns, and borrowed a pair of granny glasses. The image of Santa arriving on a topsail schooner had left a vivid impression on the children who lived near the harbor. Now, on a warm April day four and a half years later, one of those children was hoping that Santa Claus had sailed back into town. But this time, Sugar had no presents and the *Pride* was merely the latest in a succession of big sailboats to pull into the Port Elizabeth harbor to fill up on water and fuel. As each arrived, little boys in small boats rowed out to greet the crew, offering their services and trying to sell limes and other local treats. Some of the boys would sing, usually quite badly, and the sailors would be compelled to pay them to shut up.

The *Pride*'s overnight sail from Barbados to Bequia had been a grueling one. In steep, confused seas, a topsail ripped, the rigging strained and groaned, and Armin had kept the whole crew working until almost midnight. In the morning, a torrential rain pelted the boat, which lumbered ahead under engine power alone. Patience wore thin and several of the crew were left muttering about their shipmates.

Once the boat reached the protected waters of Admiralty Bay, where a handful of other schooners were anchored, moods brightened. This was familiar ground for the *Pride*, which had often made winter stays in Bequia. The crew embarked on yet another round of maintenance and repairs, painting, tarring, and varnishing. But this was more of a nine-to-five routine, not the around-the-clock commitment required when the boat was sailing. There was plenty of time to explore, drink, or hang out on the white-sand beaches under sun shelters built from branches, palm fronds, and sheets. The other crew members took notice when Vinny and Nina walked down the beach together one afternoon and built their own palm hut.

Despite weeks at sea, some of the crew hadn't had quite enough of sailing. A couple of people purchased brightly painted, eighteen-inch wooden boats modeled on a Bequia design, and took turns pushing and blowing them around the placid waters off the beach. One evening, the crew decamped for a beach barbecue. Coconut trees provided the backdrop, and a pig tied to a rope that had somehow gotten tangled up in a tree provided some diversion. (The crew freed the pig.) Some locals showed up to cadge free food and play Frisbee with the white sailors. A tropical sunset was capped with the "green flash," the spark of green light jumping from the sun's upper edge as it hits the horizon. That night, many crew members took blankets up on deck and slept under a clear, starry sky until a rain shower sent them below around four a.m.

After ten days in Bequia, the *Pride* made its way up to the Virgin Islands, cruising most days and dropping anchor in a different spot each night. Armin was in heaven and shared the pleasure in a letter to Jennifer: "This slippery, sexy schooner is just great fun to sail (when the conditions are right)."

The conditions were indeed idyllic, but Leslie McNish wasn't particularly enjoying the stay in the Caribbean, due to a persistent stomach problem. She visited a local doctor who gave her medicine, but it remained so bad that she could barely eat when she and Sugar went out to dinner in late April to celebrate an important milestone—her thirtieth birthday. It was one of the few negatives during an otherwise splendid sailing adventure for the couple.

Leslie had begun sailing as a kid, taking lessons in Marina del Rey, California, and later joining anyone who had a boat. In college she was offered the chance to sail from Hawaii to Alaska on a forty-foot ketch with a family friend. It was a grueling but exciting trip with an unexpected benefit: Leslie, who suffered from bothersome allergies on land, could breathe freely in the middle of the ocean.

After finishing college at the University of California in Santa Barbara, where she got a degree in biochemistry and molecular biology, Leslie immediately returned to the sea as a deckhand on a new ninety-foot French schooner. She ended up going through the Panama Canal, across the Caribbean, and on to St. Tropéz, France— all while being paid fifty dollars a week. That experience opened doors to a series of jobs in some of the most beautiful places in the world. She crewed through the Mediterranean and taught sailing to Club Med members in Martinique. She later trekked down to New Zealand to do some boat building, before finding gigs that took her to Tahiti and Hawaii.

By the time she reached her mid-twenties, Leslie was a veteran ocean sailor; however, after years of working in Europe and the Pacific, she had yet to do much professional sailing in the United States. A photograph of and article about the *Pride* in a sailing magazine tweaked her interest. The idea of working on a historic vessel was appealing, as was the prospect of sailing with a crew of twelve instead of the smaller crews she was used to on modern yachts and schooners. As a non-drinker, she sometimes felt on the outside looking in on hard-partying crews. Plus, as a young woman in an industry dominated by men, there were always sexual issues to be navigated. With a bigger crew, she figured, she could just be one of the gang.

Leslie's application to sail on the *Pride* landed in front of Armin as he was planning the West Coast trip, and he hired her without an interview. Leslie not only had a Coast Guard license, she had plenty of knowledge about sailing in California. She was introduced to Sugar when she arrived in Baltimore a few months later and fell for his competent, unthreatening manner. Four years later, they remained a couple. As with Armin and Jennifer, their future together was hazy but only in its details. They were sure of two things: they would be together and they would be sailing.

In late April and early May, the *Pride* worked its way up to the Virgin Islands. The conditions were so perfect that Armin called for a photo shoot on May 6. The crew took the *Pride* out into the blue-green water of Drake's Channel in the British Virgin Islands and set a dozen sails. Crew members took turns getting into the ship's inflatable motorboat, with Vinny doing the driving, and cruised along snapping photographs of the impressive schooner; the lush green hillsides of the Caribbean served as a backdrop. The ship fairly glowed in the crystal clear light, sails puffed out proudly, pennants dancing in the breeze. The inflatable, with its outboard motor, had a hard time keeping up with the fast-moving schooner. It was a dreamy afternoon to be a sailor, but Barry, in particular, couldn't hide his delight in the *Pride*.

Later, Armin found a phone and called in a report to WFBR, the Baltimore radio station. "We have been doing some sail training here, practicing setting and striking all of the *Pride*'s *twelve* sails," he said in a deep steady voice, clearly proud of the intricate ship handling. "We also had one magnificent day for a photo session with all sails set. Now we are preparing and provisioning for our final leg to the Chesapeake Bay of about twelve hundred miles. We'll be home soon."

The final week in the Caribbean provided a chance for last-minute phone calls and letters. On May 8, Nina, who had turned twenty-three a week earlier, sat down in the tourist-clogged port town of Charlotte Amalie, in St. Thomas, to finish a letter to her mother. Roma Schack was planning to drive from Baltimore to Virginia to meet the *Pride* when it arrived in fifteen days and Nina asked her to bring more clothes—her pink sweater and something dressy to go out in. After two months on the *Pride*, Nina also gave her mother a rundown on the crew, each of whom got one sentence or less; there was one exception.

"Then the engineer, Vinny Lazzaro. I really like him," Nina

wrote. "He's twenty-seven and he's a fisherman. He's got blue eyes, dark hair, and [is] about six feet. Well, we will see what happens. He invited me to visit Connecticut. Maybe I will." It was unusual for Nina to share that kind of sentiment about a man with her mother. But the next comment was unheard of: *Vinny is a man I could marry.*

The next day, Nina found a phone and called Roma and the conversation soon turned to Vinny. He's so wonderful, so handsome, Nina cooed. Then, she whispered, "But I can't talk anymore; he's coming."

Despite his clear interest in Nina, Vinny was ready to get off the *Pride.* He was now in his fifth month on the ship, compared to two for Nina, and he had little stomach for the laid-back Caribbean atmosphere. *I'll be happy to be back in the North before I atrophy, too,* he wrote in a letter home. As for the sailing, it had been okay, he said, but nothing compared to what he got on a windy day on Penobscot Bay in Maine. There was no mention of the cute woman he had met on the boat.

As the May 11 departure approached, Armin took care of his last chores. He finished up his trip log: "What lies ahead is unknown— a source of mystery and apprehension—perhaps the allure of the sailing life—always moving, always changing, always wondering what the next passage will be like and what we will discover at the other end," he wrote. "This time our destination is home—the Chesapeake Bay and Baltimore. It is always a relief for the captain, and I suspect, the ship, to have our lines ashore and fast where *Pride* is safest—the finger pier at the Inner Harbor."

Armin assembled the trans-Atlantic logs he and Scott had kept, Barry's videotapes, and some film the crew had shot and mailed the package to Baltimore; the office staff was eager for promotional material to be used for the homecoming.

Armin, the prolific correspondent wrote to Jennifer, who was by then, somewhere on the east side of the Atlantic. He figured she would get mail whenever *Te Vega* got back to the United States. He also did something unusual: he mailed a postcard to Liza, his exwife up in Massachusetts, letting her know the boat's schedule. While the postcard was odd enough, Liza was also struck by the postmark—St. John, the place where she and Armin had spent their honeymoon nineteen years earlier.

Finally, Armin reached Gail by phone to discuss the trip. One detail to nail down was how often he would call on the way home. On the eastbound Atlantic crossing, Jan Miles had resorted to calling in the middle of the night, when radio traffic was lighter. Coming west across the Atlantic, Armin had attempted to reach the *Pride* office by radio at least every three days, but even that had proved to be a problem. This time, Armin and Gail agreed there was no real need to talk regularly. It was mid-May, well before hurricane season, and the trip north was one the *Pride* had made many times before. For the first time in recent memory, the ship would have no pre-arranged communication schedule and Armin would call only if there was a problem. Barring that, he would check in when the *Pride* was nearing the coast of Virginia.

By departure time, an unfortunate incident had been all but forgotten. It began on a Virgin Island beach on a splendid afternoon a few days earlier, as Armin skillfully maneuvered *Irie*, the wooden sailing skiff he had built years before. Armin marveled at the way the skiff handled; she was scooting along so nimbly she seemed alive, he thought.

From the beach, Scott admired the captain and his small but elegant sailboat, with its low freeboard and high-peaked gaff rig. Later, Scott got his own chance to sail *Irie*. The evening was warm and Scott was thrilled to be on the water alone—in control after weeks of taking orders. Sailing no more than three hundred yards from the anchored *Pride*, Scott was gliding along in a gusty wind. In the dark, he attempted a jibe to come off a broad reach. The small sailboat changed course, but Scott mistakenly held the sail too tight. The wind overwhelmed the small boat and, as if in slow motion, *Irie* simply blew over.

Scott plunged into the water and clung to *Irie*, which had completely flipped. Mortified, he had no choice but to shout for help. "Ahoy, *Pride of Baltimore!*" Others heard the cry and three people set out in the inflatable dinghy to tow the flooded sailboat back, where it was bailed and brought on deck. Scott went below, changed into some dry clothes, and went back to talk to Armin, who was clearly annoyed. Scott knew he could only blame himself for failing to ease out the sail when the wind threatened to knock over *Irie*. Other crew members talked with him about it; the embarrassment eventually faded.

I practiced good seamanship, Scott decided, *but just got overwhelmed by circumstances.*

CHAPTER 13

May 11, 1986
St. John, U.S. Virgin Islands

After a rainy night, the *Pride of Baltimore* motored out of the St. John harbor at 10:30 on an overcast Sunday morning. The crew had disposed of the garbage, lashed the anchors, and stowed the canvas awning that had provided some protection from the sun and rain while the ship was anchored. The day before, the ship had stopped at a marina in the picturesque port of Charlotte Amalie, on the nearby island of St. Thomas. They topped off the two large diesel containers lashed on deck, as well as all of the water containers—some on deck, some stowed below. It had been exactly a month since the *Pride* had arrived in the Western Hemisphere and it was time to go home.

Over the last few days, the *Pride* crew had done little but practice sailing—an almost unheard-of luxury for a ship used to scurrying to make scheduled appearances. The practice had been valuable; Sugar thought that after a good two months of sailing the crew was starting to click. He and Armin also shuffled the watch assignments to give everyone a chance to work with different watch mates during the trip home.

As the boat motored out to sea, Armin reminded everyone that they were in a busy shipping lane and to stay alert for other vessels.

The course for Norfolk and the Chesapeake Bay was close to zero degrees, almost a straight line to magnetic north, or about ten degrees west of the physical North Pole. It would take roughly twelve days to cover the twelve hundred miles; of course, this depended on the weather.

Thick clouds covered most of the sky, but the northern horizon looked to be clearing, an encouraging sign. Armin had the engine turned off and three sails—the mainsail, the staysail, and the rectangular foretopsail—set; once again, the *Pride* was sailing. By evening, though, the winds vanished and the engine started. Through the night, the ship pushed ahead on diesel power.

The next day, a Monday, the wind remained a no-show. After hours of motoring, Armin decided to give everyone a chance to take a last swim in the warm Caribbean water. There were some solid swimmers on board. Nina had been a lifeguard in Baltimore and Susie had been the captain of the women's swim team at Bucknell. (She could also do an impressive one and a half dive off of the *Pride*'s bow.) Someone scampered up into the ship's rigging to keep an eye out for sharks and most of the crew piled into the sea. Barry, who couldn't swim, stayed on board. During shower time on deck, his shipmates had learned that he hated even having water poured on top of his head. While he would sometimes do a modified doggie paddle around the ship's ladder, he was definitely not a swimmer. Joe was the complete opposite; he loved the smooth water and swam far from the *Pride*, marveling at the big ship as he headed back.

After seventy days on the *Pride*, the newcomers to the crew had run into only a handful of problems; the rough first day coming out of Malaga, the unplanned jibe coming across the Atlantic, and a nasty squall or two in the Caribbean; none had been particularly serious. That was unusual for the *Pride*, which had come through many nerve-racking moments in nine years of sailing.

During its history, there had been injuries: at least one mangled finger, a broken back, sprained ankles, and the gashed face on the ship's first day out in 1977. But the real problems surfaced when the boat tried to cope with harsh weather. Anyone who spent more than a little while on the boat had a story.

For Leslie, the moment came in 1983 when the *Pride* was sailing near Costa Rica's Golfo de Papagayo, and she and a shipmate named Charter Kays climbed out on the bowsprit extending in front of the boat to secure a loose jib sheet.

The two hung on tight as the head rig was dunked under three consecutive waves in the stiff wind. The Pacific finally proved too strong on the last dunk and washed Leslie off the rig and sent her sprawling into the safety net below, with Charter falling on top of her. Both were fortunate the net was there, since Melbourne Smith had not put one on the boat when it was built, figuring the weight of the net would put too much drag on the bowsprit and jib boom in high seas.

Storms often disrupted the ship's plans. In October 1978 the *Pride* headed south for the winter and ran into all sorts of trouble. On the way down, the ship was blown out to Bermuda, hundreds of miles from its intended destination of Puerto Rico. Two months later, the boat was twelve days late reaching Santo Domingo, on the south side of the Dominican Republic. The *Pride* tried to run the gap between Haiti and Cuba but couldn't overcome the strong head winds. The ship tried but failed to go between the Dominican Republic and Puerto Rico, and was finally forced to pull into Mayaguez, on Puerto Rico's west coast, to wait for a break in the weather.

The boat ran into more trouble in the Caribbean the following November. Daniel Moreland, making his only trip as captain on the *Pride*, was sent south for the winter. With no firm itinerary, the trip to the islands was designed simply to keep the boat operating and the crew working. Sailing around the small island of Nevis one morning about two a.m., the *Pride* ran smack into "a black, black squall" with heavy rain and winds Moreland estimated at fifty to sixty knots. The *Pride* tipped sharply, approaching forty degrees, putting the cap rail in the sea and sending water rushing over the leeward deck.

Moreland had two options: round off and run with the wind or head up and beat into it. He decided to handle the big schooner like an oversized dinghy and headed up. He ordered the crew to

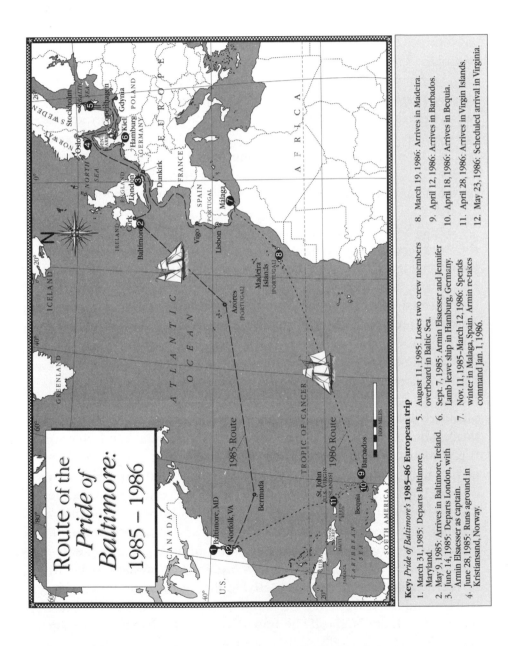

Route of the *Pride of Baltimore:* 1985–1986

Key: *Pride of Baltimore's* 1985–86 European trip

1. March 31, 1985: Departs Baltimore, Maryland.
2. May 9, 1985: Arrives in Baltimore, Ireland.
3. June 14, 1985: Departs London, with Armin Elsaesser as captain.
4. June 28, 1985: Runs aground in Kristiansand, Norway.
5. August 11, 1985: Loses two crew members overboard in Baltic Sea.
6. Sept. 7, 1985: Armin Elsaesser and Jennifer Lamb leave ship in Hamburg, Germany.
7. Nov. 11, 1985–March 12, 1986: Spends winter in Malaga, Spain. Armin re-takes command Jan. 1, 1986.
8. March 19, 1986: Arrives in Madeira.
9. April 12, 1986: Arrives in Barbados.
10. April 18, 1986: Arrives in Bequia.
11. April 28, 1986: Arrives in Virgin Islands.
12. May 23, 1986: Scheduled arrival in Virginia.

loosen the headsail and the *Pride* turned into the wind. The sails and rigging rattled and shook ferociously in the oncoming wind but nothing broke. The memory of that steep heel stayed with Moreland, who was still sailing more than two decades later. "I've been in similar vessels that I don't think would have leaned so far," Moreland said.

Armin's worst moment, at least before the Baltic, came during a stormy April night in 1981 on his first trip with the *Pride*. He had taken the *Pride* on a grueling voyage through the Caribbean, to Grenada and Venezuela, and back up through the Gulf of Mexico to Galveston and on to Louisiana. One anxiety-producing highlight came as the *Pride* motored 110 miles up the Mississippi River, dodging an astonishing number of boats all the way to the French Quarter.

Weeks later, on April 11, the *Pride* was making the turn around the southern tip of Florida, heading into the Atlantic, when the boat was hit by twelve-foot seas and a stiff wind gusting to forty knots. The size of the waves wasn't particularly troubling—the *Pride* had pushed through twenty-five-footers in the ocean on the trip south the previous fall—but they were pounding the *Pride*'s bow in rapid-fire sequence, too quick to allow the boat to fully recover before the next onslaught. The *Pride* surged along with almost the bare minimum of sails—a double-reefed mainsail and a triple-reefed foresail. About three a.m., the *Pride*'s jib boom once again plunged deep into an oncoming fifteen-foot wave. This time the lumber did not spring free. The weight of the sea cracked it in two, leaving a twenty-foot piece of wood dangling into the water and attached to the ship by a tangle of rope and wire. When the jib boom snapped, it led to a chain reaction high up, since it helped secure the foretopmast high above the deck. The foretopmast, a thirty-six-foot-long piece of wood nine inches thick, also snapped and fell backward. Snagged in the rigging, it hung ominously over the deck.

Looking into the dark sky, Armin ordered the crew to move aft on the deck in case the topmast fell. He then turned the ship northeast toward Key West, only ten miles away. Fortunately, the jib boom hung far enough off the bow that it wasn't banging into the ship's hull, a potentially dire situation that would have required crew members to venture out on the bowsprit in the storm and cut the whole mess free.

Despite the damage the ship was able to plunge ahead using only lower sails and soon limped into Key West. "Your first concern is the safety of the crew," Armin told a reporter when describing the incident. He added, "I don't want to go through that again." In a report to the home office, he later called the jib boom "so fragile and vulnerable" and suggested the boat carry a spare.

Jan Miles was the skipper two and a half years later when the *Pride* ran into a similar problem heading down the west coast of Central America. On an October afternoon, Miles was down below when he heard a bang and felt a jolt that was followed by a dire scream, "The jib boom broke!" This time, the wood snapped in two places, sending a chunk of the boom plunging into the Pacific Ocean. But Miles was more worried about the now-weakened top-mast. He had the crew move quickly to loosen the aft rigging before the topmast toppled backward onto the deck. Unlike the mishap off Florida, the *Pride* was sailing in moderate weather off of Central America, with seas of about four feet and winds of only twelve to eighteen knots. In that sense, it was more troubling as it was probably caused by a design flaw, poor wood quality, or some combination of both. "Thank the stars it did not break with five crew out there getting the jib in," Miles wrote that night in his log.

On the same trip out west, Miles was forced to call for Coast Guard help when the schooner sailed into disastrous conditions and nearly ran out of fuel heading up the California coast. Beating against what the crew called "a snotty nor'wester," the *Pride* took three tries to get out of the San Francisco area. Miles watched with dismay as the seas pushed the *Pride* up so high that the ship's propeller popped free of the water.

"You plunge down into the next trough and wonder if you're going to come out again," Miles recalled. In all, the *Pride* required eight days to cover the 280 miles to Eureka; by the end, the galley was down to rice and Spanish omelet mix. Things got so bad that Miles had to summon the Coast Guard to tow the *Pride* to the mouth of Humboldt Bay in northwest California. Near the bay, Miles once again turned on the engine and used the last of the fuel to allow the *Pride* at least the dignity of motoring in on its own.

Minor crew injuries, broken jib booms, and fuel emergencies were the kind of problems that happened quickly and could be more or less handled on board. By the time the public found out—and some of the incidents received little or no publicity—the drama was over. But in early April 1979, the *Pride* was the star of a highly public misadventure. It began when the boat left Wilmington, North Carolina, a day behind schedule, after waiting for a storm front to move through. Under the command of Charles Whitcomb, who had taken over only a few days earlier, the boat was due to reach Norfolk, Virginia, in three days following a trip around the tricky shoals off of Cape Hatteras.

The second day out, the wind filled in from the east, propelling the boat up the coast on a pleasant broad reach, with dolphins, flying fish, and at least one whale making appearances. The next day, a Saturday, the wind picked up significantly—reaching more than twenty-five knots—and the ship continued to make good time. Sunday brought a red sky in the morning, and this time, the "sailors take warning" adage proved on target. A storm with winds gusting to more than fifty knots blasted down from the north-northwest. Whitcomb struck all sails except for the tiny storm trysail as the wind pushed the *Pride* out to sea at a seven-knot clip. Waves reached thirty feet and pummeled the ship, one bearing down so hard it cracked the rowboat stored at the stern. It took two people to hold onto the *Pride*'s huge tiller, which was arcing dangerously back and forth, and the deck was often under a foot of green water. The crew had little choice but to ride out the miserable storm as the temperature dipped into the forties and salt water soaked everything on deck and below. Provisioned only for a short hop up the coast, the ship ran low on fresh water; by Sunday night, the only things left to eat were dehydrated instant mashed potatoes and condiments such as mustard, salt, and syrup.

The storm raged through Monday, pushing the *Pride* farther out to sea, but, fortunately, well north of the Hatteras shoals. Finally, after two days of nasty weather, the winds eased Tuesday afternoon and Whitcomb turned the boat westward toward New Jersey, the nearest landfall. The mood turned brighter, with even some singing and dancing on deck, and crew members aired out their soaked clothes and sleeping bags.

By then, the *Pride* had been at sea for a week and was four days late arriving in Norfolk. Equipped with only a VHF radio that could reach no more than fifty miles, the *Pride* had not made contact with anyone either on land or at sea in days. (It was discovered later that the ship's radio antenna had been damaged early on in the trip, making communication all but impossible.)

While the ship headed back toward land, *Pride* officials in Baltimore grew anxious and finally reported the overdue schooner to the Coast Guard, which dispatched two C-130 planes to search a two-hundred-mile stretch of the coast. Word of the hunt soon reached the media and the "missing" *Pride* became big news. The search grew to include a Coast Guard cutter and six planes searching some sixty-four thousand square miles of ocean—at a cost of thousands of dollars an hour. The Coast Guard instructed all ships in the general vicinity to keep an eye out for the distinctive topsail schooner.

Meanwhile, the *Pride* sailed obliviously back toward New Jersey. On Thursday, the ship had two unlikely visitors—a woodpecker and a sparrow. The birds landed on deck and promptly died, exhausted after being blown out to sea by the storm. In the cabin, food and water were running low, and the crew was forced to use old copies of the Tampa *Tribune* for toilet paper. On Friday, after crew members discovered and repaired the malfunctioning antenna, the *Pride*'s radio finally made contact with the Coast Guard station at Cape May, New Jersey. Only then did Whitcomb find out about the ruckus back home and he assured everyone the boat was fine.

But the ordeal wasn't finished. As the *Pride* motored into the Delaware Bay, another storm bore down. The ship had to fight stiff winds and waves that grew worse as the day wore on. That night, the wind continued to howl; it was so strong that it pushed the schooner out of the ship channel. Whitcomb dropped one of the *Pride*'s two anchors and revved the engine, but the wind proved too much and shoved the ship into shallow waters. About 10:30 P.M., the *Pride* banged into the Delaware shoals, about ten miles northwest of Cape May. The waves and wind repeatedly thumped the boat into the hard sand beneath the bay, jarring the hull and throwing crew members off their feet. A Coast Guard helicopter flew over and lowered an extra pump to help cope with the water flooding the ship, but for a tense few minutes it looked as though the *Pride* would sink in Delaware Bay. The crew prepared to abandon ship, but within an hour of the grounding, the wind shifted and pushed the *Pride* back into deeper water. Whitcomb was finally able to drop the *Pride*'s second, heavier, anchor and the ship spent the windy night secured in the channel. Conditions abated the next day and the *Pride* finally made it to a nearby dock—towed ignominiously by the Coast Guard cutter.

The exhausting trip gave the public its first glimpse of the ship's true vulnerability. The second-guessing of Whitcomb and the *Pride* soon followed. Melbourne Smith, the builder, told reporters that the ship was delicate and dangerous and should never have sailed around Cape Hatteras in the spring with its entire rig up. Tom Gillmer, the ship's designer, responded with a blast at Smith, his former partner. "It must be finally said that the *Pride* is not a 'dangerous' ship. What is dangerous? Crossing the street can be dangerous, but calling the *Pride* dangerous is to condemn all ships."

As the sun rose over the Atlantic on Tuesday, May 13, the *Pride* continued to motor along. The soothing trade winds that had pushed the boat so easily across the Atlantic were a distant memory, as were the pleasant tropical breezes the crew had enjoyed in the islands. The light winds were no surprise to Armin and Sugar, veterans of the trip to and from the Caribbean. But so much motoring was a bit of a concern, and the two men kicked around the possibility of a detour west for an unplanned pit stop to refuel in the tiny island of San Salvador in the Bahamas.

Armin worked the radio and made contact with a friend heading north on a yacht named *Kestrel*, about one hundred miles ahead of the *Pride* on the way back to the mainland United States. Aboard

Kestrel, the captain reported decent wind coming from the northeast, a good sign to Armin. By the afternoon, the *Pride* found enough wind that the crew was able to set the foresail. Armin changed plans and took a course of twenty degrees, slightly east of due north. That way, when the *Pride* reached the northeasterly winds, the ship could turn back to its planned course and sail more comfortably. By 7 P.M., as the sun was setting, the winds grew strong enough that Armin turned off the engine for the first time in two days. The crew was pleased to be rid of the drone.

With only ten days to go before reaching Virginia—and reunions with family and friends—the crew knew the ocean adventure would soon be coming to an end. Susie, in particular, had grown a bit wistful. Like Nina, she grew up in North Baltimore, and like Chez and Vinny, she had gone through the Outward Bound sailing school at Hurricane Island. She had done some sail training on a schooner during high school and had served for several weeks as a deckhand on the *Pride* after college. But those sailing experiences along the East Coast paled in comparison with the trip from Europe. This stint on the *Pride* could well be her last big sailing adventure before she settled into a more conventional career.

As the *Pride* headed north on May 13, the twenty-three-year-old deckhand talked with Armin about the trip. She told him she wasn't sure she had fully experienced ocean sailing. "Armin, you know I almost feel like I haven't done a transatlantic crossing. It was just too easy."

CHAPTER 14

May 13, 1986

Tuesday night, the *Pride* moved easily under four sails and trailed a foamy wake. The overcast sky shielded the stars; the new moon had already disappeared for the night. Armin kept a close eye as the wind climbed to at least twenty-five knots, or about thirty miles per hour. Just before midnight, he called for all hands. It was the first such call in the middle of the night since the *Pride* ran into the storm leaving Malaga two months earlier. Armin wanted to reduce the sail area for the rest of the night and ordered the crew to put a double reef in the mainsail, which involved lowering the top edge of the sail a couple of notches and tying off the excess. With Susie at the helm, the *Pride* eased westward from its intended course by twenty degrees to take pressure off the sail while the crew wrestled with it. The crew spent several minutes scrunching and tying and Sugar pronounced it a good reef. Armin excused everyone except Sugar and his eleven p.m. to three a.m. watch—Susie, Barry, and Nina. Armin also stayed on deck for a while, talking to Susie at the helm. As they chatted, a wave unexpectedly shot over the windward rail and hit the two of them square in the face—a wet, early-morning slap.

Just before three a.m., Leslie emerged to take command of the boat from her boyfriend. Robert and Scott came up the ladder from the main cabin a few minutes later. Both wore foul-weather gear and both slipped on safety harnesses, which they clipped into safety lines when venturing around the boat in the dark. Given the healthy wind and seas, Leslie opted to place watches on either side of the boat, rather than in the bow, which was the normal practice. Steering slightly west of due north, at 350 degrees, it took more than the usual effort to keep the *Pride* within five degrees of her course. Down below, Armin lay in his bunk and listened to the water wash over the deck, wondering if the boat still had too much sail up. Just then, Leslie popped down the aft ladder and found him awake. "We're shipping a lot of water; I thought you'd like to know," Leslie told him.

"Do you think we should shorten sail?"

"I don't think so," she said. "We'd just be stuck in the swell if we do."

Despite Leslie's reassurance, Armin eased out of bed and came up into the cool night air to check on things. He agreed that no sail changes were needed and advised Leslie to try to fall a bit more off the waves, to reduce the water coming on board.

As the early morning wore on, the wind eased a bit and the clouds broke. Robert looked up at the spring sky; Libra and Virgo were visible among the multitude of stars. As the shift wore on, the *Pride* took on more than the usual flow of seawater as it worked through the waves. As with any wooden vessel, water in the bilges was a constant headache for the *Pride*. While those on watch were normally supposed to pump out the bilges at least every hour, Leslie had her crew pumping every five minutes or so.

At five a.m., Chez rolled awake, slipped on his wire-frame glasses and a pair of shoes, and stepped into the dark *Pride* galley. With six of the crew in their bunks only a few steps from the kitchen, he worked quietly to make coffee, home fries, and scrambled eggs—enough to feed the crew beginning at 6:30.

Chez had been making breakfast on the *Pride* since before New Year's and the thrill of cooking three meals a day for eleven others had long since vanished. The ship's galley could be unbearably hot, and Chez wore only a T-shirt and a pair of gray gym shorts. Standing six feet tall, he barely fit in the galley and had learned to duck under the low-hanging deck beams as he moved around. When the boat heeled, as it usually did while underway, Chez could still use both hands for cooking by wedging the top of his head up under one of the beams.

Chez tended to complain and there was plenty to complain about; at the top of the list was the balky diesel stove that he had to lean down and reach behind to light. The galley had almost no countertop space to work on and only one small sink. All in all, though, the twenty-four-year-old was pleased to be at sea. It was a nice diversion from his life in New Hampshire building houses, sculpting, and taking some college classes.

A native of Brooklyn, New York, where his father taught economics and kept beehives on the roof of their building, Chez had done some sailing over the years, including a semester on the water through the SEA program at Woods Hole, Massachusetts. During that time aboard *Westward*, Chez watched with awe one day as the *Pride* pulled up to a dock in Bath, Maine. *Now that's a boat I'd like to sail on,* he decided.

But instead, Chez headed to the mountains to do some climbing, eventually scaling several challenging peaks in the Canadian Rockies. There were mountaintop moments that stayed with him, including the time he treaded along on a ridge no wider than his boot knowing that his life depended on the care he took with each step. One of his climbing friends was seriously injured in a mishap; other climbers he had heard of died on mountains. He eventually gave up the sport.

The trip across the Atlantic had fallen into his lap almost at the last minute, when a friend who had signed on to do the cooking opted out. She called Chez to see if he wanted to apply; he did. With experience cooking in restaurants in Wyoming and Maine, including Alice's Restaurant in Jackson Hole, Chez was offered the job. He eagerly accepted it, thinking he might find a way to sail around the world before heading back to carpentry work.

Unable to shop for days or weeks at a time, Chez could do only so much to vary his meals. He served countless pasta dishes and flank steak, as well as endless helpings of unpleasant tasting mystery meat from Spain that was made palatable only with heaping quantities of spices. He had also taken merciless teasing about the "chicken parts" he had somehow purchased in bulk in Malaga. Not much of a Spanish speaker, Chez had inadvertently instructed a butcher to sell him many kilos of *chopped* chicken parts instead of the usual cut-up chicken pieces. The chicken parts had indeed been chopped, and the pieces of bone and meat were diced so small that the crew could hardly tell which part of the chicken they might have evolved from.

"Don't worry about it," the deadpan Joe instructed the others. "Parts is parts."

The cook's job was surprisingly stressful, as food was a crucial element of a long cruise. Over the years on the *Pride,* a number of cooks had simply walked off the job when they got sick of the demands. One quit on Armin years earlier after the crew complained about all the corned beef and cabbage being served.

For his part, Chez had a disturbing dream in which he ran out of pasta while the *Pride* trudged along in the middle of the ocean. Armin occasionally added to the stress. There was the time in Malaga when the captain instructed the cook to have lunch ready at two p.m., following what was to be a busy morning of work. But the morning's work was finished more quickly than anyone had anticipated, and Armin called for lunch to be served earlier than planned. Chez reluctantly obliged, knowing that the soup wasn't ready. "The least you could do is *cook* the soup," Armin admonished him. Later, in the Caribbean, Chez had been flummoxed when Armin informed him that the pile of receipts he had brought back from food-shopping trips in Malaga, Madeira, and the islands was unacceptable and had to be reorganized and itemized before the ship arrived in Baltimore. Chez, who had an aversion to paperwork, was unsure about how he was going to accomplish this task.

Chez tolerated the cooking but lived for the sailing. Although it wasn't part of his job, he happily pitched in whenever he could. Fortunately, he had found the opportunity to do plenty of work on deck and had pulled enough rope to give his hands thick calluses; they were so thick that one day he picked up a hot skillet and barely felt the heat. Later, he was amazed to see that the heat had seared an imprint of the skillet handle in his leathery palm.

* * *

Shortly before six o'clock, the sun peeked over the eastern edge of the ocean as Chez worked in the galley. In the aft cabin, Sugar awoke to listen to the early weather forecast coming out of the Portsmouth, Virginia Coast Guard station: some low pressure in the general vicinity, but nothing to worry about.

By 6:30, breakfast was ready and some crew members emerged from their bunks. Danny grabbed a plate and sat down on one of the sea chests around the galley table. Joe rolled out of bed, noticed the main hatch was closed tight, and figured the weather had turned rougher since the sail handling at around midnight. He put on a garish, green and orange flannel L.L. Bean work shirt his mother had found for him at a Goodwill store in Baltimore and sat down with Danny. He doused his helping of hash browns with ketchup and dug in.

Up on deck, Scott was at the helm for the last few minutes of the four-hour watch. With easterly winds of more than twenty knots, the *Pride* was moving briskly and heeled noticeably to port. The waves came quickly, putting the *Pride* into a rolling pattern. Scott relied on the large, old-fashioned compass located directly in front of the tiller to maintain the course. About eight inches across, the brass compass had blue diamonds and triangles indicating the various compass points and a simple fleur-de-lis indicating due north. The compass sat in a varnished wood box attached to the aft cabin trunk, which rose about eighteen inches above the deck. Even so, the sea and air had given the compass's brass frame a rich, greenish patina.

The trick for the helmsman was to keep the *Pride* angled so that the stern absorbed most of the impact of the waves, not her sides. It wasn't easy. Despite Scott's best efforts, the *Pride* took a decent-size wave on the starboard quarter—the corner of the boat near the stern. A second wave came quickly after and dunked the starboard rail. Water rushed over the deck and sent a brief shower into the aft cabin through the open passageway.

Down below, Armin felt the roll and saw the water splash into the cabin; he quickly came up to see what had happened. The companionway opening was a little more than two feet square, and was offset to the boat's port side. The opening could be covered with a heavy, sliding hatch made of solid wood. There were also wooden slats that fit into a grooved channel at the rear of the hatch to keep water from slopping off the deck and down into the cabin. Irritated, Armin slipped two slats into the hatch and instructed Leslie to batten down the ship's other hatches before her watch came off duty.

Off-center hatches such as the one near the *Pride*'s tiller have typically been unwelcome on sailing vessels for a basic reason: when a ship gets pushed over, an offset opening is likely to flood more quickly than one on the center line. But in designing the *Pride*'s deck layout, Tom Gillmer located the hatch on the port side of the center line. That freed up space for the large compass to rest directly in front of the tiller area. During construction of the *Pride*, some of the workers in Melbourne Smith's crew spent considerable time figuring out how to build the aft hatch, among them Allen Rawl, a forty-one-year-old building contractor.

The hatch cover was a heavy piece of wood that had to fit snugly but still be able to slide open and shut. It also had to be sturdy enough so crew members could stand on it without causing damage. And since it was going to be varnished and not painted, Rawl couldn't use a carpenter's best friend, putty, to fill in any ugly gaps or holes. As Rawl finished work on the hatch, he, like others on the work crew, wondered about the wisdom of an off-set companionway. But as the ship took shape, he figured it was just one of those things that the ship's crew would have to be aware of.

With all hatches except the aft companionway battened tight, and the bilges pumped one last time, Leslie turned the boat over to Joe and his seven a.m. watch mates, Danny and Vinny. After being on deck for a busy four hours, Robert grabbed breakfast before heading to his bunk to read and sleep; the good news was his watch wouldn't be on duty for twelve hours.

Vinny wore an orange foul-weather top over blue pants and his usual choice of thigh-high boots. Danny had slipped on sea boots, and wore his foul-weather pants and jacket over a pair of long pants and a flannel shirt. He wore a belt with a knife around his waist. Joe also wore a knife and a marlin spike in a leather belt he had fashioned and sewn himself. Joe had blunted his knife's sharp tip, turning it into a combination screwdriver and scraper. He and Sugar had also devised lanyards that attached both the knife and marlin spike to their belts so they wouldn't turn into lethal weapons if dropped from the rigging.

A few minutes later, at around eight, Sugar rolled out of his bunk and ventured up the aft companionway to check the weather. The wind had increased and was blowing at a good twenty-five to twenty-eight knots. Sugar could see some squall lines on the horizon but nothing too threatening. With only a week or so before the *Pride* reached the East Coast, Sugar wanted to try to get some photographs of the ship with the new camera and zoom lens he bought in Europe. The conditions were perfect for some action shots, and he tried to capture an image of the spray blasting over the leeward rail as the *Pride* surged ahead.

Within an hour, Sugar had taken enough pictures and retired below. On deck, the crew watched a couple of squalls build and pass around the *Pride*.

About two hundred miles to the south that morning, a Coast Guard pilot, Lieutenant Steve Eddy, put on his flight suit and prepared to fly out of Puerto Rico.

Eddy would later recall seeing a profusion of waterspouts and squalls clinging to the water. He figured a shift in the jet stream a few days earlier was partly responsible for the odd conditions. It was, Eddy decided, the weirdest weather he had witnessed in two years of flying in the area.

CHAPTER 15

Susie woke up at around ten a.m. in a dank, stuffy cabin that had been all but sealed up for hours. After going off watch at three a.m., she had slept through breakfast but wanted to go up to get some air. Wearing a T-shirt and shorts, she made her way to the aft cabin and climbed up through the companionway. Susie often wore a bathing suit and shorts to sail, but today it was too cloudy and a T-shirt felt right. She figured she would hang out on deck for a while before lunch.

Chez appeared on deck at around the same time. Like Sugar, he wanted to take some pictures of the boat working through the foamy waves. He could see dark clouds off the stern to starboard, but otherwise, the weather looked fine. Down below, Armin was in the aft head using the sideband radio to talk to other boats in the area. The weather report, which had come in a little before six that morning, was mildly promising but hardly precise. South of thirty-degrees and east of seventy-degrees, the forecast called for easterly winds of up to twenty knots and seas reaching seven feet. Of course, that forecast covered an area of thousands of square miles, forcing Armin to try to reach other captains to see what was really happening more locally. In mid-May, the *Pride* was far from alone heading north from the Caribbean to the East Coast; several other sailboats had left the Virgin Islands at about the same time. The weather was finally warm enough for sailing up north, and hurricanes would not threaten the Atlantic until the summer. For the second day in a row, Armin reached an old friend on *Kestrel,* which was making better time than the *Pride* and was 150 miles ahead. *Kestrel* reported strong winds from the northeast but no sign of storms. After comparing notes, the two captains made plans to talk by radio again in six hours, at four p.m. Armin reached three other sailboats in the general vicinity; one was off Guadeloupe and two others were also heading back to the East Coast. None reported any problems.

On deck, Joe was in charge and kept an eye on the wind. If it started blowing any harder he knew the jib would have to come down, and he asked Vinny to get a line ready to tie up the sail. The conditions—winds of about twenty-five to thirty knots from somewhere between east and northeast—had held steady for a while. Waves were averaging six feet, as Danny stuck to a course of 350 degrees, slightly west of due north.

Finished with his radio calls at around 10:30, Armin climbed back on deck and took a look.

"Why didn't you tell me about this?" he demanded of Joe.

Curiously, it seemed that the wind had picked up almost the moment Armin set foot on deck. As captain, Armin was supposed to be kept informed of any significant change in the weather.

"It just happened," Joe told him and Armin let it pass.

But the captain had another concern. "Why aren't you using harnesses?" he asked. Joe was astonished. The conditions had seemed fine, with no need for harnesses.

But Armin persisted. "We had five people over the side of this boat. Put your harnesses on and use them."

Armin didn't have to explain what he meant by "five people over the side." Joe had left the *Pride* a few weeks before the Baltic, but he had, of course, heard about the saga of Sarah Fox. It was strange, Joe decided, that Armin had two major problems on the same trip. Besides the Baltic, he had also been in charge when the ship ran aground in Norway; this was something Joe *had* witnessed. To be sure, Jan Miles was the more aggressive captain but it was the far more cautious Armin who kept running into trouble. Something wasn't fair about that, Joe figured. While the harnesses seemed unnecessary, Joe and his men strapped them on and clipped in.

With Armin raising hell about the harnesses up on deck, Chez decided he had taken enough pictures and went below to make lunch. Susie also headed down and found Nina, who would be going on watch with her after lunch. The two women talked for a while and bantered with Chez while he worked. Susie begged him to make tomato soup for lunch. Fine, said Chez, who had grown tired of planning menus for every meal. It would be easy enough to peel some canned tomatoes and cook them.

On deck, Armin said little. He stood at the starboard rail for a long while studying the seas and the dark clouds off the quarter, the right rear of the boat. After eleven, Armin had seen enough and took over the helm from Danny.

Armin didn't like the amount of sail the boat had up but he waited for a while to take any down. If possible, he wanted to wait until closer to the one p.m. watch change. Such changeovers provided natural opportunities to handle sail, as at least two-thirds of the crew was already on deck and fewer sailors would have their routines disrupted.

By around 11:30, Armin decided to go ahead and reduce sail. He told Joe to bring up the standby watch—Sugar's four-person group. But a few minutes later, Armin amended his order, calling for all hands. There were two kinds of "all hands" calls: one was an immediate summons for emergency help; another was when there was time to spare. The latter was the case now. Vinny went below to rouse Sugar in the aft cabin and to tell the rest of his watch to get on deck with harnesses.

Sugar went up immediately and Armin, as Joe had figured, told the mates to strike the jib. Moments later, he changed his mind and instructed Sugar to prepare to double-reef the foresail instead; that is, take it down to about half its normal size.

The rest of the crew got ready quickly. Already awake, Susie and Nina slipped on their yellow foul-weather tops and boots. Nina also pulled a pair of yellow rain pants over her shorts and strapped on her folding knife. The two women headed up on deck.

Leslie stirred in her bunk with all the commotion. Wearing just underwear and a T-shirt, she grabbed her foul-weather gear, which she had shoved under her bunk earlier that morning, and slipped it on. When she couldn't find the smaller knife she usually wore in a sheath around her waist, she grabbed her larger rigging knife, shoved it in a pocket, slipped on a pair of tennis shoes, and headed aft to reach the deck. Robert, who was also asleep, heard the "all hands?" call and sat up. He, too, put on his weather gear and sea boots and made his way aft to the companionway, right behind Scott. Emerging up on deck, Robert was surprised the conditions had changed so much since he had climbed into his bunk only four and a half hours earlier. The boat was still clipping along nicely, but there were more clouds and the sea was rougher.

With the *Pride* heeled noticeably to port, most of the crew took positions to reef the foresail up toward the bow. At the tiller, Armin eased the boat to about three hundred degrees, to take pressure off the sail once the crew began taking the reef. Sugar instructed the crew to prepare the halyards and brails, a series of lines used to hoist and gather the sail. Crew members carefully laid them out on deck in figure-eight patterns, which would allow them to run free when the sail came down.

"Sugar, why is it taking so long? Get it down!" Armin shouted from the helm.

Even as the sail began to drop, Armin decided that double-reefing it would still leave too much sail up.

"Just strike it," he shouted. There were two options for striking the foresail. The crew would usually haul it back up and yank it tight to the foremast and the wooden gaff that angled aft. Instead, to save time, Armin said to drop it to the deck, the first time during the entire trip that the sail had been handled that way. The crew hauled it down quickly and left a huge pile of wet canvas covering mid-ship. They struggled to yank the heavy sail into a manageable roll and lashed it to the deck, next to *Irie*.

"Is that good enough, Sugar?" Robert asked.

"It's good enough for now. I just don't want it flogging around the decks catching water." They could neaten it up when things calmed down. With the foresail down, the boat was left with a double-reefed mainsail at the aft end and two sails at the bow, a staysail and a jib.

Armin's next order came quickly and was not a surprise.

"Sugar, get the jib down." This would be trickier as the jib flew out over the water between the jib boom and the foremast. A half-dozen crew members lined up at the bow to pull on the downhaul line. Barry alone handled the opposite line, the halyard, to make sure it didn't jam as the jib came down. The crew members pulled as one and the jib, newly made of a synthetic canvas earlier that year in Maine, collapsed to the boom while the waves lapped up eagerly from below.

It was imperative to tie up the triangular sail as quickly as possible because the waves were high enough that the jib boom was spearing the water. It would take four people to secure the sail; Sugar decided it was a job for the most experienced sailors. He, Leslie, and Joe ventured out on the bowsprit and boom, along with Vinny, the strongest of the others. The wind whipped the sail around and the four struggled to pull it down into a manageable pile. Robert hustled back to the helm to see if Armin had instructions.

"Tell them to hurry up. Clip in out there." Armin didn't like having four people out on the head rig in the rough conditions.

Sugar decided it would be dangerous to lash the jib to a boom already crashing through waves. He knew that the extra weight of the sail could snap the boom. Instead, Sugar decided to trice up the sail—tying it into a roll like a sausage—and yank it up, suspended from the foremast. The four sailors struggled to secure the line around the wet sail as the *Pride* bounced over the waves.

At the helm, Armin instructed Robert to ease out the mainsail by three or four feet to try to keep the bow out of the water. Even so, the four got soaked by the waves and spray, and water ran down into their boots. With the tricing under way, Leslie climbed off the boom and went aft to talk with Armin, who was not pleased that it was taking so long. He wanted the ship to be ready when the storm hit.

"Sugar, what's taking so long out there? Get off the head rig," Armin shouted. His voice had grown anxious, and for the first time all morning, Robert noticed things had gotten more serious than he realized. Again, Armin ordered the mainsail let out a little more. Finally the tricing was finished, and Sugar, Barry, and Dan hauled the tied-up sail above the boom and out of the reach of the ocean.

The three mates then gathered at the tiller with Armin to assess the situation. The east wind had climbed to a blustery thirty-five knots and threatened to build. The squall line hung ominously to the east. Tired from wrestling with the jib, Joe sat down near the helm. The boat was still sailing a good bit west of its intended course of roughly due north.

"Are the waves too high to return her to the original course?" Joe asked Armin.

He seemed to ignore the question, instead instructing Joe to tighten up the portside-running backstay, a part of the rigging that had loosened up while the foresail was coming down. Joe headed to the leeward side of the *Pride* to take care of it.

At about 11:45, Chez popped his head through the aft companionway and found Sugar.

"What time do you want lunch?"

"Another fifteen minutes," he answered and Chez headed back to the galley to keep an eye on the soup.

The boat was sailing along nicely, with foamy water splashing off the bow. At the helm, Armin and Sugar discussed their options if the wind increased any more. The mainsail, now down to about half its normal size, could be reefed one more time or taken down altogether. They could also remove a piece of the staysail known as the bonnet, to reduce its expanse. Finally, if the wind picked up substantially, they could strike both sails and go with only a storm trysail—just enough to keep the boat under some control.

With the sail handling complete, Robert and some of the others not technically on duty were wondering if they were still needed.

Normally the on-duty watch would take care of the cleanup, and Leslie was already thinking about climbing back into bed for a couple of hours before her next shift began at seven that night. But Armin made no move to excuse anybody.

Around the deck, crew members fanned out to clean up the mess of lines left over from the sail dropping. Lines were coiled in neat piles to clear them from the deck and the scuppers, the small slots along the edge of the deck through which seawater flowed off the boat. Sugar realized the bilges hadn't been pumped in a good forty-five minutes and told Vinny to take care of it. The engineer went to the hand pump at mid-ship and began pumping.

"Use the Lister," Sugar told Vinny, referring to the ship's small generator, which also powered a mechanical pump. The water was surely high in the bilges, and it made sense to let the generator do the work. Vinny headed down to the engine room, switched on the pump, and came back up.

A short while later, with the pumping complete, Vinny climbed back down and went into the engine room to turn off the pump. Next door in the galley, Chez heard someone in the engine room. He ducked in and asked Vinny what was going on. Vinny told him about the foresail and jib coming down and headed back up on deck. Chez followed him through the engine room and the aft cabin to see how things looked. From the ladder, he saw the waves had picked up and clouds had moved in.

"Looks like you're going to get wet," Chez told Vinny, who silently climbed back onto deck.

Soon after, Sugar popped down into the aft cabin to check the ship's speed and position and recorded them in the log. The boat's location was roughly twenty-three degrees north, sixty-seven degrees west, and about three hundred miles north of Puerto Rico.

Twelve hundred miles to the north, the staff of Pride of Baltimore Inc. worked on the guest list and sent out invitations for the Welcome Home ceremony planned for June 14. The ship would be returning to the Inner Harbor under rather inauspicious circumstances because of the cancellation of the Mediterranean cruise, but a celebration was still needed. This one would include a parade of sail, the U.S. Army Field Band, fireworks, and a gala dinner.

That would be the official homecoming. The unofficial one would come much sooner, around May 23, when the *Pride* would reach the Norfolk area and friends and family could visit.

CHAPTER 16

May 14
Noon

Flying only the staysail and a double-reefed main, the *Pride* still clipped along nimbly on the brisk easterly wind. Clouds blanketed the sky and whitecaps dotted the Atlantic. Opposite the wind, the schooner's port side was awash in water that streamed aft from the bow and slowly drained off.

At mid-ship, Nina and Susie stayed together on the starboard rail with their backs to the stiff breeze, coiling lines and talking about the hectic few minutes of sail handling, some of the best action the crew had seen during the entire trip. Joe and Barry cleaned up lines near the foremast, Leslie and Danny were on the leeward side by the mainmast, and Scott and Robert were close by at mid-ship.

Wearing yellow foul-weather gear and dark brown sea boots, Armin stood to the right of the polished rosewood tiller, which he controlled with a line that fed through a block-and-tackle assembly. He glanced to starboard and saw that the dark clouds that had been keeping the *Pride* company had rolled closer. The conditions remained steady: six-foot waves and a thirty-five-knot wind, but things were about to change.

"Sugar, get up here." Recording the ship's position in the aft cabin, Sugar stopped what he was doing and hustled back up to deck. As he emerged, he could tell instinctively that the boat was about to get hit by a storm.

"Stand by the main sheet," Armin told his first mate.

Sugar moved into place near the main sheet, the thick rope that ran from the main boom around the back of the boat to the starboard side. The wind from the east picked up noticeably and wisps of foamy water blew across the waves.

There was no time to drop more sail and the *Pride* was in a vulnerable position, with the wind roaring in at almost a ninety-degree angle to the boat's starboard side. Armin had two choices: He could make a right turn, face eastward, and grind head-on through the squall until conditions eased; or he could let out the sails, turn to port, and run with the wind until the squall blew itself out. Running off a squall can be problematic near coastlines, but this time the nearest westward landfall was three hundred miles away. The decision boiled down to a gut call: How would his boat best handle the wind?

With the wind hitting from slightly behind the *Pride*'s mid-ship line, Armin opted to run off rather than make the slightly longer turn and head upwind.

The decision made, Armin yanked the tiller hard to starboard to force the *Pride* downwind to port. "Clip in! Hold on!" he shouted; it was the same warning he had given nine months before in the Baltic.

In an instant, the squall was upon the schooner. A misty blast of wind and water exploded over the boat and strained the two sails. The world suddenly became a blurry sea-spray watercolor and Sugar couldn't see anything in the distance. The *Pride* heeled sharply to port, water streaming down the port side, but it chugged ahead. The drops—were they sea or rain, it was impossible to tell—pelted Danny as he glanced over the starboard rail to see what was going on. A distressing high-pitched whistle sang out from the rigging, the same sound the wind makes roaring through urban canyons.

"Oh my goodness, what is this?" Nina yelled over the roar, as she turned her back and braced herself against the wind. Robert looked up at her and smiled, a silent teasing about her nervous reaction. He glanced over the rail and was hit with a cold pinging, perhaps hail, but didn't worry. *This is nothing,* thought Robert, who had lived through a typhoon off of Japan.

Near the helm, Sugar went to his knees to un-cleat the line to allow the mainsail to swing wider. The sail propelled the boat forward, but because of the angle of the wind, the sail was also working to turn the boat upwind. The boat was fighting itself: the rudder was trying to push the boat to port while the mainsail was serving to turn her the opposite way.

Armin realized the boat wasn't turning and shouted: "Let go of the sheets!"

Sugar let the mainsail sheet run. If the sail flared out farther, the wind would spill out and allow the boat to turn downwind. Forward on the boat, the staysail also held taut; it, too, needed to go free to allow the *Pride* to run.

But easing the mainsail out did not turn the boat and the wind slowly powered the boat farther to port. Suddenly the fifty-foot-long main boom hit the surface of the water and dragged through the Atlantic. The boom had hit the water often, but this time the wind kept the boat angled over and the corner of the sail remained pinned to the ocean.

The ship was in trouble; it was still sailing, but barely. There weren't many options now.

"Someone get the staysail sheet!" Sugar shouted over the wind, which he figured had zoomed up to a hurricanelike sixty or seventy knots—Force 12 on the Beaufort scale, the highest. The boat was going over, unless the sails somehow sprang free.

"Blow out," Sugar shouted to the mainsail, which was still attached securely to the main mast and the ship's aft end. But the countless hours that he and the crew had spent repairing and strengthening the rig were working against them now. The boat's sails, lines and wire rigging, all of which were stronger than what would have been found on an 1812-era clipper, were handling the relentless wind all too well.

For a split second, Sugar's mind raced back to the Long Island Sound and the countless times he and his friends capsized small sailing dinghies for fun. *This feels just the same,* he thought. The misplaced memory evaporated immediately, though, as he glanced down to the leeward side and saw Leslie being pulled through the water. Moments before, Leslie had unclipped to try to move forward to reach the staysail but had been pushed back by seawater cresting up the deck. She grabbed hold of the main shrouds—the thick rigging supporting the main mast—and was being dragged along.

Hold on! she told herself. *This boat will not be coming back to get anyone who falls off.*

Robert didn't hear Sugar's order over the howling wind, but he knew without being told to cut the staysail. Without quick action, the boat would be over on its side. It was risky, as cutting the line would turn the staysail into a deadly weapon, a flapping piece of heavy canvas and rope, but there was no choice. Steadying himself to avoid falling off the tilting deck, he glanced forward and saw, as Leslie had, that the sheet and cleat were well under water. It was too late.

Nearby, though, Danny unclipped his harness and crept forward toward the staysail sheet. Water covered the lower half of the deck, and the wind blew sharp, hissing spray over the ship. Danny was farther forward than Leslie and inched ahead through the thigh-high water by grabbing hold of the rolled-up foresail stowed a few minutes earlier.

For about twenty seconds, the boat stayed upright, but barely; it could go either way.

"Come on! Come on!" shouted Susie, willing the boat to right itself. She unclipped from the starboard rail and eased down to where *Irie* was lashed to see how much water was on deck. The dark water had submerged the two-foot-high rail and was creeping up the port side, advancing farther than it ever had before. Near mid-ship, Scott watched the rising water with awe. "Oh, my God, it's going down!" he shouted.

Farther forward, Barry couldn't believe what he was seeing. "Oh shit," he shouted, as he struggled to hang on to something, anything, to stay out of the water.

Frantic voices shouted, "Get the staysail! The staysail!" Danny tried to creep forward but the water on deck threatened to take him with it. He clipped in again and leaned his head down into the flow, trying to feel for the deck and the submerged staysail cleat. It was impossible to see anything through the water, and his hand couldn't find the line. The water knocked him off his feet as the boat rolled farther to port, and Danny thought he was falling overboard. Tossed by the turning boat, he suddenly found himself well under water, his glasses washed away. He made out light above, unclipped his harness, and kicked to the surface a couple of nerve-wracking seconds later. Breaking through, he breathed deep, and watched in shock as the *Pride*'s huge foremast smacked into the water in front of him—close enough to touch. The boat shuddered to a halt. The staysail sheet was still firmly attached to the cleat, but it didn't matter anymore.

Leslie held on to the main shrouds as long as she could, but finally dropped into the ocean, plunging perhaps thirty feet down because of her boots and heavy foul-weather gear. As she swam up toward the glimmering light, she saw the eeriest sight: the *Pride*'s two wooden yards—booms normally high above the deck—floating on the surface of the water above her. Leslie bobbed up near the stern and spotted Sugar near the tiller. She shot him a look that said silently: *You, you stay alive.*

Nearer the bow, Barry was suddenly in the water, too. He struggled to stay afloat and instinctively kicked off his sea boots. He hated swimming but had no choice now; he did what he could to keep his face out of the waves.

From the helm, Armin saw the *Pride* lying on its port side. In the Baltic, the big schooner had threatened to roll over; this time, it did.

In slow motion, the easterly blast of wind overwhelmed the *Pride*, sending it sprawling in about seventeen thousand feet of water. After months of treading the *Pride*'s deck and coming to know every inch of pine board, most of the eleven people on deck found themselves trying to navigate a boat turned sideways.

At the helm, Armin steadied himself on the leeward rail; the water was already up to his waist. Around the submerged deck, it was pandemonium. Leslie and Danny were in the water while others scrambled up the deck, now a vertical wall, to reach the starboard bulwarks.

"I want a head count!" Armin shouted frantically from the stern. "Where is everybody? I need a head count!"

"There's six up here," Scott shouted back.

Only a few feet away from where he balanced, Armin could see the real problem—the aft companionway, left of center and now submerged. If the boat had blown over to starboard, the offset opening might have remained out of the water. But the wind was from the east, the *Pride* sailed north, and the boat was on its port side. The ocean cascaded into the *Pride* through the offset hatch that had been built so lovingly a decade earlier in the Inner Harbor.

Nobody had to remind Armin that the *Pride* had no watertight bulkheads down below. She was essentially one big space, separated by thin walls and doors that did little to stop water. The water streaming into the aft cabin would meet no resistance and would quickly pour through the entire ship. The old admonition remained true: *Don't leave the boat until the boat leaves you.* This time, the boat was surely leaving.

"Abandon ship!" Armin shouted. At mid-ship, the words chilled Scott. Standing on a deck cleat, the blond deckhand glanced back at the helm and caught a glimpse of Armin. The expression on the captain's face said it all: catastrophe.

When the squall hit, Joe was coiling lines on the port side, not far from Barry and protected from the weather by the two small boats stacked on top of each other—*Irie* and *Rhino*. With little warning, the water was quickly up to his waist and the deck was tilted to an alarming angle. Like Robert, he had grown up sailing on the Chesapeake and his instincts were sure: *This is not coming back. Up! I've got to get up.*

First he had to free himself from the boat. Like the others, he wore a harness with a five-foot tether leading from the straps around his torso. Unlike some harnesses, which had clips at each end, the ones on the *Pride* had a clip only at the end that attached to the ship. Rather than attempt to reach the clip, which was now under water, Joe pulled out his knife from its leather sheath and sliced through the webbed tether. Now free to move around, Joe climbed up the deck and reached to grab the starboard rail, which now extended sideways overhead.

"Cut your harnesses! Cut your harnesses!" he shouted as he climbed. Muscular from months of working on the boat, Joe pulled himself up and over the rail. He clambered up on the starboard bulwark, which was normally on the outside of the boat but was now hanging horizontal to the ocean. Looking down, he saw that some of his shipmates just below were still clipped in as they tried to stay out of the rising water. Knowing that anybody who remained clipped in would be dragged under with the sinking boat, Joe reached down and grabbed a couple of the harness tethers. As he took his knife to cut them, an odd thought popped through his head: *These are expensive harnesses.* The notion vanished just as quickly and he finished slicing through them.

Robert shouted up to Joe, "Give me your knife." The request gave Joe a visceral jolt; how could he give up his *knife*, something he always carried on the boat. *Where's your knife?* Joe thought to himself. But he fought off the instinct to say no, and handed down his well-used knife, first cutting through the lanyard attaching it to his belt. "Don't lose it," he shouted down to Robert.

Robert turned and tried to cut through the ropes that held the two ship's boats to the now-upright deck. But with half the lashings already under water, it was impossible to cut them all and Robert gave up.

Nearby, Susie slipped her harness over her head and turned to Nina.

"We have to climb."

The two women grabbed a line above them and looked for a foothold to get high enough to climb up and over the rail.

"Susie, put your foot on that cleat," Nina shouted. Susie put her right foot on the deck cleat, reached up to grab the rail, and held on for a moment. She couldn't pull over the rail, though, and she felt herself plummeting into the Atlantic. Her heavy sea boots and the suction caused by the sinking 120-ton vessel dragged her perhaps 20 feet deep. Next to her, the *Pride* was halfway submerged and filling fast. Susie, who had swum countless miles as a competitive swimmer, kicked as hard as she could.

Nina, too, disappeared into the waves and struggled to find her way to the surface.

As the boat went over, several crew members had the same thought: Chez.

"Chez is down below!" "Chez! Get out!"

Vinny had seen him in the aft cabin just a couple of minutes earlier. "Looks like you're going to get wet," Chez had teased him. Now the cook was somewhere in the cabin, trapped in a knocked-down, flooding boat with only one open hatch.

Vinny, who had calmly survived the sinking of the *Coastal I* just a year earlier, was determined to make sure Chez escaped. He unclipped his harness and scrambled along the deck, now a vertical wall. He worked his way to the nearest hatch, the one leading to the engine room, which was next door to the galley. The hatch had a canvas cover, which was battened down using old-fashioned boards and straps. When Leslie's watch sealed it early that morning, they used a little rubber mallet to wedge in the battens. Vinny wrestled with the straps, but without the mallet, he had no chance of getting the hatch open before the boat sank.

"Chez!" The shouts rang out again and again.

Several feet forward, Robert tried to get the cover off the main hatch but realized there wasn't time to undo the fastenings. Despite his earlier bravado, he realized this storm was indeed something like a typhoon; the winds topped sixty knots, maybe even seventy, he figured. Abandoning the hatch, the former merchant seaman's mind clicked back to his abandon-ship assignment: get the medical kit. But that was impossible; the kit was stowed below. Instead, he realized he was only a few feet from the emergency food stored inside *Irie*. He reached into the small wooden skiff, now turned sideways, and grabbed one of the two milk crates that had been there since Spain, both stuffed with food triple-wrapped in plastic bags. The provisions included peanut butter, condensed milk, canned food, and some oversized European chocolate bars that the crew members had somehow restrained themselves from eating on the Atlantic crossing. Robert reached down into the boat to grab the crate, then tried to creep aft through the seawater to where the life rafts were kept. He made it a few steps, trying desperately to hold onto the awkward load while all but swimming. Moments later, he lost his grip on the crate and the food plunged into the ocean.

Vinny also gave up on the engine-room hatch and began climbing up to the starboard bulwark. With everyone else making their way aft, Vinny headed forward on the side of the boat toward Nina.

Two months earlier, at the Malaga dock, the mates had explained what was supposed to happen in an abandon-ship situation. Each person on board had an assigned task, which had been easy enough to fulfill during the dockside drill. But this was no drill, and things were in chaos.

Sugar knew his assignment—launch the life rafts—and he was actually in a position to try to do it. After being inspected and repacked in Spain, the two rafts had been secured side by side in a rigid plastic cover under the tiller. From his position at the starboard rail, Sugar slid around the tiller and dropped down into the water to try to reach the release that would free the life rafts, a release that was on the port side. But he was too far away—the release was just out of reach unless he went down into the water. Sugar took a deep breath and lowered himself into the sea. He reached for the release but suddenly the thick wooden tiller swung down hard and cracked him in the side. At the stern, the wind and waves were whipping the ship's exposed rudder, which in turn was pushing the long tiller in wild arcs. Sugar gave up on reaching the life-raft release for fear of getting pounded again by the out-of-control tiller. Besides the manual release, there was also a hydrostatic release that was supposed to free the rafts when fully submerged. The crew would just have to wait for the water to do its job.

Sugar fell back into the water, and in a heartbeat found himself a good eight feet under the roiling surface. He kicked off his sea boots, which had quickly become water-logged, and swam furiously upward. It seemed to take forever—perhaps thirty seconds—to go eight feet. Was it the suction of the huge ship sinking? Whatever it was, the thought crossed his mind: *I might not make it.* Finally he broke the surface and gasped for air. He was right next to the boat and grabbed hold of a safety line, which ran above the cap rail, and held on. Above him, Armin clung to the bulwarks and shouted: "Get the life rafts! Somebody get the life rafts."

A couple of others had made their way to the area—Sugar couldn't see who—and he yelled for them to steer clear.

"It's too dangerous! Don't go down there." Moments later, the hydrostatic release did its job, and miraculously, with a whoosh of water, the two life rafts bobbed to the surface.

After scrambling to the bulwark and cutting harnesses, Joe quickly headed aft, where he saw the life rafts pop free from under the tiller. There were still people struggling on the boat, but Joe jumped into the water and swam through the waves toward one of the rafts. While the wind remained ferocious, the waves were not overwhelming—like a rough day at the beach. Joe lost sight of the raft when he bobbed into a trough, but could spot it again when he reached a crest. As he swam, the second mate felt his sea boots slip off. Joe had deliberately bought them two sizes too big, thinking he would want them to fall off in just such a situation as this. But now that he was in the moment, Joe wished his boots had stayed on; surely they would come in handy as the disaster unfolded. Joe chased through the waves after the still-folded raft, which had not inflated and was being blown by the wind. When he reached it, the CO_2 cartridge did its job and the black and orange boat automatically unfolded and filled with air. As Joe held on to a line, two stacked pontoons took shape and then a little roof. And then, *Phooosh!* The raft's air plugs popped free and the CO_2 rushed out of the pontoons. Joe was left treading water in the storm, with no boots, holding onto a slowly deflating blob of black and orange plastic.

*   *   *

As the boat went over, Scott clung to his perch on a deck cleat, his body curled up under the starboard rail. He watched Susie drop off the boat; moments later the water was so high that he, too, had no choice about staying out of it. He was in the ocean and pushed off the deck to get away. After a few seconds of stroking, he broke through the waves and experienced an amazing thing: silence. The storm was raging on but he heard nothing except a voice in his head saying: *It's not your time to die.* He wasn't a churchgoer, but Scott simply accepted the message. *Was it the voice of God?* he wondered. The message calmed him, and he swam aft, looking through the seas for his crew mates.

Just below him, the suction action created by the sinking schooner pulled firmly at Susie as she stroked as hard as she could to reach the surface. One . . . two . . . three strokes, but she was still under water. *Stay calm, keep trying,* she thought. One more stroke, then another, and, finally, she bobbed up through the waves and gulped a breath. The world was wet, gray, and confusing; horizontal white spray whipped over the surface. Susie couldn't make out anything or anybody, but heard a voice: "Life raft! Go to the life raft!"

Then a hand on her yellow slicker hood grabbed her and turned her around. *Scott. It's Scott!* And there, about fifty feet away, was a black and orange life raft. The two deckhands navigated the rolling waves and swam toward the colors.

Farther forward, Barry tried to stay afloat and managed to wriggle out of his heavy foul-weather gear. The waves pounded him and he swallowed water, but he somehow stayed afloat.

Near the stern, Sugar grabbed the second raft. Its CO_2 cartridge discharged and the raft quickly filled with air. Immediately, the wind pushed it westward toward the steadily sinking *Pride*. Sugar held on and hoisted his 225 pounds up onto it.

Over the last few chaotic minutes, the wind had kept the *Pride* pinned to the surface of the water. Now, with the hull steadily filling, the forty tons of ballast—lead, iron, and old paving blocks—finally did its job and re-righted the schooner. The two great masts climbed slowly back to vertical as the ballast turned the hull bottom-down.

Sugar had climbed the *Pride*'s rigging many times. Now, in the most surreal of moments, he found himself up in the rigging one last time, but floating in a life raft. The wind pushed the little boat toward the mainmast rigging, eventually shoving it into the taut collection of wire and rope, and Sugar realized some lines were tangled around his ankle. Desperate not to be dragged under with the boat, he pulled free of the ropes and pushed the raft clear of the top-mast rigging as it descended. Sugar watched with awe as the *Pride of Baltimore*, once again upright, descended majestically into the Atlantic, her pennants flapping until they reached the water.

Moments later, Sugar realized he was sinking, too. When the raft brushed up against the rigging, something had happened and the craft was deflating quickly.

Instead of life rafts, the crew of the *Pride* had two plastic blobs.

CHAPTER 17

May 14
Noon

Down below a few minutes earlier, Chez watched Vinny head back up the aft ladder. The cook figured he should get back to the galley to keep an eye on the soup simmering on the diesel stove. But he lingered to watch the stark scene unfolding outside. The sliding hatch cover was pushed open a couple of feet; with the boat sailing on a steep heel, Chez could see a wide expanse of overcast sky. Windblown water raced over the waves.

Then the real wind hit. Chez watched in awe as the boat leaned ever farther to port. He braced himself against the unnatural tilt and watched the water creep up the deck as the ship's port edge dipped under the Atlantic. Before long, he saw that the *Pride*'s entire railing was under water, and he knew things were going very wrong. For a few stomach-churning moments he waited for the *Pride* to right herself as she always had before. This time she didn't manage it. Chez saw the main boom splash through the sea, and before long, the ship stopped moving forward and collapsed on its side.

Chez struggled to keep his balance; he was now standing on the wall, not the floorboards near the companionway. Furniture, books and gear flew across the small cabin as the *Pride* rotated ninety degrees to the left. The sea level quickly overwhelmed the aft deck and water rose to the opening of the companionway. In a flash, water began pouring through the opening and into the cabin. Unless the boat somehow righted itself, nothing could possibly stop the water from filling the entire cabin. The water gushed through the opening and into the cabin. Chez had only one thought: get out of the boat.

Outside, Armin screamed for a head count and others shouted for Chez to get out. But it was too late for anyone to come below to help him; half of the crew was already in the water and the rest would soon be.

With the *Pride* now on its side, the ladder leading to the aft end of the deck was also turned sideways and useless. Instead, Chez reached up and grabbed the port edge of the companionway opening, a solid piece of varnished wood, and tried to pull up through the onrushing water. It was impossible. The force of the water pinned him against the port side of the opening, pounding his chest against the hard wood. The force fractured four of his ribs and sent a burning pain through his chest. He dropped back down and then reached up to open the polished-wood hatch cover a bit to make more room for an escape route. The bigger opening allowed more water to pour in.

Chez steeled himself and tried to pull through the opening a second time. The water repelled him again and sent him sprawling into one of the officers' bunks. He took a moment to regain his breath as water filled the cabin.

He tried a third time, desperately attempting to pull himself far enough through the opening so that he could use his legs to push out. But again, the water was too powerful, sending him back and taking his shoes and thick glasses along the way. Chez was half-blind and wearing shorts and a T-shirt.

Through the cabin's skylight, he saw nothing but water—it looked like an aquarium—and briefly wondered if there was some way he could break through the window to escape. Countless gallons of water flowed in every second and was soon up to Chez's chest. His mind began to race frantically and he dredged up a claim he had once heard: "Drowning is supposed to be a good way to die," as it was relatively painless. The thought was somehow comforting. But then he thought of his mother. *I can't do this to her.*

Only a couple of minutes had passed, but water had already filled much of the aft cabin. Farther forward, water also streamed into the boat through cracks and seams, and seeped through the battened hatches. Water poured down into the galley through the stove's chimney, which jutted well above the deck, but like the aft companionway, it sat on the *Pride's* now-flooded port side. While the chimney opening was sometimes closed in rough weather, it had been open that morning since Chez was using the stove.

In the darkened swamp that the aft cabin had become, Chez figured he had time to make one more try. Water was only inches away from filling the entire space; once it got much higher, the *Pride* would sink like a boulder. He craned his neck above the water and gulped a breath, sending a painful jolt through his broken rib cage. He grabbed the edge of the opening with both hands and pulled most of his body up through the companionway. Straining against the force of the ocean, he finally secured enough leverage to get his legs up over the edge. He held firm and wriggled his legs outside the boat. The rush of water, though, tugged his gym shorts down his thighs and Chez reached down instinctively to pull them back up, using the other hand to hold on to the boat. His shorts safely rescued, Chez finally escaped the flooded cabin. With the *Pride's* hull almost fully under water, Chez emerged from the cabin more than ten feet under the surface of the Atlantic. With his bare feet, he pushed off the *Pride*, still sideways in the ocean, to get clear.

His heart racing with the adrenaline rush of the escape, Chez swam through the gloomy ocean as much as fifteen yards from the companionway, heading aft to avoid the ship's rigging and sails, which had become potential traps for the twelve people on board. He reached the surface spluttering with exhaustion and kicked hard to keep his head above the cresting sea. For a moment, he forgot about the broken ribs and felt exhilarated to be alive. It had been close. Had he gone back to stir the soup instead of lingering at the companionway, he would never have gotten to the aft cabin in time to escape.

As Chez caught his breath, the *Pride* pivoted for the second time in the last several minutes. The ship was once again upright, only now it was mostly under water. Without his glasses, Chez couldn't make out much as he struggled to stay on top of the waves, which swelled to about eight feet. But several yards away, Chez saw an orange blob and realized it was a life raft. He took a few strokes toward the raft and could make out somebody—was it Sugar?—sitting in it. The raft floated toward the *Pride*'s main mast and brushed under one of the ship's thick shrouds. Chez didn't want to go near the rigging of a sinking ship and stopped. He looked around desperately and spotted the second orange raft; he began swimming for it. As he stroked, he found Danny in the water; he, too, had lost his glasses. Chez pointed out the raft.

As he swam, Chez suddenly remembered the EPIRB. In the minutes he was trapped in the companionway, he had been within easy reach of one of the *Pride*'s emergency beacons. It would have taken only seconds to grab the EPIRB from its bracket under the companionway opening, turn on the signal, and somehow shove it out into the ocean. The EPIRB, though, had been the last thing on his mind and now it was quickly sinking to the bottom of the Atlantic, still turned off.

Chez swam through the waves, and he and Danny finally reached the raft that Joe had commandeered. As he approached, Chez realized it was barely inflated.

Others reached the raft and were relieved to see that Chez had escaped from the aft cabin. Scott and Susie climbed in over the edge of the raft, only to discover how little air it held. But while he was perched slightly above the surface, Scott could see a little farther over the waves. Off in the distance, in the direction where the *Pride* had gone down, Scott caught sight of something in the foamy water: splashes of orange and bright yellow. Vinny and Nina! Minutes before, Vinny had headed forward on the *Pride*'s starboard bulwark toward Nina and finally reached her in the water.

Vinny made his way over the waves to the young woman he had so impressed during their ten weeks together. Scott watched them come together and grab for each other, struggling to stay afloat. It was hard to see what they were doing, but there was no mistaking them. Vinny was the only one on board with orange foul-weather gear, and Nina wore yellow.

With no warning, Vinny and Nina disappeared behind the waves.

After floating through the rigging, Sugar jumped out of his deflating raft and swam it over toward the one Joe had grabbed. Once they were near each other, Sugar used a line from one to tie the two together. By then, eight of the twelve had made it to the vicinity of the life rafts. Along with Chez, Susie, Scott, Leslie, Danny, and Robert had swum clear of the sinking schooner. Vinny and Nina were some distance away, behind the waves, but nobody seemed to know where Barry had ended up.

Soon after spotting Vinny and Nina, Scott caught sight of a yellow rain slicker several yards away: Armin! The captain who had frantically tried to account for his eleven crew members minutes earlier now had his hands out of the water and was waving above his head, apparently signaling to someone—Vinny, maybe? Moments later, Armin began swimming—not toward the rafts, but back toward the place in the waves where the *Pride* had gone down. The lanky captain wasn't particularly athletic but was strong in the water. He and Jennifer had often swum hundreds of yards into shore from boats moored off beaches. Armin moved methodically over the waves, his arms reaching out of the water again and again.

"ARMIN!" Susie bellowed as she watched him swim. Scott and others joined in, beseeching the captain to come to the raft.

"Armin, over here!" But he continued off to the west and the shouts drifted into the still-howling air.

Sugar watched Armin disappear into the distance. *Turn around, Armin,* he thought. If Armin would only glance in their direction, he would certainly see the rafts.

"ARMIN!"

The wind continued to churn the sea, and spray blotted the horizon. With each cresting wave, his confused crew could see Armin for a moment. If Armin saw something in the distance, nobody else did. Eventually, the shouting stopped.

Armin was gone.

CHAPTER 18

May 14
Noon
In the water

At any other time, the sight of Armin disappearing into the waves would have been profoundly disturbing. But at the moment, his eight crew members were numbed by a dire instinct to save themselves. Each had taken a different path off the *Pride*'s pine deck boards and into the Atlantic. Susie, Leslie, and Chez had almost been sucked down by the plummeting schooner; Joe, however, had escaped and reached the rafts without much struggle.

Huddled around the lashed-together rafts, the eight concentrated on staying out of the waves. Joe had heard the plugs blow on the one raft. The second one, Sugar's, had also lost its air, although he wasn't sure why. But even deflated, the rafts maintained some of their buoyancy. The crew grabbed on to an edge or one of the raft's ropes, and kicked their legs to tread water. It took concentration to rise with swells that were several feet high. Every so often, a bigger wave loomed over them and someone shouted, "Breaker!" giving everyone a second to gulp a breath before getting pummeled.

Many of the supplies that came in the rafts had spilled into the waves. Looking for an air pump, Susie used her knife to cut open a pouch inside one of the rafts. To her dismay, it turned out to be food rations—important provisions but a hassle to hold on to while treading water. Some of the supplies floated away or sank, but others bobbed on the water and the crew scrambled to save as many of them as they could. Susie spotted two signaling flares and grabbed both; Sugar plucked another one and shoved it down into his foulweather gear as he swam. Moments later, he reached a flashlight and shoved that into his pants, followed by a second small bag filled with food rations. Leslie, meanwhile, found perhaps the biggest prize—a five-gallon jug of fresh water that had been stored on deck for just such an emergency.

Joe reached a five-gallon bucket that had washed off the *Pride*'s deck—a wonderful find, as it could hold air to help keep someone afloat. The air pressure inside the overturned bucket kept water from rushing in and created a buoyant flotation device that someone could hug for support in the ocean—at least until the bucket tipped too far, allowing the air to bubble up and water to rush in. Joe also spotted two small cans of fresh water and a gray bag with medical supplies, both of which had fallen out of a raft; Danny saved another can of water.

After giving up on the unwieldy crate of food that was stored on deck, Robert had made his way aft on the ship and had safely reached the deflated rafts. Along the way, he grabbed the *Pride*'s long boat hook and a two-gallon plastic bucket, which he used for flotation. Robert looked over the waves and saw one of the fishing kits from the raft floating away; it wasn't worth the risk and he let it go. Likewise, the wooden paddles from the rafts seemed inessential and they, too, were allowed to float off.

Finally, Danny spotted one of the pumps for the rafts. Joe took a look at the small device but couldn't believe it: The pump was a cheap plastic gizmo with a bellows, the kind of thing one might use to inflate a beach ball. Without a hard surface to push against in the water, there was no way to create enough pressure to make air flow. The thing was useless, and he threw it into the waves.

About then, something yellow came into view several yards away. Gathered around the raft, the sailors noticed the foul-weather gear.

"Nina!" Robert announced, as he looked out and saw her going in and out of view beyond the cresting waves. Leslie, though, had already gotten a better look and broke the news.

"She's dead," Leslie said quietly. Nina had been a lifeguard and taught swimming in the chlorinated waters of middle-class Baltimore, but she had not survived the sudden fury of an Atlantic storm. Vinny had tried to reach her, but something had happened.

"Oh, my God!" Susie said as she saw her friend's body. One moment they had tried to climb the deck together, the next they were separated. Now Nina's body was floating face down toward her shipmates, slowly drifting in the waves. Until that moment, it had not dawned on Susie that some of the other four crew members might not have survived.

The horrible reality set in. Sweet Nina was dead. Treading water, nobody said anything to mark the loss. It was beyond words.

The squall had overwhelmed the *Pride* sometime around noon. The heavy wind continued for no more than fifteen minutes before easing up. Whatever had hit them had come and gone in a flash. By 12:30, the waves subsided to a few feet. The skies were overcast but there was no hint of another storm.

As the two uninflated rafts drifted along, Nina's body floated nearby. It was disconcerting, but there was nothing to be done about it.

The water temperature was in the low seventies, not immediately dangerous but cool enough that hypothermia would set in before too long. For Chez, an uncomfortable thought surfaced and he finally broached the subject.

"What should we do about Nina's gear?" he asked the others.

While his shipmates had all put on foul-weather gear that morning, Chez was wearing nothing but shorts and a T-shirt in the cool water. They could be in the water a long time and Nina didn't need her yellow slicker and pants anymore. He knew, though, that it was a sensitive subject.

"Get real," snapped Joe McGeady. "She's dead. That gear will save somebody's life."

The no-nonsense answer dissolved any sentimentality about Nina's clothes. Chez swam over and carefully removed the yellow slicker and pants, the extra-small ones Nina had spent days hunting for in Baltimore, along with her single-bladed knife, which was attached to the pants with a lanyard. He tried not to think about what he was doing; this wasn't about Nina, it was about the clothes. Treading water, he managed to remove the top and pants without looking at Nina's face.

Fourteen inches taller than Nina, Chez barely squeezed into her slicker; the end of the sleeves reached only his forearms, but it was a help against the chill. Eventually it fell to Joe to give Nina's body a farewell push away from the group.

Some of the eight did a mental head count. Nina was now, sadly, accounted for and Armin had swum off mysteriously. But where were Vinny and Barry?

Staying in the water would surely mean more deaths. Everyone knew that there was only one realistic hope for survival; inflating the rafts. But it was impossible to imagine how they could accomplish that without a pump. In the meantime, the only goal was to keep everybody afloat. Someone suggested using Joe's bucket to scoop some air *under* a raft to create a buoyant bubble. Treading water, Joe pushed the overturned bucket straight down through the water, then pushed it sideways until it was under the raft. Once the bucket was in place, Joe tilted it to allow the air trapped inside to bubble up and create a pocket under the bottom of the raft. While he did that the others held down the edges of the heavy raft to try to keep the air pocket trapped underneath. It worked. The air bubble provided a good bit more buoyancy to help keep everyone afloat, at least until a wave came along and allowed the air bubble to escape or until someone leaned too hard on one side and pushed the air out.

Sometime after 12:30, with the wind dying down, Leslie and others heard something that sounded like moans and then spotted Barry in the water several yards away, his arms moving awkwardly above his head.

"Barry! There's Barry!"

This had to qualify as a miracle. The worst—and most terri-fied—swimmer in the bunch had survived for at least half an hour in the fierce storm, alone with nothing to hold on to. Sugar, the ranking officer in Armin's absence, volunteered to go get him but he wasn't venturing out without a safety line. He grabbed a rope at-tached to the rafts, tied it around his waist, and swam out toward the carpenter. But even Sugar had a hard time pulling two rafts and several clinging people. Despite his cracked ribs, Chez swam out with Sugar and helped haul the load toward Barry. Slowly they made it over the waves and got within a few feet of Barry. Chez had brought along the *Pride*'s boat hook and Sugar extended it. Half-drowned and confused, Barry grabbed the hook and Sugar pulled him close.

Sugar and Chez grabbed Barry, keeping his head afloat and talk-ing to him. Barry could barely speak but could nod his head. He had kicked off his dark boots and was wearing only shorts and a T-shirt after stripping off his safety harness and foul-weather gear to help stay afloat. His dark brown eyes were alert, but he was ob-viously in great distress. Behind his reddish beard, his face was pale and his lips were a bluish purple. Frothy spittle oozed from his mouth and his bloated belly made clear that he had swallowed a lot of seawater.

The two men did a sidekick and brought Barry back to the group, increasing the number of crew members at the rafts to nine. Saving his life became the crew's primary focus. Beginning with Scott and Danny, they took turns supporting his body to keep his face out of the water, a grueling task in the waves.

"You're going to be all right. Just hang on," Scott told him with all the conviction he could muster. What Barry needed was CPR and fresh water to combat dehydration brought on by the saltwater he had taken in.

Perhaps the strongest swimmer in the group, Sugar took long turns holding Barry. In his near-drowned delirium, Barry kept pushing down on the bigger man and struggled to rise out of the water. Moving instinctively to save himself, Sugar ducked out of Barry's grasp and swam down and away.

"Stop it, Barry," Sugar shouted, when he re-emerged.

As the afternoon wore on, the crew searched for ways to help keep Barry afloat. Joe had used his bucket to scoop air into Leslie's foul-weather top to add buoyancy, while Scott and Danny fashioned life preservers out of their foul-weather pants by tying the legs together and putting air in through the waist. Somebody suggested doing the same for Barry. But it was clear that Barry wouldn't have the strength to hold onto the makeshift life vest.

The shipmates realized they were caught in a nightmare. They could do nothing about inflating one of the rafts because they were spending all of their energy either tending to Barry or keeping everybody else afloat. Every so often, Barry tried to climb up on one of the rafts, only to slide back into the water. Each time he did, the raft's air pocket would disappear, and the others would have to use the bucket to add more air underneath. Occasionally, a six-foot breaker would drench the entire group, and Barry, physically unable to fight off the oncoming waves, continued to take on water.

Sometime around three p.m., the life seemed to flicker in Barry's dark eyes, and he vomited up more seawater. "He's going out," Scott said.

"Chez! He's not breathing, what do we do?" someone shouted to Chez, a trained paramedic.

"Let him go," Chez said quietly; this was it. Another wave crested over the group and swamped Barry. This time, with nobody holding on, he was swept away. Robert, who had not noticed, turned around moments later.

"Where's Barry?" he asked Sugar. The quiet look in Sugar's eyes answered the question.

Adrenaline and survival instincts had helped the eight sailors shut out the horror of what was happening to them—the sinking and Nina's death. But they had worked hard to keep Barry alive and had failed. It was a huge blow, and nobody said much for a while. Privately, some had the same thought: at least we can worry about ourselves now.

* * *

Not long after Barry's death, someone noticed, for the first time in hours, something besides sea and sky—a jet flying miles overhead.

"Should we fire a flare?" someone asked. It was a long shot, but the group quickly decided there was no other option. It would be absurd to drown with flares in their pockets, instead of at least taking a chance.

Sugar grabbed one of the parachute flares, which were slightly narrower than a paper-towel tube. He pulled on the launch cord and the flare shot high above the ocean, exploding in a brilliant shower of red flame lasting half a minute. As the bright flare dropped slowly to the ocean, the eight looked upward and waited for something to happen. But the momentary burst of optimism fizzled as quickly as the flare. The SOS was laughably inadequate; the jet was far too high for anyone on board to notice such a distant signal in the daylight. Sugar figured they'd have to be more prudent with their remaining flares.

By mid-afternoon, the waves had moderated but the seawater was cooling everybody down. Danny, bony to begin with, was shivering in the water without his pants, which had washed away, and some of the others took turns trying to encourage him.

Sugar and Leslie, after finding each other near the *Pride*'s stern during the sinking, were determined not to be separated. They clipped their safety harnesses together, to make sure a wave didn't wash one away. Somehow, neither of the two had begun to panic. Even during the crucial minutes when the *Pride* was blowing over, things unfolded rather neatly as each of them went from task to task. *What should I do next?* Leslie kept thinking. In the heat of the moment, she had tried to reach the staysail sheet but had been pushed aside by the water. *Okay,* she figured, *you better at least hang on to the boat.* That proved impossible and she found herself under water. *Okay, time to swim to the surface.* Once she reached the surface, she had to find a life raft. Finally, she had reached the rafts—as useless as they were—and, to her relief, Sugar. She realized that during the storm she had been working with instinctive blinders on. While the wind that knocked over the big schooner had surely been an intense one, she had no memory of its strength.

Once the boat was gone, Leslie shifted into survival mode. She tied the hood of her yellow foul-weather poncho tightly around her head and got some air from Joe's bucket to add buoyancy to her top. To save energy, she put her face down into the sea and resorted to a dead man's float from time to time. It wasn't so bad unless a big wave crashed on top of her.

But all that was about coping. Two, perhaps four, of their shipmates were dead. The way things were going, they would all drown soon enough. If ever there was a time for final requests, this was it and Leslie decided she had one for Sugar—just in case. Raised in a traditional two-parent family in California, Leslie had opted for an utterly non-traditional life throughout her twenties. She had sailed for most of the decade and seen the far corners of the world. Now, at the age of thirty, she was floating in the middle of the Atlantic, tethered to the love of her life. She looked into the eyes of the man who had so impressed her years earlier.

"Sugar," she said matter-of-factly. "I don't want to go through life without being proposed to."

Sugar had not expected that one. He and Leslie were obviously committed to each other but had not talked much about marriage, something Sugar considered more of a formality than anything else. But it was also clear that Leslie was serious. He couldn't exactly go down on one knee, but Sugar managed to coax out a proposal of sorts.

"Sure, Leslie," he said. "If we survive, we'll get married."

"Just keep swimming," he added, first mate to bosun.

As the eight drifted in the water, holding on to the two shapeless rafts, news of the engagement spread and wedding plans were discussed. There would be a big party, with plenty of music and sailors. Giuseppe, as Sugar called Joe, would be the best man; Susie, the maid of honor. For a moment, the future didn't seem quite so bleak.

CHAPTER 19

May 14
Late afternoon

After several hours in the water, Robert analyzed the situation and considered himself fortunate, at least relatively. Unlike Chez and Danny, he had on full foul-weather gear. Like Joe, he had a bucket that was helping him stay afloat without relying too much on the rafts. Using the bucket as a seat, Robert bobbed along and held on to the sea anchor, a piece of nylon fabric extending off of a rope from one of the rafts. In the short run, things were under control.

Yet he couldn't help but contemplate death. It wasn't cowardly, simply pragmatic. The sun would set at around seven, and if they were still in the water by nightfall, things would go from bad to ghastly. It would be exhausting trying to hang on to the raft all night while treading water. Sleeping would be out of the question, and if they got hit with another storm—a distinct possibility—the eight crew members could easily be separated. Then there was the unspoken worry about sharks. All in all, he knew it would be ugly once the sun set.

If we don't all get into this raft by night, he figured, *we won't all be here in the morning.*

Robert tried to picture what his death would mean in the larger world and his mind flashed home to Virginia and his sister Leslie.

She was eight and a half months pregnant. She may have already had the baby while they were sailing north from the Virgin Islands. If he was going to drown in the ocean, the thought of a new baby taking his place on Earth provided some comfort.

At the same time, his mind clicked through a list of the people who would grieve his death, including, of course, his sister. The thought of so many people back home stirred up his resolve and he steeled himself for a night in the water. He would set a simple goal: to survive until sunrise. He would worry about tomorrow in the clear light of morning.

Others weren't feeling much better. Chez's rib cage ached; Scott had gone temporarily blind from all the saltwater in his eyes, and he, like several others, was shivering after being in the cool water for hours.

Joe had also been thinking about dying. Like some of the others, he saw Armin swim off into the storm and couldn't make sense of what he had seen. Surely Armin had seen something in the distance. But Joe couldn't entirely rule out another possibility. Had Armin been so devastated by the sailing disaster that he had swum off in profound despair? The idea was utterly counter-instinctive. And yet, to his surprise, Joe himself found that the notion had some appeal. If he just pushed away from the others and floated away on his bucket, he could separate himself rather quickly and would surely drown eventually. It would be a lonely death, but at least it would be quick, Joe figured, not the drawn-out ordeal he knew they were all in for.

Why not just make peace with it instead of prolonging the struggle? Joe asked himself. But the notion of swimming away, of ending it all, vanished just as quickly as it surfaced. He was in, and he would stick around for whatever was in store.

The doubts that plagued Joe and the others remained unspoken. It made no sense to fret about the obvious. Instead, the group tried to stay focused on whatever task was at hand. Just keeping the raft buoyant and everyone afloat was hard work and left little psychic energy for worrying. The determination of the eight also reflected an attitude that all good schooner sailors took to sea—that they can handle just about anything the world throws at them.

*   *   *

"Hey, Chez. What's for lunch?" Sugar shouted to the cook at mid-afternoon.

The gallows humor provided some momentary relief. It was also a natural subject as nobody had eaten since breakfast, and they had been swimming, or at least treading water, all afternoon. They had a small amount of the emergency food rations but there was no practical way to open any of it while they were in the water.

The crew had also found several small cans of fresh water, as well as the big jug that Leslie had rescued. With that much fresh water on hand, it was an easy decision to go ahead and drink some to combat the dehydration that was already setting in. The fresh water rations came in $10\frac{2}{3}$-ounce tin cans. Someone used a knife to pop a hole in one and passed it among the eight. Each person was allotted a little more than an ounce, scarcely anything after pickling in the salt water for hours.

After Barry's death, the eight shipmates turned their full attention to the rafts. Just getting them organized was difficult since nobody had ever seen one inflated. There were ropes everywhere; some were knotted around each other and had to be untangled. One rope had a yellow rubber ball at the end to be used as a life line. It took a long time for someone to figure out which side of the raft was which; the clue was the empty CO_2 canister, which they eventually realized had to be on the bottom of the raft. With some difficulty, they managed to turn over the huge blob of submerged nylon.

Without a pump, there was only one way to get air into the thing: blowing it in themselves. Joe, Chez, and Susie set to work on Joe's raft, while Sugar, Leslie, and the others did the same on Sugar's.

That meant locating the plugs and attempting to blow into one. For someone treading water, it was almost impossible to get enough of a grip on the raft to be able to blow air through the valve. Sugar eventually figured out how to lift the heavy raft far enough out of the water to reach the plug with his mouth. Gradually, the others realized he was making slow progress and Joe's group stopped its efforts on the other raft. Susie was exhausted and cold, and she and Chez huddled together, wrapped inside the shapeless raft to try to stay warm.

Sugar pressed ahead and developed something of a rhythm. Using his legs to do a vertical frog kick, he took deep breaths and exhaled into the valve with each kick. He would snatch a breath on the way back into the waves. Leslie or one of the others did what they could to help by supporting his head in the water. Every so often, he had to stop blowing to help while Joe or someone else used the bucket to scoop more air underneath.

Sugar kept at it for a couple of hours, but the raft was showing little sign of inflating. Finally, sometime after five o'clock, he gave up. *The damn thing must have a hole*, he realized. Two hours of grueling effort had been in vain. The revelation was crushing.

Five hours had passed and they were still in the water. In their frustration, everyone had the same thought.

We've got to get this done before nightfall.

Chez had seen enough.

"Fuck it," he said. Two people were dead; Armin and Vinny were missing. He was the cook, the low man on the sailing totem pole, and with a bunch of cracked ribs he was probably in the worst physical shape. But somewhere inside he discovered a reserve of adrenaline and went to work on the raft he and Susie had been using for insulation. Climbing up on the partially inflated raft, he found one of the air valves and began blowing furiously. After a few minutes, the raft seemed to be expanding a bit, although nobody was certain.

Inside the valve a plastic membrane was supposed to re-seal and prevent air from leaking out, but Chez could tell it wasn't working. Taking his mouth off the plug to gulp breaths allowed too much air to escape from the raft. That forced him to keep his mouth on the valve stem and to breathe in through his nose—and do his best to keep a flow of air going into the raft. Each breath in and out sent a jolt through his rib cage, but he kept going.

"Chez, let us help," someone pleaded with him.

He took a long enough break to gasp, "No! This is mine."

The raft had three compartments; two pontoons that provided the flotation and an arch that supported the canopy, which covered the raft like a pup tent. Chez went to work on the first pontoon, breathing in and out again and again without stopping. The others watched in amazement.

Soon they noticed the subtle but sure sign that the raft was finally starting to puff out. Fifteen or twenty minutes went by and the pontoon took shape. When the first pontoon had enough air, Chez replaced the gray plastic plug and went to work on the second.

Again, others tried to take a turn, but Chez kept at it; he was a man possessed. The second pontoon was somewhat easier since he could rely on the other one to help keep him afloat. One of the plugs had gone flying when the raft had inflated hours earlier, so someone ripped one off of Sugar's raft to use on Chez's. After another twenty minutes or so, the second pontoon was more or less filled.

The other seven were clinging to the sides of the raft, watching in awe as Chez turned to the canopy arch. This required him to climb into the raft itself and blow into a third valve. After several minutes, the canopy took shape over what had inflated to become, truly, a life raft.

Chez collapsed in the raft, exhausted. After hours of tending to drowned shipmates and more time spent futilely on a punctured raft, Chez, with his broken rib cage, had inflated the raft in an hour.

Off to the west, the sun was dropping fast. The raft was inflated but also halfway submerged, thanks to all the seawater that had gotten in during the previous six hours. The small rope ladder that hung into the water had torn in the chaos and was useless. Scott, one of the lightest of the crew, scrambled up over the pontoon to join Chez; he began bailing water. Leslie handed up the five-gallon jug of water she had carefully kept track of all afternoon. Others handed up Joe's bucket and all the supplies: food, water, medical kit, flashlights, and flares.

Then, one at a time, the others climbed into the tiny space, each bringing along a small flood of water from their drenched clothes. Sugar, the biggest of the eight, was one of the last to climb in and plopped his weight in the middle of the raft. Joe came last, landing upside down after being yanked up and in. The sensation of finally being out of the ocean caused Scott and Danny to vomit seawater they had swallowed.

Inside, it was wet, far too crowded, and the whole craft seemed like it could tip at any moment. Even so, an immense sense of relief settled over the eight sailors as they wriggled in together. For the first time in six hours, they didn't have to hold onto anything or tread water to stay alive. They could just sit.

Joe and others suddenly had to pee.

"What should I do?" Joe asked.

"Just pee in the raft," came the answer. Nobody had the energy to move to make room for him to pee over the edge.

The sun set at about seven p.m., not long after the eight climbed in the raft. A tiny, battery-powered light bulb in the canopy cast a faint, orange glow that provided just enough illumination to remind everyone how jammed things were. Exhausted and emotionally drained, the eight tried to arrange themselves, moving legs to accommodate one another. The eight of them were crammed into a raft meant to hold six, although even six would have been a snug fit. But there was reason to be relieved. They had dodged the horrifying prospect of a night treading water. At least eight of the twelve had survived the day; two others were missing, but were perhaps together, clinging to a piece of wood—or *something*—possibly drifting along not far from the raft.

The survivors had no motor or sail, or even paddles, although paddles wouldn't have made much of a difference. It would have been nearly impossible to row the unwieldy raft, and where would they row in any case? The nearest land was hundreds of miles away.

One thing about their predicament was absolutely clear. Sugar knew that before sailing home, Armin had canceled the communication schedule with the office back in Baltimore. He and Gail had agreed he would radio in only when he was close to Norfolk, a call she would not be expecting for at least a week. At the same time, Chez and the others were painfully aware that both of the EPIRBs had gone down to the bottom of the ocean with the *Pride*; there had been no time to grab one and set off an emergency signal.

All they could do now was sit and wait because nobody was looking for them.

CHAPTER 20

Sitting in the dark, the crew could do almost nothing to control their craft. Accomplished sailors who were used to handling a complicated schooner had become little more than human ballast, and everyone worried about the same thing—flipping the raft. It was essentially a big baggie, sealed tight except for the one triangular-shaped opening. Sugar knew that if it did flip over in the waves, there would be chaos trying to get eight people out. He preached calm: *If it goes over, stay cool, get your head into an air pocket and take a breath before trying to get out.*

Despite their exhaustion, the crew slept fitfully. The raft leaked and the rising water forced the crew to bail every half hour or so, an operation that disrupted everybody's rest. After midnight, the temperature dropped into the fifties and the small light gradually petered out, leaving the raft sloshing in disorienting, sometimes terrifying darkness. From time to time, someone asked plaintively for a little light from one of the flashlights.

* * *

Finally, the sun peeked over the horizon a little before six a.m. and light slowly worked its way into the raft. Those near the zippered flap looked out to see an immense, calm sheet of sea that provided no hint of the previous day's terror.

The eight were in varying degrees of distress. Scott had taken his pants off to use them for flotation and had spent the cool night in only shorts. At least he had his pants, though; Danny's had disappeared. And Chez was shivering in his shorts, with Nina's tiny top pulled tight across his broad shoulders.

After just one night, the raft was a mess. It smelled of plastic, and the eight sat in an acrid pool of seawater, urine, and vomit. There was nowhere to put the five-gallon bucket and large jug of water except in someone's lap. To get the raft cleaned up, Sugar, Leslie, and two others had no choice but to ease back into the ocean. While they were out, the other four bailed using the only tool they had—an empty gray plastic bag that had held some of the raft supplies. During the cleanup, someone blew into the pontoons to give the craft a little more buoyancy.

After the storm, the crew had tied the two rafts together and the second one had stayed attached all night. After unsuccessfully trying to inflate it after the storm, Sugar was determined to try one more time to see if the raft would hold air. Back in the water, he spent a good fifteen minutes blowing into one of the valves, but the raft remained a shapeless blob and he gave up. If the repair kits hadn't disappeared during the storm, they might have been able to find the hole in the raft and patch it, but that was a moot point. They were going to have to survive in one raft, although they decided to leave the useless one tied behind to add weight and stability to the functioning one.

After a half hour of bailing, the good raft was as dry as it was going to get and the four climbed back in. Suddenly, as Scott pulled himself over the pontoons, the crew heard an unmistakable whooshing. The air valve was located right in front of the only entrance and Scott had accidentally pulled the valve plug free while climbing in. Someone quickly stopped the air flow and the pontoon was reinflated yet again. It was just one more discouraging revelation about their new home.

*   *   *

Any hope of dividing the eight of them among two life rafts had dissolved. They were stuck in a six-man raft that was, in effect, a tiny, floating cell. Made by the Zodiac company, the raft measured six feet seven inches in each direction. Two flotation pontoons formed the walls; the bottom pontoon measured ten inches in diameter, the upper one slightly narrower at seven inches. The space enclosed by the pontoons—the actual sitting area—measured fifty-nine inches in each direction. Eight people crammed into twenty-four square feet, a space slightly bigger than a single-bed mattress.

The raft was made of black nylon coated with neoprene; during construction, its seams had been sealed a second time with glue to ensure air-tightness. Both in and out of the raft, a thin orange safety line wrapped around the lower pontoon. The small nylon drogue anchor was attached by rope at one side.

Above the stacked pontoons, the tentlike canopy angled in on all four sides to a height of about four feet above the floor. The sloping ceiling forced all eight to keep their shoulders stooped and heads bowed. The canopy, which was supported by an inflated arch, was made of orange nylon on the outside and white on the inside, and had been waterproofed with a sprayed-on coating of polyvinyl chloride.

There was nothing waterproof about the floor. Despite their bailing efforts, most of the eight were sitting in cool seawater, and every square inch of the floor was covered by butts and legs. The raft's structure itself was also waterlogged. The valve plugs had been dislodged for hours in the waves and a good amount of seawater had trickled through the valves and into the pontoons, making the raft ride lower in the sea than it should have. The water in the pontoons also tended to shift away from the wind and waves, giving the small craft distinct windward and leeward sides. The crew decided to try to keep the opening to the raft on the windward side. The leeward side—away from the wind—became the bow. Sugar, the heaviest of the bunch, agreed to provide some stability by remaining on the lower side of the raft, meaning his bottom was constantly under water.

*   *   *

That morning, a Thursday, the crew took stock of where they were. Sugar remembered the position he had recorded minutes before the boat sank: twenty-three degrees north latitude and sixty-seven degrees west longitude. Most of the eight had sailed in the Caribbean before and they pieced together the geography of their situation. The *Pride* sailed north-northwest from St. John before sinking in the Sargasso Sea, roughly 280 nautical miles north of the nearest land: the northwest corner of Puerto Rico. The Turks and Caicos Islands—a small chain known for mangrove swamps and idyllic scuba diving—were about the same distance to the west, while Bermuda was several hundred miles to the northeast. Otherwise, there was nothing but water.

The *Pride* went down inside the infamous slice of the Atlantic known as the Bermuda Triangle. There are no official boundaries for the triangle, but it is most often defined as the area formed by lines connecting Bermuda, Miami and San Juan, Puerto Rico. The lore of the Bermuda Triangle took on new prominence in the 1960s when wide-eyed authors recounted tales of ships and planes that disappeared in clouds of mystery. Among them were some believable accounts of magnetic compasses going haywire and odd power failures, suggesting that some unexplained electro-magnetic phenomenon may have been at work in the region. But there were also more prosaic reasons that ships ran into trouble in the triangle. The area was often wracked by hurricanes and fierce, unpredicted thunderstorms. Tricky shoals near the islands of the Caribbean played havoc with boats.

The experienced sailors knew that the prevailing current was pushing the raft westward. The best estimate put the current at somewhere over a knot per hour, meaning the raft could drift about thirty miles a day, as long as the winds remained out of the east. The long string of the Bahamas was about three hundred miles to the west; with any luck the sea might take them there. The closer they got to the islands, the better their chances of coming across a boat—perhaps a fisherman or a charter boat.

But if they missed the Bahamas, there was a very bad worst-case scenario: the raft could end up in the Gulf Stream. The fast-moving river of warm ocean water ran past Florida and up along Cape Hatteras, before turning across the Atlantic and over toward the British Isles. Joe, the only one of the eight who had gone east on the *Pride* the year before, figured he could end up in Ireland a second time. But such a trip could take months; the idea of being in the raft that long was impossible to contemplate. They needed to find a boat.

The crew took another look at their meager store of supplies. There were some treasures: the two remaining flares, two waterproof flashlights, and a first-aid kit. There was also a laughably useless plastic knife—"the butter knife," someone dubbed it—that was tied in place inside the raft. The two fishing kits were gone, unfortunately, as were the raft-patch kits, meaning a puncture to the raft would be devastating. With that in mind, Joe took the marlin spike off his belt and lashed it to the outside of the raft. That left him with nothing strapped to his side, his knife having disappeared in the sinking.

As for food, Robert had been unable to hold onto the crate of rations from the deck—the chocolate bars!—but somebody had salvaged one packet of emergency food. Inside were twenty shrink-wrapped protein bars, each the size of a candy bar. Along with the jug of water, the crew had held onto six white cans of "Purified Drinking Water," each holding 10⅔ ounces. US Coast Guard Approved was labeled on each, just above a wavy pattern of blue, green, and yellow squiggles.

As they contemplated their rations, the crew tried to answer a crucial question: How long could they expect to be in the raft? The *Pride* staff back in Baltimore had no clue the schooner had gone down and was busy preparing for the ship's return sometime around May 23, eight days away. The folks in Baltimore probably wouldn't begin to worry for a couple days after that, meaning the *beginning* of any search for the *Pride* and its crew was at least ten days off. It sounded like an eternity, but it gave the crew some rationale for a survival plan. They decided the rations would have to last ten days.

That meant they would divide two of the food bars each day, sharing one for brunch at ten and one for dinner at six. But everyone agreed to fast for the first twenty-four hours to stretch out the supply.

Having salvaged the jug, the eight seemed better fixed for water than food. But the first sip from the jug was jarring. The container had lost its cap during the sinking and the water inside tasted brackish—not as salty as seawater, but definitely not fresh. Drinking ocean water would be disastrous: the high salt content would lead quickly to dehydration as the body moved to expel excess salt. But Leslie and Sugar, who had read many accounts of survival at sea, suggested the group should drink some of the brackish water early on to help their bodies adjust to the higher salt content. The first day, the crew gave themselves a couple of sips of both brackish and fresh water. For a cup, they used the clear plastic cover taken off the non-working light inside the canopy. The small cover resembled a cap from a large soda bottle, or a communion cup.

Sitting so low in the covered raft, nobody could see much of anything except for the never-ending expanse of water through the canopy opening. Their best hope for rescue was to be spotted by a boat of some kind, but unless a boat somehow ended up nearby, the tiny raft was all but invisible in the water. The crew attempted to establish a regular watch system; several wore wristwatches with alarms that could remind them to scan the horizon. Every thirty minutes, someone took a turn and poked through the opening to look around. Danny and Chez couldn't help with this chore, having lost their glasses in the sinking. It was decided that Sugar (and his heft) should stay seated to keep the raft stable, so the others took turns.

By noon on Thursday, the sun was blazing and the temperature inside the raft was sweltering. Joe gingerly eased out of the opening and looked around.

There it was! A ship heading west, clearly visible. Joe could see that it was a cruise ship: the white superstructure above the deck was clearly for passengers, not cargo. Joe provided a running narrative.

"We're on his starboard bow," he announced. The cruise ship was passing close by—close enough to spot people leaning on the passenger rail. Scott peered over the waves and heard the faint sound of music.

"I can see people . . . nobody's looking," Scott said. For the others, it was like listening to a radio play-by-play.

When it seemed the raft had gotten as close to the ship as it would, the eight quickly agreed that it was time to use one of the remaining flares. Surely someone on the ship—a watch officer or even a passenger—would notice the flare.

Suddenly things looked very promising. A rescue seemed possible—and a rescue on a cruise ship of all things. Not a bad way to get home, under the circumstances. Joe took one of the flares and jerked the firing cord, sending a red beacon high above the ocean. For a few beats, everyone waited for something to happen—some indication that the ship had seen the flare. They even joked about it. Sugar imagined a little old lady in tennis shoes trying to convince the skeptical captain that, yes, she really had seen a raft off the starboard bow. As the minutes passed, Joe took off his yellow foul-weather gear and waved it frantically to try to get someone's attention. The ship, though, continued to head westward.

Shoot the other one! someone suggested. Again, the group agreed. It was the last flare but there was no telling when such a good opportunity would come along again. Joe fired the second one, with the ship still tantalizingly close. Again they waited for some sign that the ship was turning around, or perhaps some kind of signal acknowledging their distress. The eight sat quietly, waiting to hear the ship's horn: five blasts would mean the ship had seen their emergency signaling. But no horn sounded over the ocean, the music faded, and the ship slowly disappeared. It was a crushing blow. The three flares were gone, used up in two fits of undue optimism. The crew realized, belatedly, that they should have saved the flares for nighttime signaling.

Scott sank back into his corner of the raft and cried. *If they're this close and didn't see us, how close do we have to be?* he wondered to himself. *Do they have to run us over?*

*   *   *

The afternoon dragged on. Snippets of conversation occasionally broke the silence. Someone brought up Armin and Vinny. Both were strong, and Vinny had calmly survived the sinking of his fishing boat only a year earlier. If anybody could make it without a life raft, it would be Vinny. Huddled in the raft, it was comforting to imagine that ten people had survived the sinking of the *Pride* and were now in two groups: eight in the raft and the two others somewhere else.

Maybe they're clinging to a piece of debris, kicking together toward land, someone suggested. It was a long shot but not inconceivable. Furthermore, the location of the sinking was along a well-traveled route from the Caribbean to the upper East Coast. There were plenty of boats in the area.

Sugar remembered *Kestrel,* the yacht that Armin had radioed a couple of hours before the sinking. The two captains had promised to talk again at four p.m. that afternoon. It was conceivable that the *Kestrel* captain, after not being able to reach the *Pride,* would have contacted the Coast Guard. For all the *Pride* crew knew, the Coast Guard could already be scouring the area.

Occasionally, the conversation turned back to the disaster. There wasn't much to be said about Nina and Barry; it was too painful. Danny, for one, couldn't shake the image of the life leaving his old sailing friend, Barry, next to him in the water.

Instead, the sailors talked about the list of things they had lost. *The sextant,* Joe remembered. *Eamonn's not going to be happy.* This, of course, was a joke. Joe had borrowed the sextant from his uncle, Eamonn McGeady, a Baltimore businessman who was utterly devoted to the *Pride* and had served on its board of directors for years. Chez remembered his Moroccan purchases.

Then, out of the blue, someone remembered the cats. Tuck and Bill had also gone down with the *Pride.*

Someone suggested singing. It was a corny idea, but they didn't have anything else to do. The only problem was finding the right songs. The Beatles's "Yesterday," seemed fine until they got to the line, "All my troubles seemed so far away / Now it looks as though they're here to stay." "American Pie" worked until they reached the lyric, "This'll be the day that I die."

Simon and Garfunkel worked, as did a couple of Grateful Dead songs, a tribute to Barry. "Puff the Magic Dragon" also worked well. There was also some optimistic wedding planning for Leslie and Sugar. And finally the others confessed to Scott about the trick they had played on him with the mustard crock that never seemed to empty out.

That night, no one could see anything. Outside, the ocean rose and fell, sloshing against the raft incessantly, and the wind picked up enough to be heard occasionally. Inside, the space was filled with the sounds of breathing, rubbing, and shifting as eight people tried to stay warm and perhaps get comfortable enough to sleep. Once in a while, someone would go stir-crazy from being confined in such close, dark quarters.

Can you turn on the light for a second? someone would plead.

The group decided to try to conserve the flashlight batteries. The yellow D-cell flashlights, the only source of illumination available, were worth their weight in gold. Even so, if the request was desperate enough, nobody objected to a quick flick of the light to give everyone a peek at their surroundings.

Thursday night, as the waves picked up, Sugar hunkered down in his spot in the middle of the raft and listened to the pointed conversation. Everyone, it seemed, was bickering.

Can you move over?

I need some room. Your elbow is grinding into me.

There was something different about the whining, though. People were talking faster, almost frantically. And there was something else. Sugar noticed that everyone was breathing heavily—including himself. Then he realized that the only opening to the outside was zipped tight. They were suffocating.

"There's no air in here! Open the door," Sugar shouted. Someone pulled up the zipper and fresh air flooded the small space. With the door snugly zipped, the interior space was nearly airtight, thanks to the thick plastic coating on the canopy and the tightly glued seams.

Wouldn't that be perfect, he thought. *We survive a shipwreck and then suffocate in the life raft.*

CHAPTER 21

Friday
May 16, 1986
On the raft

Thursday night was no better than Wednesday. The moon was half full but did little to illuminate the raft. Inside, the eight sat hunched in gloomy silence, unable to see anything.

During the night, the wind built, the waves grew, and the raft rocked back and forth on the Atlantic. It was disconcerting to be trapped inside with no sense of how big the next wave would be. Water cascaded over the canopy and down the sides, and Susie began to worry.

"I'm afraid the roof on the raft is going to collapse," she whispered tearfully to Leslie.

"Hey, it's not so bad," Leslie tried to reassure her. "You're going to be all right."

Scott dreaded the moment it came time for him to sit in the corner, in water up to his waist and far from the opening. Hunkered in there, he became almost paralyzed with fear. The waves pounded one after the other over his back and pushed the canopy down over his head and shoulders. The power of the ocean was being held back by a thin sheet of plastic. Scott knew he was helpless, a feeling aggravated by his inability to see in the complete darkness or tell how high the waves were: the next wave could be two feet, or it could be ten feet; there was no way of knowing.

The hours ticked by; once in a while, someone looked outside to see if there were any vessels in the vicinity. There weren't. In the morning, the crew noticed that water had condensed across the inside of the canopy, and they happily ran their fingers along the plastic and sucked off the water. This was a freebie that didn't count against their daily ration and momentarily eased the dry mouth all were experiencing. Chez leaned his head back and licked the droplets but nearly choked on the nasty taste left by the plastic.

Given the tangle of bodies, it took several minutes in the morning for everyone to pee. There was no pretense of privacy anymore, but the group decided it was worth the effort to keep the wastewater out of the raft, if possible. The six men used an empty water can. Leslie and Susie could make their way to the opening of the raft and dangle out over the ocean.

By ten o'clock, it was time for brunch. Somebody unwrapped one of the protein bars and used the bottom of a sneaker as a cutting surface on which to slice the bar into eight portions. The trick was to keep the bar from crumbling and falling off the shoe sole and into the wet raft. The label on the food had washed off in the storm, so they weren't sure what was in the bars. They tasted faintly of chicken, or maybe chocolate. The one-eighth share was tiny, but it was something. When some of Sugar's crumbled out of his hand and into his thick beard, Leslie vacuumed out the pieces with her mouth.

The terror of the night made the days seem easier. Scott tried to focus on the positives. *We have a raft and we have a plan for making the food last until we'll be missed. Plus, nobody is about to die*, Scott thought. It made no sense to think too far ahead, he decided. He focused on getting through the day.

Mercifully, it rained on Friday, which meant a good drenching of pure fresh water. Someone held the bucket out through the flap and caught a few ounces of water to be shared before the clouds passed perhaps fifteen minutes later.

Then, a ship appeared; it was well off in the distance, though. Like the cruise ship the day before, it lumbered on without slowing.

As the raft bobbed steadily westward that day, the weather remained calm but the tight quarters made everyone miserable. Elbows and hips ground relentlessly into each other. They had two choices: keep their knees tucked tightly to their bodies, or stretch out and become intertwined and nestled with others. No one could stretch or move without disrupting the entire group.

The crew decided the big water jug and the five-gallon bucket took up too much space and had to go outside. Leslie did what she could to plug the jug to keep out more seawater and she used her safety harness to attach the jug and bucket so they dragged along behind. That meant the raft towed a second raft, a drogue anchor, the jug of water, and a bucket.

Later in the day, Scott, who was sitting near the open flap, felt a snap and could tell that something had broken loose. He turned and saw that the entire load had come loose and was slowly being left behind.

He turned to Robert and asked whether he should get the stuff. "No," Robert answered. "It's not worth the risk."

But Scott couldn't stand the thought of losing the extra gear. He quickly took off his yellow foul-weather gear and rolled out of the raft into the water. He swam to the second raft, by then about forty feet away, and turned to pull it back to the inflated raft. But the thing was so heavy, he could barely move it. Robert leaned out through the opening and saw Scott struggling to swim with the load. He was falling behind.

"Scott! Come on back. Forget it," he shouted.

It wasn't that simple. Freed of the excess weight that had been attached, the raft and its cargo of seven people quickly picked up speed. Scott reluctantly let go of the second raft, put his head down, and began swimming hard to catch up. Despite being a solid swimmer, Scott tired quickly in his weakened state and resorted to a modified breast stroke, keeping his face out of the water to catch his breath.

"I'll catch up. Don't worry," he shouted to Robert. A few moments later, he put his face back in the water, did a determined crawl, and finally reached the others. He held on to the raft for a few seconds, then pulled back over the pontoons; by then the red jug and second raft had bobbed far from sight. The eight were down to less than two quarts of fresh water.

"Do you think there are any sharks around here?" someone asked. It was an innocent question.

"NO!" replied several others in near-unison.

But by the second day, someone noticed something ominous swimming below the raft. It turned out to be not sharks but dorado, or dolphin fish. Known in some restaurants as mahi-mahi, the fish often congregate under boats and rafts and are easy to recognize with their distinctive yellow and green coloring. Four years earlier, American sailor Steven Callahan survived seventy-six days adrift in a life raft after his small sailboat sank, in large measure by eating dorado. Callahan, though, had a spear gun that he used to catch fish.

Despite losing its fishing gear, the *Pride* crew decided to try. Someone fashioned a hook from a safety pin and lowered it down on a string. It dangled among the dorado for a few minutes, but without any bait, the fish weren't interested. The crew gave up rather than risk puncturing the raft with the pin.

Eager for anything else to eat, Scott later scooped up some seaweed and suggested they try it. The stuff was horrible; it was too salty and hard on the stomach. But it was psychologically reassuring that there was food out there that could be eaten if things got dire enough.

Among the eight on the raft, many had read sea survival stories such as Callahan's, whose book hit the bestseller list at about the time the *Pride* sailed from Spain. One of the best-known adventures was that of the Robertson family, whose staysail schooner was knocked over by a pod of whales as the boat headed across the Pacific for the Galapagos Islands in 1972. Five members of the family and one crew member drifted for more than five weeks in a raft and dinghy before being rescued by a Japanese fishing boat.

The next year, Maurice and Maralyn Bailey survived 117 days in a dinghy and life raft after a whale banged a hole in their small sailboat in the Pacific. Circumstances differed in each of the three stories, but not the bottom line: everyone made it home.

Another brief rain shower blew through Saturday, but without a bucket, the crew had to improvise using Nina's foul-weather pants, which weren't being worn. Someone tied off one of the legs and fashioned a bright yellow funnel to catch the water dripping off the zipper in the raft's doorway. The water trickled steadily down through the pants leg and they were able to catch about twelve ounces of fresh water in an empty water can.

Around mid-day, another ship emerged over the horizon. The flashlight was useless, so someone took a turn waving foul-weather gear. The ship cruised on, oblivious. Three ships in three days kept hope simmering, but none had noticed the little raft.

Most of the conversation centered on the mundane details of getting by, although there was a loosely enforced rule against whining. Whose turn was it to watch for ships? Can somebody give me a little room for my leg? The group discussed the first food they would have after getting back to dry land: coffee ice cream and pizza topped the list.

Occasionally someone brought up the sinking.

The one question nobody could seem to answer revolved around Armin. Where was he going when he swam off? Maybe Armin had tried to grab something in the water. Maybe he had seen Vinny and attempted a rescue.

Why did the boat sink? was the larger question; it was also hard to answer. Not the mechanics, which were fairly straightforward: The intense wind had developed so quickly the boat had been overwhelmed. But that didn't mean the sinking was simply an act of God. The question hovered unasked: Was someone to blame?

While at the Merchant Marine Academy, Robert had studied admiralty law and he tried to sort out the possible legal issues. He knew there was no workers compensation for this kind of maritime accident; an injured party in such a case would have to sue for compensation. But it seemed clear that *someone* was responsible for their predicament.

"I don't know if we'll get out of this, but if we do, we'll be okay financially," Robert told the group.

Chez suggested that the company that made the life rafts could be liable for the sorry performance of its products. But the discussion of fault and payouts fizzled. Given the circumstances, it felt good to be alive and anybody who made it home would have plenty of time to learn the ins and outs of maritime law.

Sugar was holding up well, despite enduring the worst conditions of the eight. Acting as ballast, he shifted his weight from one side of the raft to the other at regular intervals. That gave everyone at least some relief from having to sit in water—everyone except Sugar. His back was starting to ache from the cool water and the constant pressure against the pontoon.

Joe grew quiet, put off by the constant rocking of the raft and the incessant rubbing of body against body. And he balked at helping with the regular bailing that others insisted on, deciding it created unnecessary agitation. He didn't say much, but Joe was determined to make it home. His fleeting contemplation of sacrificing himself in the water had not returned. He remembered that his mother's favorite uncle had been killed during World War II, and he knew what a loss it had been for her. Like Robert, he had a sister—two, in fact—pregnant back home. *If he died, the two babies would grow up thinking of him as this mysterious Uncle Joe who was lost at sea,* he thought. He hated the idea.

Robert didn't complain much but his body was a tender mass of sores and scrapes. His Gore-Tex foul-weather pants, with their stiff lining, felt like sandpaper on his legs and butt. Scott and Susie, both Outward Bound graduates, seemed to be doing well. Susie adopted the attitude that this was a group effort. If she focused on others, she would not worry so much about herself. *A team only moves as quickly as its slowest member,* she thought. The idea of teamwork was easy enough for the group to embrace. They had already spent ten weeks working as a team in the tight confines of the *Pride*. The conditions had become considerably tighter, but the principle was still the same.

Whatever the principles, in reality, Chez was suffering. He couldn't see much without glasses, and his ribs ached. For a couple of days he had been stuffed in Nina's foul-weather top and had gone without pants, and now his legs were developing ugly sores from the water and constant scraping against the stiff nylon raft. Robert had tried to help by stripping off the pair of cotton pants he wore under his foul-weather gear and giving them to Chez; Scott agreed to trade foul-weather tops, donning Nina's and giving his to Chez. The change of clothes provided some relief, but his condition continued to deteriorate.

Danny was also starting to become a concern. He, too, was hobbled by the loss of his glasses. Without foul-weather pants, he was colder than the others. Everyone knew about his brush with a hurricane nearly two years earlier, and nobody had forgotten his screaming fits on board. Now he was living a nightmare, cooped up in a claustrophobic raft that could be capsized at almost any time.

Danny and Chez grumbled the loudest about the conditions. When they sat next to each other, the combination proved unbearable as the other six had to listen to the two bicker about everything—elbows, knees, whatever. Leslie watched them go, aware that these guys, both active and energetic, were not suited to this kind of hibernating. Finally, the group separated them.

When Danny was forced to shift into one of the raft's wet corners, he groaned: "There's water down here."

"Christ, Danny! Just sit there and shut up," Joe erupted.

As the days went by, modesty grew less important. Almost unable to move, Chez's bladder was on the verge of exploding, but he couldn't physically manage to pee because he was scrunched up so tight. Finally, after warning everyone, he un-tucked his body and lay out over the other seven sets of legs and relieved himself. Nobody said a word.

While the space crunch was unrelenting, water was now a far more important concern. The human body normally needs roughly sixty-four ounces of water per day to stave off dehydration. But each crew member was getting no more than an ounce or two per day.

The effects of dehydration can be deadly serious. In 1982, five crew members from a sixty-foot yacht that sank off the coast of North Carolina were cast adrift in a rubber dinghy. Two of the five, including the captain, were so thirsty they drank seawater. The excessive salt intake screwed up their brain chemistry and addled their thinking, and the two jumped in the water to swim to shore. Both were killed by sharks. A third crew member died from deep cuts she suffered during the sinking; the other two were picked up by a Russian freighter after five days.

On the *Pride* raft, everyone had grown parched and fantasized about something to drink. Susie dreamed about guzzling water from a big pitcher. In Robert's version of the dream, the raft floated up to a marina bar in the Caribbean filled with cold beer. But when the crew discovered that the person they were looking for—a creation of Robert's subconscious—was not at the bar, they were forced to push off the dock and drift away in their raft again, still thirsty.

By the third night, Chez was hallucinating.

"Can I get a drink of water?" he asked one night. He was completely serious.

"No, Chez," came the answer.

A minute or so passed. "Okay, how about a beer?"

Aside from the strange requests, Chez began receiving strange visitors—at least in his mind. In one dream, an elegant little man wearing a dark suit walked slowly through a Japanese garden. Sculptures lined the walks and candles filled the space with delicate light. In his hand the man carried clear pieces of ice; one at a time he placed them in small stone structures, where they held their shape before dissolving into streams of the purest water. The scene was one of perfect simplicity—just ice, stone, and candlelight.

As Chez's condition deteriorated, Susie took pity and used her body as kind of a blanket to warm him. In his confusion, Chez thought there was something sexual happening. "Can't we go up on deck and be alone?" he wondered.

At another point, Chez imagined he was at the *Pride*'s galley table and tried to push away to go get cabbages. The weird hallucination spooked everyone, including Chez.

"I think I'm going crazy," he announced in a moment of surprising lucidity. Hearing this, Danny erupted in his own fit of anxiety.

Things got desperate on Saturday night when Chez, imagining himself in downtown St. Thomas, pushed up and tried to get out of the raft to go for a walk; they quickly pulled him back down and talked him out of a stroll. Chez didn't try it again, but it was clear the others would have to watch him closely. Tall, strong, and delusional, Chez would be hard to stop.

Leslie and Sugar's engagement provided occasional diversion as the others helped them with their wedding plans. *If you had gotten the other raft inflated, you could have had a honeymoon suite,* someone teased Sugar.

Although Leslie wasn't one to complain much, she was hurting physically. At one point, the salt water caused her vision to go so cloudy she couldn't stand her assigned watch. Her stomach problems also persisted, causing bouts of diarrhea, which the others simply had to accept as part of being adrift in a small raft.

She also developed a urinary tract infection that caused her to lose control of her bladder. By Saturday night, Leslie was in agony. Her hips were tender from the constant friction of rubbing against the raft and her crewmates; her back was raw from all the chafing. It was all but unbearable when the urine-soaked seawater washed over the open sores along her backbone.

"Sugar, I got holes in my back and my kidneys are on fire," she said mournfully, her eyes flooded with tears.

With help, Leslie peeled off the foul-weather gear she had worn for more than three days straight. Susie and others ripped up a T-shirt to dry off her back and Susie applied ointment from the first-aid kit, which eased the pain. The sores needed to air out, but it was too cold to leave the gear off all night and Leslie was forced to put the thick pants and poncho top back on.

By Saturday night, their fourth on the raft, the ten-day plan they had charted optimistically on Thursday morning seemed unrealistic. Nobody was thinking much about reaching the Bahamas, much less the possibility of a good blow up the Gulf Stream to Ireland. The raft had probably drifted one hundred miles or so in a westerly direction. They were still many days away from landfall, if they were lucky. But the problems of the last twenty-four hours made it clear that all eight were not going to last that long.

CHAPTER 22

Sunday
May 18, 1986
On the raft

On land and sea, life in the sailing world went on as usual.

The *Westward* returned to its home port on Cape Cod, completing another semester of sailing for college students. On *Te Vega*, somewhere in the Atlantic, Jennifer and the rest of the crew were in the home stretch of their tour of duty with the high school kids. And in Massachusetts, naval architect Roger Long spoke over the weekend to a gathering of sailors about the stability study he had worked on—the study that had raised doubts in the mind of Armin and others about the *Pride*'s ability to withstand the worst of storms.

But the most important news in the world of sailing—the sinking of the *Pride of Baltimore*—was being held tightly within the orange and black raft bobbing slowly westward over the Sargasso Sea. Nobody had made a distress call and no ships had witnessed the sinking. The still-raw memories of that day belonged solely to eight people. The fury of the wind, the split-second decisions at the helm, Danny's determined but unsuccessful attempt to reach the staysail sheet, and, finally, the sight of the *Pride*'s flapping pennants disappearing under the waves were details yet to be shared with anyone. The raft's eight passengers had replayed the sinking in their minds as often as they could bear it, and they had said their own private good-byes to Nina and Barry. Now on their fourth full day adrift, the crew looked ahead with a grim quiet.

There was little talking and less laughter in the raft, which smelled stale and salty. Memories of that first day and the giddy thought that they might get to ride home on a cruise ship had long since disappeared by Sunday. The reality was that they could be floating for days to come.

Joe's teeth chattered; Chez's feet had ballooned and the sores on his legs had grown even more alarming; Robert could barely stand because of the abrasions on his legs; and Danny seemed lost and fragile and had barely looked outside the raft in days.

Brunch was served as usual at ten a.m.—yet another tiny piece of the food bar and a sip of water. Saturday night had been hard. They all were exhausted and had sometimes gone an hour or more at a stretch without bothering to push up through the doorway and scan the horizon for ships. It was an ordeal to reach the opening and get up on one's knees, an ordeal that disrupted all eight on board. Once the lookout made it to the opening, one or two others had to hold on from behind to make sure the lookout didn't flip out of the raft.

Even harder was trying to push aside seven sets of bottoms and legs to find enough room to sit down again once the watch was over. There was little need for anyone to order the others around; the raft had become a pure democracy. But Sugar didn't like what was happening and decided to exercise a bit of authority.

"We have to be more regular with our watches," he told them. From now on, he said, there must be a watch every half hour in the daytime, and every fifteen minutes at night. An hour was simply too long between lookout watches, he said, since a fast-moving ship could pass them by, unnoticed, in that time.

The hours ticked by as the sun beat down on the raft, sending the temperature inside soaring. The monotony finally broke at around six o'clock when they ate dinner. Since their first raft meal Thursday, the crew had stuck to its rationing plan; someone cut open the seventh food bar, leaving thirteen in the supply bag. Water, though, was a concern, given the contamination of the big jug and the modest amount of rain. As for the raft, it was starting to deteriorate. Under the pressure of eight bodies, instead of the normal load of six, some of the raft's seams were starting to pull apart. The flaws weren't yet critical but it was clear the little boat wasn't going to hold together forever.

As the sun dropped in the west, everyone realized the nighttime terrors were about to begin again. Susie dreaded the prospect of another night in the claustrophobic raft.

We can't keep this up, she thought. *Please, God, send us a rescue boat before dark.*

Shortly after dinner, Scott took the watch and excitedly broke the news that another ship was off to the east, the fourth in four days.

It's a freighter, Susie said, peering out over the water. It was hard to see above the waves, but she could make out white smokestacks above a black hull. The ship appeared to be at least two miles away, perhaps close enough to be seen. The problem was the setting sun, which was behind the raft in relation to the ship. Scott realized that the flashlight would be useless; anyone looking westward from the freighter would see nothing but the sun. By the time the sun was below the horizon, the ship would be too far away for anyone on board to spot the flashlight. The only hope was to attract attention and Scott began vigorously waving a foul-weather top back and forth and shouting into the twilight. He kept at it for several minutes, desperate for somebody to see him over the waves. For the fourth time in four days, a boat cruised on, oblivious.

Early on, Leslie had tamped down any expectations by recounting a sea adventure she had read while crossing the Indian Ocean. Photographs in the book included tiny, barely visible dots in the ocean, dots that turned out to be life rafts. Everyone realized that it would be near-miraculous for someone to spot a six-and-a-half-foot-square raft sitting only a few feet high in the water, particularly in daylight. Even so, each of the ship sightings had caused a stir on the raft and the crew tried everything they could think of. During one, Robert used the top of a water can as a mirror to try to attract attention; someone else used the metal reflector from the flashlight. Nothing worked and each sighting ended in disappointment.

After this most recent one, with the sun gone in the west, the temperature dropped and the crew resigned themselves to a fifth night of darkness and fear.

Leslie struggled to poke through the raft opening at about ten p.m. The air had turned cool and a new moon did little to illuminate the great Atlantic. Hungry, tired, and sore, Leslie scanned the horizon in all directions. Then she saw it: another ship. The lights were unmistakable but it was miles off in the distance. She watched for a while, long enough to realize the ship was not coming much closer. She turned back to confer with Sugar and Robert, the former merchant marine.

"I think it's too far to signal," Leslie said wearily. The batteries in the two flashlights wouldn't last forever. Already, someone had to take out the batteries and rejuvenate them by rolling them around between their hands. Sugar and Robert agreed it would be unwise to waste them trying to signal a ship that was so far away. The decision was sound but once again disappointing: one plane and five ships had now passed nearby but failed to see their flares, light signals, or waving.

In the raft, the usual discomfort played itself out. This time it was Scott's turn to plead for help; he was tired of sitting in the water and asked to move. The others let him sit near the doorway, where it was dry. After a round of grumbling and shifting, the eight settled into place. The watches continued on schedule—11:00, 11:30 and so on—as the crew fell in and out of sleep.

Around 1:30 A.M., Leslie pushed herself through the opening and peered over the waves for any sign of another vessel. Then, she saw it: another set of lights.

"I see something," she said softly to Robert, who sat next to the opening.

"Don't say anything." There was no sense stirring everybody for no reason, he figured.

Perched on her knees and leaning out through the flap, Leslie watched and waited for the vessel to come closer. This one looked to be passing a good bit nearer than the others as it headed south. How far was it? A couple of miles, maybe. In any case, the night was clear and the waves weren't all that high so Leslie grabbed one of the flashlights and began signaling. She used the flashlight to send out a steady S-O-S, with Robert helping her with the right sequence—three shorts, three longs, three shorts. As she signaled, Robert's mind flashed back to the countless hours he had spent learning signals at the academy—something all graduates had to master before they could receive a license.

Leslie's fingers soon ached from pressing the flashlight button on and off, so she resorted to using her hand to block the beam and create the appropriate sequence of lights. She couldn't make out anything about the ship, except for its lights.

"I can see the range lights," she told Robert, referring to the two white lights that large commercial ships run at the bow and stern. The stern light sat well above the one at the bow, creating an angle that showed which direction the ship was heading. Soon, Leslie could make out a green running light on the ship's starboard side. The white and green lights made their way southward as Leslie continued signaling. The drone of the huge ship's engine rumbled over the ocean and Leslie shouted back: "Hey! Over here!"

Minutes ticked by and Leslie kept signaling, switching between the two flashlights when one faded. Behind her, the others had caught on that there was a ship and they took turns warming up the batteries with their hands. Joe leaned into Sugar and whispered: "I hope this is it. This *better* be it." The nighttime provided the best opportunity for being seen but there was no guarantee they would have many more chances before their flashlight batteries faded entirely.

Leslie watched in dismay as the green running light moved ever southward. Scott peered out around Leslie's legs and could make out the ship's stern light, meaning the ship had passed. This one wasn't stopping either.

CHAPTER 23

Monday
May 19, 1986
1:40 A.M.
Aboard the M.V. Toro Horten

John V. Andersen sipped a cup of coffee on the bridge of the *Toro Horten* and stared out into a pretty spring night. The temperature hovered in the sixties; there were few clouds and a new moon was setting. All in all, these were perfect conditions. As one of the ship's first officers, the thirty-six-year-old Andersen had command of the early-morning watch.

The Norwegian oil tanker had cruised out of New York harbor three days earlier bound for one of the busy oil terminals in Amuay Bay, Venezuela. The three-year-old tanker was enormous, able to carry more than 375,000 barrels of crude oil and make nearly 16 knots in good seas. From end to end, the *Toro* was 680 feet long and its superstructure soared five stories above the deck. The tanker plowed through the Atlantic with such steady effortlessness that you could forget you were on a boat.

The *Toro* carried a crew of nineteen: fifteen Norwegians, three Spaniards, and Andersen, a native of Denmark. The oldest was a fifty-seven-year-old mechanic; the youngest a shy twenty-one-year-old female radio operator from Oslo. The crew was happy to be working following the bankruptcy of the *Toro*'s previous owner and the generally lousy condition of the Norwegian shipping industry.

The monotony of the run down to Venezuela had been broken the night before when much of the crew stayed up to celebrate Independence Day, a Norwegian national holiday. But now, a good twenty-four hours later, it was back to the routine, with only a skeleton watch on duty and the rest of the crew asleep. On the bridge, Andersen stood watch with Jesus Marino-Varela, a deck-hand from the coast of Spain who had turned fifty a week before. The two men chatted in Norwegian, a second language for both, keeping an ear open for the radio and scanning the dark seas ahead.

As the ship cruised south, the two men noticed the faint light of a fishing boat off the starboard bow, perhaps a few miles to the southwest. Staring intently over the water, the two men could make out the light blinking, which was standard procedure to alert the huge tanker to watch out for the much smaller vessel. They gave the fishing boat little thought as the *Toro* pushed ahead. The run from New York to Amuay Bay took the boat almost due south, and the boat routinely encountered big commercial vessels, as well as the occasional cruise ship, fishing boat, or yacht.

As the tanker moved steadily southward, Andersen's eye kept returning to the blinking light, the only other vessel visible. There was something odd about the white light off in the distance. It seemed to disappear again and again behind the waves. He stared. It wasn't just the waves causing the light to flicker; the light seemed to be flashing in a pattern, but not a regular one. If this fishing boat was trying to signal the tanker, it was not being very precise about it.

Andersen, as the ranking officer, reached for the ship's radio and tried to hail somebody on the fishing boat to figure out what was going on. Andersen's radio call met with silence. Finally, the radio crackled with a response, only it came from a ship one hundred miles north, which was apparently the only other vessel in the general vicinity. After establishing that this was not the nearby boat, Andersen glanced back down to the odd light off to starboard. He checked the *Toro*'s radar but saw no indication of a boat of any kind. Andersen left the bridge and stepped out into the cool spring air to get a better look, taking a bullhorn with him. Using the bull-horn, Andersen again tried to hail the boat, or whatever it was. He got no response but the signaling continued, still in an irregular and perplexing sequence. On the *Toro Horten*, as on any boat, a mate had only so much authority. Andersen concluded he had done all he could on his own; he would have to wake up the captain to fig-ure out what to do about this curious light.

Coincidentally, the ship's captain, forty-nine-year-old Arne Ros-tad, was having trouble sleeping and had just walked onto the bridge to get his own cup of coffee. Andersen explained what was going on and he and the captain, along with Marino-Varela, stared intently at the flashing light.

Finally Andersen figured out the pattern.

It looks like an SOS, he told the others; three short lights followed by three long and three more short, the international signal of dis-tress. Watching the pattern, Rostad agreed. He knew the *Toro* was due in Venezuela, and time was money in the shipping business. But the rules of the sea dictated his next move.

We're coming about, the captain told his mate.

On the raft, Leslie couldn't take her eyes off the ship's disappear-ing lights. Robert, who had sailed around the world on an oil tanker, urged her not to give up hope just yet. He knew that if the crew had spotted her light—and that was a big *if,* given the distance—it would take several minutes for the ship to slow and turn back.

Then it happened. Across the waves, Leslie suddenly spotted a tiny speck of red—beautiful, glowing red. The red was the portside running light and it meant only one thing: the ship had turned! She waited to be certain, signaling all the while. Then she shared the news with the others.

"It's coming to get us!" Leslie shouted. Others craned out to take a look at the ship. The lights told the story: this vessel—what-ever it was—had turned around. Suddenly, after four days and four-teen hours, someone had spotted them.

Giddiness took hold among the eight; even Chez came out of his stupor to celebrate. Then someone suggested drinking the water.

They popped open a couple of cans and took real swigs of water, their first in almost five days.

The *Toro* made a wide U-turn, coming about to bring up the blinking light on its port side. Inside the raft, Sugar tried to cool the excitement, urging everyone to stay calm during the next several minutes. He warned them that it would take careful choreography to avoid capsizing as they left the raft. Leslie continued her signaling to guide the big ship, while Scott and others peeked through the triangular opening.

Robert tried to prepare the others for what awaited them, reminding them that the freighter crew might not speak English. "Don't forget that we're guests on their ship," he added.

After a few minutes, the view of endless sky and water that had been their only touchstone with the world was suddenly transformed into a wall of rust-streaked orange metal that blocked everything else from view. The sea turned calm as the ship blocked wind and waves. When the ship's searchlight fixed on the raft, the elation inside turned feverish.

They've got us!

Rostad, the *Toro*'s captain, summoned another first officer, Frank Amundsen, out of his cabin to lead the investigation of the distress signal. Only twenty-eight, the officer was about the same age as Barry and Vinny. Amundsen prepared to launch the *Toro*'s small diesel-powered boat, which was lowered to the water by mechanical lift. He and Marino-Varela, who had spotted the light in the first place, put on life preservers and set out in the small motorboat. They pushed off from the *Toro* and with Amundsen at the wheel, motored out to find out who was signaling. They quickly reached the orange and black raft bobbing in the waves, circled once to see what they were dealing with, and then pulled close.

Amundsen shouted in English, "How many are in there? Are there three?"

Leslie shouted back, "No. There are eight of us."

"Oh, shit."

Amundsen pulled the launch close to the raft and cut the engine, allowing the motorboat to drift over. Marino-Varela and Amundsen reached out and pulled Leslie up into the boat. One by one, the two men hauled the others up on the launch, as well as their meager but well-rationed cache of supplies and food, including Nina's pants.

Then came a decision: What to do with the raft, their tiny, stinking home. It was too large to fit on the launch and Amundsen decided to sink it rather than allow it to float in the ocean and attract attention. Before the *Toro*'s Spanish deckhand could plunge his knife into the raft, Joe shouted, "Wait!" He reached down to grab his spike, which was lashed to the outside of the raft; he wasn't going to leave both of his tools in the Atlantic. Then, several of them punctured the raft, and the air that Chez had blown in nearly five days earlier finally escaped. The little boat slowly sank.

Amundsen's crowded launch headed back to the *Toro*'s port side and pulled up alongside a Jacob's ladder dangling down from the huge tanker's deck. Amundsen told the *Pride* crew that most of them would have to climb up to the deck, as the *Toro*'s lift was not powerful enough to hoist the launch and all eight survivors. From the deck, crewmen lowered a safety harness for the raft's passengers to use while climbing, but the *Pride* sailors, as usual, opted not to bother with it. As they began the climb up, Sugar warned his crew mates: "Don't try to walk," but he needn't have bothered.

Joe went first, and despite the fact that he hadn't used his legs for four and a half days, he scrambled up the rope ladder in an adrenaline-fueled push. He collapsed the second he hit the deck. Scott followed and he, too, fell down. One by one the others climbed, falling into a rapturous pile on the metal deck, laughing and crying at once. The horror of the sinking, the five days of floating and worrying, the unspoken fears, all dissolved in a moment of pure joy. The Norwegians watched the unexpected scene with bemused delight. Chez, who could barely move, stayed in the launch for the ride up to the deck. Once there, a burly bearded *Toro* sailor grabbed and lifted him on to the deck and kept an arm around him.

Hakon Tonder, the *Toro*'s forty-four-year-old chief first officer,

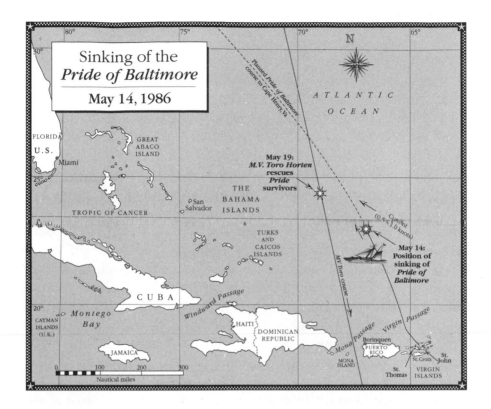

Sinking of the
Pride of Baltimore
May 14, 1986

took a good look at the eight newcomers and could see that all were exhausted and hungry, and all had rashes of some kind. One of them—Chez, he would learn later—looked terrible. It was a good thing the *Toro* had found them, Tonder decided. That one would not have made it much longer.

Crew members helped the eight make their way to the galley. "Is it me, or is this boat rocking?" Joe asked, to the amusement of the Norwegians. On the way to the galley, the crew spotted a stainless steel water fountain. Chez, who had dreamed about cool, clear waterfalls on the raft, stood and stared with wonder. Sugar leaned in and gulped down water, as did others.

In the mess hall, pitchers of cold water and juice waited on the tables and *Toro* crew members set out Ritz crackers. The eight *Pride* sailors guzzled the juice and feasted on crackers; nothing had ever tasted so good.

Captain Rostad and a communications officer joined the eight survivors in the mess hall, and Sugar provided the basic information. By three a.m., an hour and twenty minutes after the *Toro*'s watch spotted Leslie's SOS, the tanker had turned around and was once again heading south toward Venezuela. An hour later, Rostad sent a telex message about the rescue to the Coast Guard in New York, and alerted the *Toro*'s owners in Norway about the ship's passengers.

After their meal, the eight made their way through the ship's narrow passageways to cabins, and the crew found jumpsuits for them to wear. Most of the *Pride* crew members collapsed into beds made up with flannel sheets and covered with soft down comforters. There was a God.

Alone in his small berth, Chez, his chest aching and his feet a swollen, tender mess, carefully peeled off Scott's foul-weather slicker. He took off his shorts and T-shirt, stepped gingerly into the shower, and luxuriated in the flow of water; it was cool but fresh, at least. Minutes passed as the water rinsed off the thick crust of salt, dirt, and bodily fluids. Later, Tonder, who was also the medical officer, stopped by to wrap Chez's cracked ribs with a bandage. Finally, the cook climbed carefully into bed and snuggled under a down comforter. He woke a little while later, needing to pee, but his body refused to sit up. Struggling to get out from under the covers, Chez felt the ointment and open sores on the lower half of his body clinging to the sheet. He delicately pulled back the sheet, somehow rolled over, and fell out of bed onto the hard floor. He inched his way to the head on hands and knees, before creeping back to bed.

In another cabin, Scott pulled off Nina's foul-weather top and his clothes. A stench he had not noticed over the last several days nearly overwhelmed him. After a shower, he couldn't sleep so he asked a *Toro* sailor for paper and pencil. The deckhand, who had kept a log since Malaga, had a lot to write. He knew there would be questions about the disaster and he wanted to record everything he could remember about the previous five days. He produced five pages of notes, including one quick sketch of the *Pride* blown over in the water and another detailing where he and four others were standing when the squall hit. The sinking had produced an out-of-body sensation, Scott wrote, as if he were "an outsider watching T.V."

He also wrote down what he remembered of the worst moments: Armin swimming away, and Vinny and Nina in the water. Finally he fell asleep.

CHAPTER 24

May 19
Baltimore

A ringing phone jolted Emily McGeady from sleep in her home in a suburb south of Baltimore; it was 4:30 A.M. The mother of seven children had been awakened in the middle of the night many times, and she quickly found the phone in the dark.

"Hi, Mom. It's Joe," came the voice on the other end. Joe, her son.

"*Joe*. Where are you?"

"I'm on a freighter going to Venezuela."

Emily tried to make sense of the words. Joe, she knew, was sailing in the Atlantic and the family had been making plans to welcome him home in a few days.

"What do you mean?" Emily asked her son.

"Mom, the *Pride* sank."

Emily McGeady was suddenly wide awake and out of bed, standing. Her husband, also named Joe, listened from the bed, trying to figure out what was going on.

On the phone, Joe told his mother to write some information down; she found a small piece of paper and began taking notes. The boat had gone down a few days before and he gave her the last location: approximately twenty-three degrees north, sixty-seven degrees west. Four of the crew were dead or missing, and he ticked off the names: Armin, Vinny, Nina, and Barry. The other eight had been floating in a life raft since the sinking. Before hanging up, Joe gave her the phone number of the ship.

Emily collected herself and shared the story with her husband. The *Pride* was gone, but Joe was safe. Emily dialed the number for Eamonn, her husband's brother and one of the founding board members of the *Pride of Baltimore* organization—the same Eamonn who had loaned Joe a sextant for the trip. He had also helped nurse the *Pride* along for most of its life: raising money, sitting through board meetings, and donating his marine construction company's time and equipment to help maintain the ship.

As Emily talked, Eamonn listened in stunned silence, writing down the names of the four who were missing or lost. Armin he knew well and liked. He had met Barry at the airport back in March, but not Vinny. And then Nina's name. Eamonn had been one of the last to hug her before she disappeared down the airport ramp ten weeks earlier. But there was no time to dwell on that. There was so much to be done, and Eamonn's old army instincts kicked in. His wife, Betsy, got out of bed to make coffee and breakfast. A few minutes later, Eamonn convened a conference call of three other *Pride* board members, including a public relations executive, Chris Hartman, and Henry Rosenberg, an oil executive and one of the city's prominent business people.

After the conference call, Hartman called Gail Shawe. "Gail, this is Chris. The *Pride* sank." Shawe couldn't believe the words. The *Pride* was her baby; she knew everything about it. If it sank, she would be the first to hear.

"How do you know? That can't be true; they would have called me."

Gail's instincts were right: she was the first person they tried to call from the tanker. Sugar and Joe tried to recall her home number, but the calls didn't go through. Joe then suggested calling his mother in Baltimore; at least he was sure about her number.

Gail got dressed in a numb panic. The *Pride* was gone and four of the twelve crew members were missing. Among them Armin, a man she had fallen for when he came to work for the ship six years earlier. Their relationship had flowered and then ended. The two had continued to work together, although it was tense. Now Armin was missing. Gail steeled herself for what was certain to be a very long day.

The loss of the schooner was a stunning blow to the city and would dominate the news for days. After nine years, the *Pride* had become a Baltimore civic treasure. In a city that had lost its football team and was battling a crime epidemic, such treasures were well loved. Unlike the Colts, who were hijacked by Indianapolis after months of debate and worry, the *Pride* disappeared with no warning. Armin and others associated with the *Pride* may have quietly wondered about the ship's stability, but the idea that it might not come back had never occurred to the public, making the loss that much more jarring.

Before dawn, an aide awakened Mayor William Donald Schaefer to break the news. A thoroughly sentimental man, Schaefer had championed the *Pride* as a grand gesture of optimism and had been the one to insist on a bell or whistle to remind the public when the ship came or went. That morning, he had his driver take him to the harbor, passing a series of animal-shaped balloons city workers had installed overnight as a promotion to help drivers locate parking spaces. At the harbor, the mayor stared out at the *Pride*'s empty pier and pictured the schooner leaving the harbor a year earlier. A short while later, he was back in City Hall, sitting down with two of his top aides to discuss what had to be done. The three sat in silence for a long time, afraid that the first word would prompt a flood of tears. By mid-day the balloons had been taken down; the silly inflated animals were inappropriate for a city in mourning.

With a little nudging from U.S. Representative Barbara A. Mikulski of Baltimore, the Coast Guard scrambled to launch a search for the remaining crew members and within a couple of hours, a jet based in San Juan took off to comb the area of the sinking.

*   *   *

Gail took on the worst job: calling the families. She reached John Elsaesser at home on secluded Salters Point and gave him the facts: The *Pride* had gone down five days earlier. Two members of the crew were dead; two, including Armin, were missing, and the Coast Guard had launched a search. The Elsaessers took the news stoically but wanted to hear directly from Armin's crew and asked about calling the survivors.

At about eight a.m., Gail reached Maria Lazzaro in the kitchen of the family's airy, wood-framed house in Connecticut.

"Mrs. Lazzaro, are you sitting down?" she asked, before laying out the news: Vinny was missing. Victor Lazzaro walked in just in time to hear his wife ask quietly, "Is there any hope?" The answer was, not much.

The news was so sudden—and so detached. Maria Lazzaro had never actually seen the *Pride* and had never spent much time in Baltimore. Now, people from the *Pride* organization she didn't even know were calling to share the worst news of her life. Maria Lazzaro hung up the phone and told her husband and daughter what had happened; the three of them hugged each other for a long time.

Gail had no luck reaching the family of Barry Duckworth and finally called the Delaware State Police.

"I don't know how to do this," she told a trooper, and asked them to locate the Jewetts before the family heard about the loss on the news.

Then Gail called Nina's mother. Roma Schack had left home early to get a good start on the week. Dogwoods were in bloom as she walked through the sprawling Johns Hopkins University campus to her secretarial job in the materials sciences department. Before nine, the phone rang and Roma answered.

"Mrs. Schack? This is Gail Shawe with the *Pride of Baltimore,*" the voice at the other end began. Then came the news: *The Pride was gone. Nina was dead.*

Roma dropped the phone, but Shawe could still hear the blood-curdling scream.

* * *

On Salters Point, the Elsaessers needed to know more and managed to patch through to the *Toro*, where a sailor summoned Sugar to take the call.

"Is there any hope?" the Elsaessers asked him, as they listened in on two phones.

Standing barefoot in the radio room, Sugar chose his words carefully.

"It's not great, but there is still a chance."

Sugar spent much of the morning on the radio, talking to the home office, the Coast Guard, and others. Somehow the phone number for the *Toro* reached newsrooms, and reporters began placing calls to Sugar.

"How's Nina?" one asked, trying to get Sugar to confirm her death, news of which was spreading although it had not been made public by the *Pride* organization. Sugar was flabbergasted that someone would try to trick him.

As the big tanker cruised south, the day was a blur for its eight passengers. Despite having spent part of the night in bed, all eight remained shaky. After writing his notes and finally getting some sleep, Scott made his way to the mess for lunch but felt nauseous and retreated to the nearest head. Inside, he got dizzy; he collapsed and passed out with one foot suspended over the toilet. After fifteen minutes, Susie and others realized he was missing and found him slumped over in the head.

Later, Sugar joined Captain Rostad in his cabin to make plans. The ship was headed to Venezuela, but would be passing close to the western end of Puerto Rico. The Coast Guard offered to send a helicopter out to the *Toro* to pick up the *Pride* crew and take them to the Borinquen Coast Guard station. It would be a fairly straightforward pickup off the ship's expansive deck, and by sending out a chopper, the Coast Guard would save the *Toro* from making a lengthy and expensive unplanned stop.

The eight survivors took turns calling home. In their dazed state, some didn't fully appreciate the enormity of the news about the *Pride*. When Leslie reached her mother in California, she blurted out the news: "I'm getting married." Only then, did she remember to mention that the *Pride* had gone down. Robert didn't call until five p.m., when his mother got home from work. He didn't realize that she had waited anxiously by the phone all day.

At four p.m., Mayor Schaefer and several *Pride* officials held a press conference in Baltimore's City Hall—in a high-ceilinged reception room with overstuffed chairs and lots of polished wood. Two television stations and one radio station carried the somber event live. Immediately after it was over, the *Pride* officials gathered with Schaefer in the mayor's private office and discussed what to do next. Gail had made plans to fly to Puerto Rico that evening; Eastern Airlines had offered her a first-class seat.

"Do you have any money? You have to go down there with some money," one of the men in the room told her. When she realized she didn't, each of the men—including some of the city's most powerful businessmen—reached for their wallets and handed her ten and twenty dollar bills. Schaefer excused himself and opened a safe tucked away in a closet; he pulled out more bills. That night, with plenty of cash, she reached Puerto Rico and made her way to Borinquen.

As the day wore on, the Elsaessers' home on Salters Point was flooded with calls—from friends and reporters. Some news people managed to find the secluded house and knocked on the door. The Elsaessers remained as upbeat as possible, talking about Armin's love of the *Pride* and holding out hope that he would be found.

Martha Elsaesser knew there was one other person she had to reach. Jennifer was somewhere on the ocean on *Te Vega* and Mrs. Elsaesser sensed that she would have no idea Armin had been in an accident. Not sure how best to reach the boat, she called Kim Pedersen, Armin's old friend, who had returned to Massachusetts after leaving *Te Vega* earlier in the spring.

"Armin's missing. We need to get ahold of *Te Vega*," Mrs.

Elsaesser told her. "I don't want Jennifer hearing about this on the radio."

Stunned by the news, Kim wrote down the basic information and called the Coast Guard. Officials there agreed to try to reach *Te Vega* every hour. But the calls never reached the boat, which sailed placidly across the Atlantic.

CHAPTER 25

May 20, 1986

Early the next day, a Tuesday, the *Pride* crew again awoke in dry beds and under down comforters, as the *Toro* steamed for the dark green waters of the Mona Passage separating Puerto Rico and the Dominican Republic. The sinking of the boat was front-page news in the *New York Times* and other newspapers around the country. Word also reached Baltimore, Ireland, which had played host to the *Pride* the previous spring, and one pub owner draped black around a photograph of the schooner.

The sun was bright and a healthy breeze whipped spray off of the waves. A little after sunrise, a Coast Guard helicopter arrived and hovered over the *Toro*, which was moving at a steady twelve knots. The Coast Guard cutter *Whitehorn* cruised along the starboard beam as an escort. Concerned about the danger of landing on the oil-filled tanker, the pilot, Lieutenant Pete Verralt, lowered the chopper to within twenty-five feet of the deck, dropped a meshed metal rescue basket, and lifted the *Pride* crew to the helicopter one at a time. Wearing an orange jumpsuit, Sugar carried a large trash bag filled with old clothes and the leftover supplies from the raft. Chez was in agony, as his ribs strained and bumped against the hard metal carrier during its ascent. It took three trips instead of two to ferry the eight back to the Borinquen air station because the Coast

Guard allowed reporters and photographers to use one of the two helicopters.

Going barefoot and wearing the blue work suit provided by the *Toro* crew, Scott was the last to be lifted off the tanker's gray deck, just after Leslie. As the helicopter turned toward Puerto Rico, he waved out the window, while Leslie flashed a V sign. Flying back to Puerto Rico, the two sailors peered out over the miles of placid blue water. Conversation was all but impossible in the noisy helicopter, but one of the Coast Guard officers slipped Scott a note, which read "Welcome Home." Scott scribbled, "Any pizza places on the way back?"

Arriving at the Coast Guard base, the eight stepped onto solid land and into the warm embrace of Gail, who had arrived the night before. The crew was examined by the base medical staff—Sugar had lost twenty-three pounds in five days—and the survivors joined Gail in a small room in one of the buildings. Jan Miles was also there after a mad dash from New England. He had gotten word about the disaster the day before, while sailing with a friend off Cape Cod. After sailing to Newport, Miles found a ride to Providence, caught an overnight train to New York, and flew to Puerto Rico, arriving by mid-day on the twentieth. Now reunited in Puerto Rico, he, Gail, and the eight survivors talked about what had happened.

Still numbed by the loss, Gail asked Sugar if there was anything they could have done differently.

"We kept thinking she was going to right herself," Sugar replied. "We should have known she wouldn't. We should have cut the lines and she might have come back up."

But, everyone agreed, it had all happened too damn quick.

The *Pride of Baltimore* officials weren't the only ones eager for information. Reporters from Baltimore and elsewhere swarmed to the Coast Guard base, only to be held at bay by Gail and given no access to the crew members. (Years later, several survivors would look with some bitterness at the careful "managing" the Pride organization began that morning.) An investigator from the company that had insured the *Pride* soon arrived in San Juan. By chance, he ran into Leslie's parents, who had flown on the first flight they could get from California; they shared a ride to Borinquen.

The Coast Guard, meanwhile, also wanted to talk to the survivors. It was a harsh blast of reality when Coast Guard Captain Michael Brown began pulling the crew members out one at a time to ask about the sinking, interviews that were videotaped. During the ten-minute sessions, Brown handed each of the eight a subpoena directing them to appear before the official Coast Guard inquiry that would convene in Baltimore. By the end of the day, five full-blown investigations were under way. A second federal agency, the National Transportation Safety Board, had already decided to look into the sinking of the *Pride*. The *Pride* organization, the company that insured the boat, and the press would also want to know what happened.

The second-guessing of Armin, his crew, and his boat, was in full swing.

Throughout the day, the U.S. military searched for the missing crew members. A Coast Guard C-130 took off from Borinquen with Steve Ruta, a twenty-nine-year-old lieutenant, at the controls. Six other Coast Guard personnel served as lookouts. For hours, they scanned the endless ocean for any sign of the four missing crew members. Four other aircraft joined in the search of one thousand square miles of the Atlantic. It had been seven days since the *Pride* sank, meaning it would be a miracle to find Armin or Vinny still alive. If they had somehow survived, the Coast Guard figured there was only a 5 percent chance that one of the search planes would actually notice them drifting in the water. A raft would be much easier to spot, but, of course, they had not reached a raft.

From one thousand feet up, the lookouts searched for colored dots: yellow for Armin's foul-weather gear; orange for Vinny's. Nothing, though, intruded on the blue, save for the occasional whitecap or the dark green of floating Sargasso weed. A huge man-of-war jellyfish and a chunk of Styrofoam prompted a brief surge of optimism, but by evening, the five planes had returned to land, with nothing much to report.

* * *

The next day, as the search widened over a bigger area of the ocean, the eight survivors prepared to go back to Baltimore. Before noon, three *Pride* board members, including Eamonn McGeady and Pete Partridge, arrived in Puerto Rico on two jets loaned by Baltimore corporations. The two men, both lawyers, flew down to bring the survivors home. But they were also there to represent the *Pride* organization in the crucial early stages of a potentially explosive legal situation. The facts were far from clear, but a boat owned by the city of Baltimore had sunk; at least two were dead and eight others had gone through five days of hell. The lawyers were well aware of the potential for expensive legal wrangling. "We pointed out to the survivors that we would do whatever they needed," McGeady said later. "Translation: we didn't want any lawsuits filed."

Around noon, the crew split into two groups of four and boarded the two jets for the long flight back to Baltimore. On one, the pilot welcomed the crew and then began his safety instructions.

"I'm sorry, folks, I have to do this," he said. "In the case of a water landing, your seat cushions can be used as a flotation device. . . ." Everyone laughed.

During the flight, Robert picked up a copy of the *Evening Sun* that someone had brought down from Baltimore. Splashed across the front page was an artist's rendition of the sinking, which included crew members flipping haphazardly off the storm-tossed schooner. While the drawing wasn't particularly accurate, it did begin to capture the chaos of the moment. *Wow!* Robert thought, as he studied the front page and the reams of coverage in the Baltimore press. *This is huge.*

The jets touched down at a small suburban airport east of Baltimore. The eight emerged stiffly from the jets, looking weather-beaten, their hair bleached by the sun and their faces bronzed. Susie waved forlornly to her family, walked over, and gave her mother a tearful hug. "I love you," Susie told her. Then, "Nina is gone."

It was an overwhelming welcome. The governor and mayor were both on hand, along with board members and family. The scene was all the more surreal for Danny and Chez, who still didn't have glasses. Wearing a dark green Coast Guard flight suit but no shoes (none would fit over his swollen feet), Chez shook hands with the dignitaries and then got a nice surprise—a warm hug from a cute blond woman who turned out to be Suzy Winter from the *Pride* office.

"Welcome home," she said, smiling broadly.

The eight survivors greeted family members in a crew lounge inside the enormous hangar that normally housed State Police planes and helicopters. After a few minutes, it was time to greet the press. Reporters had been trying to talk to the eight sailors for more than forty-eight hours but had been kept at a distance by circumstances and the careful managing of the *Pride* organization. Now there were dozens of press people waiting.

Pride officials chose to introduce the eight one at a time and have them take the stage like the starting lineup at a sporting event. Susie, the local girl, got a huge cheer from her friends and family; Chez walked slowly; and Danny soaked up his ovation, grinning sheepishly from ear to ear. Several wore jumpsuits; Leslie, Susie, and Joe had borrowed clothes from Leslie's parents. Joe, wearing rolled-up khakis and a red shirt and carrying a small bouquet from his family, looked like he was returning from a Bahamian wedding.

Seated behind a table, Sugar took the microphone and read a statement that he, Leslie, and Gail had crafted the night before. "We left St. Johns, USVI on a transit toward the Chesapeake on May 11," Sugar began, his voice steady, a trace of New England in the vowels. For a few minutes, he read a dry yet thoroughly riveting account of the five-day ordeal.

"We entered the six-man life raft with eight exhausted people. We spent four days, seven hours in the life raft. The days were barely tolerable; the nights were hell." Then, looking up, he ad-libbed: "That's an understatement." The long recounting of events gave the essence of the saga but glossed over one of the hardest details: Sugar suggested that Barry was dead when they found him, giving no inkling of his long fight to survive.

It was a painful afternoon. During their four-plus days in the raft, the eight sailors had in some sense left the tragedy behind. As awful as it had been, they had spent their time adrift wondering about their own survival. Now, the whole world wanted to relive the sinking and the deaths of their shipmates. There was also something a little out-of-sync about the homecoming event, which presented the eight sailors as heroes. But they had been on board when the city's prized sailboat was lost at sea. They were survivors, not heroes.

With a determined smile, Susie told reporters she wanted to say something to the people of Baltimore: "We're sorry we couldn't bring your boat back to you."

By late afternoon, the press conference was over, and for the first time in months, the eight *Pride* sailors were free to go their own ways. None could leave town, given the subpoenas they had received and the funerals that were being planned. Some, such as Susie, Scott, and Joe, were from Baltimore and went home. Danny's family came from Pennsylvania to pick him up. Leslie and Sugar headed off to a hotel across the street from where the *Pride* had been built a decade earlier. They, of course, had no luggage, money, or credit cards, and their hotel room had been reserved by Leslie's parents. In their depleted state, Leslie and Sugar put up no resistance when the front desk suggested they wait to check in until Leslie's parents arrived.

Leslie and Sugar found a couch at one end of the lobby and sat for an hour, waiting. Neither complained or grew antsy. It had been sixty blurry hours since they had stepped onto the solid deck of the *Toro*, and sitting alone in a quiet, comfortable hotel wasn't such a bad thing.

CHAPTER 26

May 21, 1986
Aboard the schooner Te Vega

Nothing had given the crew of *Te Vega* more trouble crossing the Atlantic than its single sideband radio. It was the boat's only link to land but had proved to be maddeningly unworkable since leaving Italy six weeks ago. The schooner had stopped in the Spanish Canary Islands off Africa and then ventured farther south to the Cape Verde Islands before heading west toward the Caribbean. Now, ten days into the Atlantic crossing, the schooner was heading northwest toward Bermuda and, ultimately, Massachusetts.

Gregg Swanzey, the ship's captain, tried often to reach a maritime operator who could patch him through to the operator of the ship, the Landmark School on the coast of Massachusetts near Gloucester. *Te Vega* was carrying about thirty Landmark students back toward New England after nearly eight months of sailing and it was important to check in once in a while. Jennifer had also been a frequent visitor to the small radio-navigation room, trying to reach Armin at noon each day. They had managed it only a few times in the last ten weeks. The conversations were short and professional, given that the whole ocean could be listening in, but still nice moments.

Swanzey stationed himself at the radio as he had so many times before. "This is *Te Vega, Te Vega, Te Vega*. . . ." His voice beamed out over the water in search of a maritime operator, but with no luck. Swanzey listened for a while to the usual maritime radio chatter—weather reports and ETAs.

Then he picked up a conversation between a distant yacht owner and a captain he knew who was sailing in the Caribbean. Talking by phone from Colorado, the owner exchanged information with the captain about the ship's passage. Then, Swanzey listened as the owner remembered he had something else to tell the captain.

"Did you hear about the *Pride of Baltimore*?" he asked. Swanzey listened intently.

"The *Pride* went down."

Swanzey wasn't sure he heard it right. The boat was gone? The voice thousands of miles away could provide only the murkiest of details: the ship had sunk and some of the crew was unaccounted for. Swanzey was stunned. He and others on board knew some of the *Pride* crew, particularly Armin, a stalwart of the historic schooner industry. Al Nejmeh, the first mate, had sailed on *Pride*. And then there was Jennifer. Swanzey realized he had to break the news to her. He called Al and found Jennifer in the deckhouse a few steps away.

"Something's happened to *Pride*," Swanzey told them. As she listened to the radio, Jennifer felt her knees buckling and she nearly collapsed. The three stared at the radio and at each other, numb to the news. Agonizingly few details emerged from the scratchy sideband, but there was a crucial one: some of the twelve-member crew was missing.

Te Vega officers tried frantically to patch through to other vessels or a maritime operator to get more information. They rotated through every radio frequency and tinkered with the antenna up on the mast, with no luck.

For days, a dark blanket of silence enveloped *Te Vega* as her crew tried to gather more information. Jennifer went through the motions of sailing, supervising most of her assigned watches, but she also spent a lot of time alone in her bunk. A letter to Armin she had begun several days before, in which she bragged that *Te Vega* was making better time across the ocean than the *Pride*, sat unfinished.

Jennifer and Al also found time to sit and talk. They had met years earlier, sailed together, and shared a realistic view of the *Pride*, having lived through the Baltic mishap together. They also shared an affection for Armin. They both knew about Armin's intense sense of responsibility as a sea captain and they both tried to imagine what had happened the previous Wednesday on the *Pride*. Although they didn't say it aloud, Al and Jennifer each reached the same conclusion: Armin was dead.

He would never have been someone to survive it, Jennifer thought. *He wouldn't want to survive it. He would be the classic "go down with the ship" kind of guy. If the* Pride *had gone down, he wouldn't have had the will to survive.*

Back in Baltimore the next morning, the *Pride* survivors adjusted to roles as reluctant celebrities. Sugar and Leslie got up early in their downtown hotel to appear as guests on "Good Morning America," with Maria Shriver marveling at their adventure. A radio station was already on the air urging Baltimoreans to send donations to help build a new *Pride*. (In only one day, the station raised an astonishing $49,000.)

The eight members of the crew made their way to Johns Hopkins Hospital for checkups. While all were still sore and worn-out, the doctors admitted only Robert and Chez, to keep an eye on the nasty sores on their lower bodies. Along with the broken ribs, Chez had trench foot; Robert had trench foot and a touch of impetigo, a bacterial skin infection.

The two received the royal treatment. Regular hospital food wasn't good enough; they were allowed to order from the VIP menu. While being pushed in a wheelchair through a corridor, and wearing just a hospital gown, Chez received a warm hug from an elderly woman who recognized him from the news coverage.

"Welcome home," she said with heartfelt joy.

Strangers sent fresh strawberries and homemade cakes to their rooms. And flowers poured in, which the two men handed over to the nurses. A stream of doctors looked in on them, including the head of the infectious diseases department and the president of the hospital. It's no surprise that Hopkins Hospital officials rolled out the red carpet; the eight survivors were civic celebrities, to be sure. But there were other considerations as well. Sugar Flanagan's uncle was C. Everett Koop, the surgeon general of the United States, in effect the nation's top doctor. It wouldn't be good to screw up care for Koop's nephew, or any of the other crew members.

Medical students also stopped by to take a look at Chez's problems—his ballooned feet and the sores on his lower body. During World War I, trench foot infected tens of thousands of soldiers forced to stand in cold water in battlefront trenches for days on end. Often it led to gangrene and the loss of toes or feet. But by 1986, trench foot was not high on the list of ailments seen in Johns Hopkins Hospital and provided a teachable moment for the students.

Later on, the two men looked up to see a short woman in her fifties; it was Roma Schack. They had never met, but Roma had taken a break in her planning for Nina's funeral to visit her daughter's two shipmates. She brought little gifts and asked how they were feeling. The three of them talked briefly and she left.

Early Friday morning, a disheartening but not unexpected announcement arrived from Miami: the Coast Guard had ended the search for the four lost crew members. Over four days, ships and planes from the Coast Guard, Navy, Air Force, and Marines had scoured a 500,000-square-mile swath of the Atlantic with no luck. It had been ten days since the sinking—far too long for anyone to survive in the ocean without a raft. The harsh news extinguished any realistic hope that Armin or Vinny had somehow survived.

Four hours later, about one hundred people walked up the steps into the twin-spire, neo-Gothic Cathedral of Mary our Queen in North Baltimore to say good-bye to Nina. Friends from high school gathered in clumps, as did sailors from the *Pride*. Emotionally drained, Gail Shawe shook like a leaf but managed to say a few words about Nina, who shared both a birthday and a date of passing with the *Pride*. Joe and Susie stood up and offered memories and one classmate, Maggie King, composed a poem about Nina that was handed out at the funeral. It concluded:

Her soul is forever a part of the sky
Her spirit alive in us all
And Nina, a lovely woman, a truly beautiful person,
Is forever young, forever beautiful.

Two hours after the tearful funeral, Sugar walked barefoot into the federal Custom House in downtown Baltimore. As the top surviving officer on the *Pride*, he was the leadoff witness in the federal investigation and officials wanted to get the probe underway. (They had tried to start the day before, but the proceedings were postponed a day because of a dispute over the Coast Guard's ban on cameras.) There was intense public interest, and investigators knew it was best to get testimony promptly after an accident, when memories were freshest. Plus, the key witnesses—the crew—soon would be scattered across the country.

Sugar settled into the witness seat in the building's ornate Call Room, once used for commercial exchanges but now a ceremonial space crammed with lawyers, reporters, camera crews, and curious onlookers. The walls were covered with an impressive series of paintings depicting the evolution of navigation. Egyptian, Greek, and Roman galleys; a sixteenth-century English warship; an 1800-era man-of-war; and a variety of steamships plied across the plaster expanses. Depictions of sailing knots—half-hitches, a clove-hitch, single and double carrick-bends, a running bowline—were displayed above some of the panels. The paintings in the room, considered one of the artistic treasures of Baltimore, were by Francis Davis Millet, a native of Mattapoisett, the small Massachusetts town where Armin Elsaesser lived before beginning his career as an itinerant sailor. Millet died in the sinking of the *Titanic* at the age of sixty-five.

The Coast Guard brass had named Commander John Maxham, an inspector based in Baltimore, to handle the inquiry, although he was by no means an expert in big sailboats. A Vietnam veteran with an engineering degree, Maxham's most recent work had revolved around inspecting cargo ships being rebuilt across the harbor at the Sparrows Point shipyard. While he had investigated a dozen accidents, they had been more mundane—barges crashing into bridges, flooded engine rooms—and none had involved a loss of life. The *Pride* case would take Maxham to a new level of complexity and public scrutiny.

Sitting next to Maxham was Paul Esbensen, a veteran investigator from the National Transportation Safety Board in Washington. While Maxham had been handed the hot potato, Esbensen had lobbied for the *Pride* case, despite the possibility of a conflict of interest. Esbensen was a good friend of Eamonn McGeady from the *Pride* board; he knew and had sailed with Joe. Esbensen had watched the schooner being built in the seventies, and the dry dock company he once worked for had done repairs to the ship after it infamously ran aground in Delaware Bay in 1979. While some officials might have disqualified Esbensen because of that close association with the boat, NTSB officials did not. (Esbensen later defended his impartiality: "We're all adults; we can do what we're supposed to be doing.")

Sugar was sworn in as a witness and the press hung on every word. Taking notes nearby were lawyers representing the many people and entities whose reputations and finances were at stake in the hearing: chiefly the city of Baltimore, which owned the boat, and Pride of Baltimore Inc., which operated it. Tom Gillmer, who designed the *Pride*, drove up from Annapolis to attend, as did Christine Parker Smith, representing her husband, builder Melbourne Smith. Armin was considered "a party of interest" in the investigation, as the inquiry could find him responsible for the sinking. His brother, Ford, an attorney practicing in Idaho, and his father, John, would sit through portions of the investigation.

For four hours, Sugar calmly recounted the last voyage of the *Pride*, as well as the long ordeal in the life raft. Things were well in hand the morning of the fourteenth, he said. He and Armin were aware of a storm building to the east, but the intensity of the wind was a surprise. "I've seen sixty knots, you know, sailing on boats before, sixty-five knots in anchorage on boats before, and this was definitely a lot more wind than I had seen before," he said. "I am not an anemometer, but I could say seventy, eighty knots, and I am not worried about over-exaggerating."

And Sugar would not second-guess his captain's decisions when the squall hit. Armin chose to try to run with the wind. He could have tried to turn the boat upwind, and some sailors were already whispering that he had screwed up by heading off.

"In my opinion, Armin's choice of heading off to try to reduce the exposed amount of sail . . . was proper," he said, when asked about Armin's crucial decision. "Exact same thing you should do, or I would do."

Even as Sugar was testifying under oath, Jennifer on *Te Vega* finally received the information she had dreaded. It had been three days since Swanzey had picked up the news about the loss of the *Pride;* then nothing. Finally *Te Vega*'s unpredictable radio received a call from Peg Brandon, Al Nejmeh's girlfriend, who was sailing on the *Westward*. Peg's news, while not entirely accurate, was close enough—and devastating. There were *nine* survivors, she told Al. Two members of the crew had died, and one, Armin, was still missing. *Armin*. Jennifer's intuition about a man she knew so well was right. That didn't make the news any more bearable and she barely moved from her bunk for twenty-four hours.

After two more anguished days, *Te Vega* reached Bermuda. Jennifer left most of her things on board and walked off the ship to catch a plane. *Te Vega* went on to New England but she flew back to Baltimore.

That same day, the Sunday before Memorial Day, Chez and Robert were released from the hospital. Later they set out in Robert's car for an important errand. After stopping at McDonald's, they found the Schack home, a comfortable cedar shake bungalow in North Baltimore. Inside, Roma looked out the window and saw the two young men heading up the walk. She could see that Chez carried a bright yellow bundle across his arms. Inside, he presented Roma with Nina's foul-weather gear. They had telephoned earlier to ask Roma if she wanted the stuff and, of course, she did. The two men also returned the folding knife Nina had taken to Spain.

Roma ushered the two men into the living room and sat across from them, the yellow gear draped over her legs. Her dark brown eyes looked over the two men, both tanned and once again healthy. At another time, the men could have been calling on her daughter.

"Did she have fun?" Roma wanted to know. Robert and Chez were pleased to remember Nina and they recounted stories from their ten weeks together. They also explained how the foul-weather gear had helped save Chez's life, just as Joe had predicted in the water on May 14. Chez had inflated the pants and used them to help float; later the pants were used as a funnel to catch rain-water. The top provided a crucial layer of warmth over his upper body; without it, Chez would surely have deteriorated more quickly.

Roma had a final question. "What did her face look like?" she asked.

"I couldn't even look," Chez answered quietly.

The two men said their good-byes. Roma had no idea what to do with the gear, so she hung the pants and jacket in the hall closet; she figured the right thing would present itself in due course.

The hearing into the loss of the *Pride* plodded along for six days. Each of the eight survivors took a turn answering questions posed by the federal authorities or the lawyers for the *Pride* and the city of Baltimore.

Raymond Biedinger, a forecaster from the National Weather Service's office in Miami, provided the weather bulletin that had been broadcast a little after 5:30 the morning of the sinking, which included an advisory that thunderstorms were possible in the area where the *Pride* went down. Such forecasts for open waters, though, were little more than educated guesses. With no radar tracking the area, forecasters relied on satellite photographs, scattered reports from ships at sea, and a computer forecasting program. While a low-pressure trough had settled in over the ocean in the area of the sinking, there was no indication that severe winds might be forming.

Biedinger discussed two weather phenomena that might have sunk the *Pride*. One, he said, was a white squall, a brief but intense wind without rain. "It's invisible, more or less," Biedinger testified.

The second weather pattern was one scientists had only recently begun to chart and was known as a microburst, a downdraft of cool air forced to the Earth's surface by fast-rising, wet warm air. The downdraft often turned into a shaft of intense wind no more than a couple of miles wide that hit the Earth almost vertically and then spread out across the surface and anything in its way. Microbursts, which were most common in the summer, brought winds ranging from forty to two hundred miles per hour and had been blamed for several airplane accidents. While their impact on ships at sea had rarely been noted, forecasters could not rule out the possibility that this kind of compact but powerful wind managed to find and sink the *Pride*.

Tom Gillmer finally got his chance to testify in the investigation on May 30. Unlike other witnesses, he prepared a defensive-sounding preliminary statement. "It should be observed that her long sea mileage provided her with exposure to the possibility of peril of the sea, but without serious incident during approximately one hundred and fifty thousand nautical miles under sail. I might add that's six times around the world," the retired professor said. Gillmer did not define "serious," and the investigators, unaware of past incidents such as the one in the Baltic, did not press him on his assertion.

Investigators did ask about the inclining tests Gillmer had supervised and the *Pride*'s stability, but the inquiries were far from rigorous. Gillmer was asked if changes were made to the vessel before it sailed to Europe. He responded that he advised the organization and skippers to remove extraneous weight and to place weight lower in the boat. He did not mention his suggestion to strike the topmasts, and nobody asked him whether such a safety precaution had been considered in advance of the trans-Atlantic crossing. Nor did Gillmer mention that he had recommended that fuel and water be stored below, advice that was also not heeded.

Then, investigators asked Gillmer how much wind the *Pride* could sustain. His answer: up to fifty knots. His assessment that the *Pride* could withstand only a fifty-knot wind was important. If that was accurate, then the boat truly didn't stand much of a chance in wind reaching seventy knots or higher.

Paul Mullen, a lawyer for the *Pride*, asked Gillmer to clarify his comment. If the *Pride* had sufficient warning, Mullen asked, "Would it be your opinion that she could indeed sustain winds in excess of fifty knots offshore?"

"Of course, but she'd have to be shortened down to practically bare poles, maybe storm trysail only," Gillmer responded.

There was also a catchall question from Mullen. Was the *Pride*, he asked the architect, "stable, safe, and seaworthy to make that Atlantic passage?"

The answer seemed carefully worded.

"Yes," Gillmer said. "As much as I could judge."

Gail Shawe followed Gillmer to the stand. Leon Katcharian, an investigator with the NTSB, asked her about Armin's letter of March 8, in which he said he was "very concerned" about the *Pride*'s stability. The letter, Shawe responded, was part of an "ongoing discussion" of the *Pride*'s stability.

"We were aware of the fact that this was a unique vessel, she is a reproduction of an early-nineteenth-century vessel, and that we had to be very sensitive to the stability of the ship," Shawe said. She made no mention of the back-and-forth between Gillmer and Roger Long about the *Pride*'s true stability characteristics, nor was she pressed for any details about the "ongoing discussion" of stability. Armin's concern was left unexplained.

A moment later, Gillmer made an unsolicited statement about the captain's unprecedented statement of concern about his vessel. "The quote 'Armin was concerned about the *Pride*'s stability'; I'd like to remind you, every captain is concerned about the ship's stability," Gillmer said.

The public phase of the investigation into the loss of the *Pride* concluded on May 30, nine days after the survivors had returned to Maryland. By then, talk of finding Vinny and Armin had long since ceased. The final count was in: eight had made it, four had not.

Two days later, fifteen hundred people gathered at Fort McHenry for a memorial service to grieve for the dead and to remember the *Pride*. Officials had proposed holding the service in the

Inner Harbor where the *Pride* was built, but it was deemed too festive an atmosphere. Instead they chose the waterfront fort with so much history associated with Baltimore clippers. The service took place on the gently sloping lawn below the brick citadel, with white and yellow flowers displayed in front of the stage. A small fleet of yachts, motorboats, and even a small raft anchored nearby to listen under an achingly pure blue sky. In the crowd were dozens of people who had sailed on the *Pride* during its nine years at sea and had returned to say good-bye.

Underlying the service was a palpable desire to turn back the clock to a time before May 14. Mayor Schaefer, an often quirky speaker, refrained from platitudes about the mission of the *Pride* and instead recounted his trip to the waterfront on May 19, the day the news reached Baltimore.

"I saw it; she was there," the mayor said, referring to the lost clipper. "The sails were billowing; the flags were waving. And she turned slowly and headed to ports unknown. And if you look real hard right now you can see her."

More than one speaker turned to Armin to help capture the *Pride*'s allure. One member of the *Pride* board recited Armin's log entry from April 2, made during the trade wind sailing west of the Madeiras and mailed home from the Virgin Islands. "Glorious, glorious sailing," he read as the audience listened in rapt attention to the lovely passage. "Now we are flying. As we come off the foamy white crests of sapphire seas *Pride* lifts her head four to five feet above the waterline. The jib boom points skyward and our ship rushes ahead throwing spray and foam, then settles back into the deep with a thunderous roar. The Power! The Energy! The giddy feeling of soaring through liquid blue space."

The wrenching service included an Episcopal boys' choir singing Psalm Twenty-three, a recitation of the Lord's Prayer, and a bugler playing "Taps." In the front row, the eight survivors sat alongside each other one more time, taking in the tributes and memories. Susie Huesman clutched the hands of Robert and Chez, as tears streamed down her face. Leslie leaned over and rested her cheek lightly on Sugar's shoulder. Jennifer sat not far behind with other *Pride* sailors.

As the service wore on, the scorching June sun took its toll. Someone produced a cup of water and the eight passed it amongst themselves.

A few days later, Jennifer received a letter in the mail and immediately recognized the neat handwriting.

"For some reason, I have been seized with the compulsion to write," Armin began his last letter to her, writing from Charlotte Amalie in the Virgins Islands a few days before the *Pride* departed. Perhaps, he said, the compulsion was due to some telepathic message she was sending across the ocean. He confided he had saved half a bottle of Gran Corona, one of his favorite Spanish red wines, to share when they saw each other in the United States.

"Did you get my poem about our reunion?" he wrote. "It's not far off now."

After more than two months apart, Armin wrote that his mental image of her was growing distressingly faint. Yet he pictured the two of them together, perhaps at sea.

"I imagine that you're on the ship or that I am on *Te Vega* (no one is aware of my presence) or that we are living together in some mythical place. Nothing really concrete, I guess, because there is so little that has been concrete in our lives together. Let's change that."

CHAPTER 27

1986–1988
Baltimore

The *Pride* crew, at least seven of the twelve, made it to New York City for the July Fourth celebration of the Statue of Liberty. The spectacular fleet of twenty-two classic vessels sailed in on a light, southeasterly wind, as countless pleasure craft bobbed in the Hudson River to watch. Joe McGeady stayed home, but the seven others accepted offers to serve as guest crew on three different sailboats. The *Spirit of Massachusetts*, the schooner Armin had captained on its inaugural sail, pulled an empty white dinghy as a tribute to the lost *Pride*.

Meanwhile, the investigations into the sinking proceeded outside public view. Luigi Colucciello, an investigator from the NTSB, flew to Spain, to visit the small company in Algeciras that serviced the *Pride*'s life rafts in February. It was an inconclusive visit. In broken English, Ernesto Ibanez, the owner of the company, told the American that he had worked on the *Pride*'s rafts personally and had taken great care with them. As a former sea captain, he said he had the highest concern for sailors and appreciated the importance of servicing life rafts. But Ibanez could not explain how things went so wrong with one of the rafts. He stressed that he had inserted the plugs into the raft's air valves and hammered them in with a mallet.

However, he also said the plugs were "no good" because of the way they set inside the valves. A burst of air pressure, he said, could pop the plugs loose, exactly what apparently happened with one of the rafts.

The small shop's documents were stored haphazardly and Ibanez could not locate the handwritten records made when the rafts were tested. A lengthy search did turn up typewritten Test Inspection Cards for the *Pride*, although the cards did not contain any record of the air pressure measured during the servicing. In other words, there was little hard evidence to confirm that the rafts had been properly tested.

Nor could Ibanez explain how the survival gear had come loose from the rafts and scattered over the waves. Each of the two bags of supplies, he said, had been tied shut and attached securely to a rope on one of the rafts. Similarly, he had no explanation for the rope ladder that was ripped and proved useless to the survivors, and forced them to flop in over the pontoons, bringing extra water into the raft.

Back in Baltimore, officials visited a shop that sold the same life raft model. The officials spent several hours inflating and deflating the raft; each time it worked as designed.

Aside from the life rafts, investigators zeroed in on another uncertain area, the *Pride*'s stability. It was crucial for investigators to determine how well the *Pride* could stay upright, or at least make an educated guess. That determination would help answer some central questions: Was the sinking unavoidable? Or was the *Pride*'s stability—and, consequently, its overall seaworthiness—deficient for the voyage it was on? Liability in the accident, along with potentially huge financial consequences, could turn on the answers.

Only weeks after the sinking, lawyers for the *Pride* watched with dismay as news reports highlighted the study of sailboat stability prepared by Roger Long and the Maine architectural firm of Woodin & Marean, which rather damningly placed the *Pride*'s stability in proximity to that of the *Marques* and *Albatross*, both also lost at sea. While the study made for provocative newspaper stories, John Maxham, the Coast Guard commander leading the investigation, quickly decided that while the study held some theoretical importance, he would not use it to guide the Coast Guard's analysis.

The Coast Guard may have dismissed the study, but lawyers for the *Pride* recognized the problems it could pose to the organization. Paul Mullen, a lawyer for the *Pride* organization, forwarded copies to *Pride* board members as well as the organization's insurers.

"It is obvious that if we get involved in litigation we are going to have to deal with the Woodin & Marean study," Mullen wrote.

In the months after the sinking, no lawsuits emerged but attorneys for the *Pride* braced for the possibility. Only days after the sinking, lawyers floated the possibility of establishing memorial scholarships in honor of those who died. But such a move required the families to waive any claims against the organization, and *Pride* officials such as Jan Miles and Gail Shawe strenuously objected to making such a request, fearing it would send the wrong signal to the families. In the meantime, though, life insurance policies paid out two thousand dollars each to the families of the four who died.

In the following weeks and months, *Pride* lawyers researched arcane areas of maritime law to assess the organization's other responsibilities and vulnerabilities. It turned out, at least on paper, that the *Pride* survivors were entitled to precious little compensation. Maritime case law held the *Pride* organization liable for the cost of any medical care and for making a "maintenance" payment, the rough value of a sailor's accommodations on an oceangoing vessel; in the *Pride*'s case, about eight dollars a day. That was about it.

As for wages, long-standing court rulings, including one stemming from the sinking of a ship sailing from Baltimore to the Far East in the early 1800s, made clear that seamen were not entitled to wages after a ship is lost. Even so, *Pride* officials opted to pay all twelve crew members (or their survivors) the income they would have earned had the boat not gone down. For the four *Pride* crew members who died, the salary payouts ranged from the $7,039 in Armin's case to $561 for Nina.

Similarly, the *Pride* organization had no obligation to reimburse the crew (or the families of the four victims) for the cost of personal belongings lost on the ship, unless it was shown that the organization was at fault in the sinking. Even without such a finding, the organization persuaded its insurers to pay the claims at a cost of more than eighteen thousand dollars. Each of the eight survivors submitted a list of belongings that they had lost—everything from Susie's dental retainer and Danny's high school class ring to Chez's treasured jalaba, valued at $20. Jennifer prepared one for Armin, a claim that included $363 for some items she had left on the *Pride* to be picked up in the United States: a wool suit, pumps, and a purse. (She had worn the outfit to her graduate school interview and had gone straight to the airport to fly to Spain for her February visit with Armin.) The board concluded it was the right thing to do for the *Pride* crew. But the lawyers also advised the board that such payouts might keep the twelve crew members and their families "friendly," thus warding off lawsuits.

There were many funerals. Four days after the tearful memorial service on the Baltimore waterfront, Vinny was remembered at a service at a church in Connecticut. Six weeks later, it was time to eulogize Armin. The service was held in New Bedford, Massachusetts, in the Seamen's Bethel—the small, white chapel made famous in *Moby-Dick*, its walls lined with black-framed marble memorials to sailors lost at sea. The service concluded with the Navy Hymn for the old Navy man, with the memorable refrain, "O hear us when we cry to thee for those in peril on the sea."

With the funerals finally completed, Sugar and Leslie could keep the promise they made to each other in the ocean on May 14. On August 30, they were married in the backyard of her parents' house in Somis, California. She wore a lacy white dress with a pink sash, he went barefoot, and the McNish family dog sat at the couple's feet during the ceremony. As they had planned on the life raft, Joe served as best man and Susie was the maid of honor. Leslie's parents picked up the cost of flying the six other *Pride* survivors to California for the wedding, and dozens of sailing friends decamped to Somis for the event.

Three days after the wedding, Sugar and Leslie were back on the water, on the schooner *Californian*, again with Joe—the three surviving *Pride* officers reunited. It was good to be working again, but the time in the Pacific stirred disconcerting reminders of the *Pride*. The *Californian* was about the same size as the *Pride*, had a similar sail pattern, and had been designed by Melbourne Smith.

"To get back on the deck of a schooner after the last one had sunk on us was hard," Sugar recalled later. "It was a challenge to get back on the horse."

It didn't help when news broke a few days later about the loss of the *Calida*. The 135-foot, full-rigged ship, which had sailed in the Statue of Liberty celebration in New York in July, sank the day after the wedding in an unexpected squall off Cape Fear, North Carolina. The five crew members managed to make it into a familiar-sounding orange and black life raft and floated for three days without any provisions. All five were rescued when the raft was spotted by a fishing boat.

"If we wouldn't have been seen for another three days, I know for sure we wouldn't be alive," the captain of the *Calida* said later, with obvious echoes of the *Pride* loss.

As the summer wore on, pressure built in Baltimore to replace the much-missed *Pride* with another boat. The movement began even before the eight survivors returned home. Not only did a radio station raise money, unsolicited contributions flowed into the *Pride* office; checks for thousands of dollars and jars of coins collected by schoolchildren. City leaders, particularly Mayor Schaefer, opposed the idea. The *Pride* had served its purpose, he figured; the city should move on. But the public all but demanded that a new sailboat be built and the state of Maryland agreed to chip in a million dollars. The *Pride* board of directors finally agreed to the idea and decided it should be called the *Pride of Baltimore*.

The news was a blow to Roma Schack—not so much the idea of a second boat, but the use of the same name.

"She cannot be the *Pride of Baltimore*, for the *Pride* rests forever on the ocean floor," Roma told a reporter. She launched a crusade, going on the radio, writing the board, and, finally, beseeching public officials for help. She found support from the parents and other relatives of Armin, Vinny, and Barry, all of whom argued that the memories of their children would be marginalized by naming the replacement boat, *Pride of Baltimore*. It would be, they argued, as though the first boat never existed.

Pride officials, though, favored re-using the name and referred to many precedents in which lost ships have been replaced with a vessel of the same name. The influential *Baltimore Sun* applauded the idea of re-using the name, but others suggested awkward compromises including *"Pride of Baltimore and Maryland."* The battle waged for months and became a public relations nightmare: the grieving mother of the lost sailor fighting against the insensitive board of directors. Finally, the board relented and agreed to a compromise that Roma could live with. The new boat would be named *"Pride of Baltimore II."*

By the spring of 1987, the two federal investigations were complete and their basic conclusions were the same: the weather had overwhelmed the *Pride*.

The probable cause of the knockdown and sinking was the "sudden onset of high velocity wind that exceeded the limits of the vessel's stability causing the vessel to heel until downflooding occurred," the NTSB found. Its report added the fact that the lack of watertight bulkheads contributed to the rapid flooding. The malfunctioning life rafts, as well as the lack of life preservers on deck, contributed to the loss of life, the NTSB concluded.

The Coast Guard report, issued shortly afterward, essentially concurred.

"The proximate cause of the sinking was a sudden and extreme wind that heeled the vessel beyond its range of stability and knocked it down. Contributing factors included flooding through the open aft companionway hatch and a lack of watertight bulkheads, which permitted the entire vessel to flood and sink in a matter of minutes."

The NTSB characterized the storm as "a sudden high wind from a gust front developed by a thunderstorm downburst." The Coast Guard estimated the wind "probably exceeded seventy knots."

The NTSB's Esbensen, despite his close ties to the *Pride*, was more pointed than the Coast Guard in his secondary findings. Esbensen's report blamed Barry Duckworth's death in part on the malfunctioning life rafts, criticized the life raft servicing, and termed the rafts inadequate for ocean service. The *Pride* crew, the report said, should have trained for a knockdown; in addition, the organization should have required its sailors to have survival swimming skills, an obvious reference to Barry's inability to swim competently. But the report stopped short of blaming the accident or the deaths on the *Pride* organization.

In analyzing the accident, the Coast Guard had to determine the stability of a ship that was sitting on the ocean floor. This forced investigators to rely heavily on the three inclining tests that Gillmer had done during the *Pride*'s nine years of sailing. However, Gillmer's numbers were far from constant, suggesting that the *Pride*'s center of gravity—and thus its stability—had risen and fallen over the years.

The Coast Guard tapped Howard Chatterton, a staff naval architect, to do a stability analysis. Chatterton determined the ship's "most likely" center of gravity and displacement numbers as it sailed north from the Virgin Islands. He estimated the ship's weight at the time of the sinking at 122 tons—more than Gillmer had estimated in either of the two last inclining tests. And he pegged the ship's center of gravity at 9.3 feet above the keel, or somewhat better than the 9.42 that Gillmer had calculated just before the *Pride* set sail for Europe.

Using U.S. Navy criteria, Chatterton concluded that on the day of the accident, with only the two sails set, the *Pride* could have withstood winds of no more than about fifty-eight knots. (If the *Pride*'s center of gravity was actually closer to the 9.75 figure Gillmer determined for the boat in 1984, it could have withstood even less wind, perhaps less than fifty-five knots.)

Chatterton used his "most likely" weight and center of gravity estimates to calculate a series of stability figures for the *Pride*. The problem, though, was finding boats to compare them to. Since the *Pride* was an "un-inspected" vessel that carried no passengers or sailing students, it did not have to meet any minimum stability characteristics. Even so, Chatterton ran the numbers to see how the *Pride*'s stability measured up against certain classes of vessels that the Coast Guard regulated. Just as Melbourne Smith had predicted a decade earlier, the analysis showed that the *Pride* had inadequate stability to qualify to take passengers out to sea, or to take sailing students off the coast with anything more than minimal sails set.

But that finding had little bearing on the matter, since the *Pride* carried only a professional crew. The Coast Guard did not take the next step and consider just how prudent it was to take the historic replica across the ocean. While there was no legal impediment prohibiting the *Pride* from taking a paid crew out to sea, should it have? Neither the Coast Guard nor NTSB tackled that complicated question. That was a matter to be decided in the court of public opinion, Maxham explained later.

The last paragraph of the Coast Guard report was the most important to the *Pride* organization. There was, the Coast Guard concluded, "no evidence of actionable misconduct, inattention to duty, negligence, or willful violation of law or regulation on the part of licensed or certificated persons."

It was an accident, an act of God.

The Coast Guard stability analysis was unsatisfying for a number of reasons.

For one, the report included no explanation of how Chatterton came up with his crucial estimates of the *Pride*'s weight and center of gravity at the time of the sinking. Chatterton later explained that he based his estimates on crew members' testimony about how the boat was loaded for the trip north from the Virgin Islands. Unfortunately, specific records of how he made those calculations have not been located and Chatterton said he had no recollection about the details.

There was also at least one significant discrepancy between the Coast Guard report and other records. Chatterton's analysis stated that Gillmer, during his 1984 inclining—the one that produced the worrisome stability figures—estimated the *Pride*'s weight at 120 tons. However, Gillmer's own memo regarding the 1984 inclining put the weight as 115.5 tons. Years later, neither Chatterton nor Gillmer could explain the discrepancy.

Investigators did not ask Gillmer or others with the organization about his recommendations for improving the *Pride*'s stability before the European voyage, and his memo on the subject was not part of the Coast Guard record. Similarly, the Coast Guard report did not attempt to answer whether the *Pride* may have survived with its top rig on deck and without fuel and water on deck—two suggested precautions that were not taken. Some sailing experts who have looked at the *Pride* sinking said it's likely that without its top rig, the ship could have survived the blast of wind. Others, including Sugar Flanagan, disputed that notion and said the extreme wind would have knocked over most any sailboat.

The Coast Guard and the NTSB cleared the *Pride* organization of responsibility for the sinking, but the Lazzaros and Roma Schack did not. They made separate claims to get compensation from Pride of Baltimore, Inc. in 1987. In their claim, the Lazzaros cited the "negligence and unseaworthiness of the *Pride of Baltimore.*"

The *Pride* organization opted not to fight the two claims in court, and after negotiations, settled both by early 1988; the payments came out of a ten million dollar liability insurance policy. A confidentiality clause prohibited the parties from discussing the settlements, but the amounts were not large—in the very low six figures. Aside from the settlements with the Lazzaros and the Schacks, the *Pride* organization made no other such payments to crew members or families, according to the organization's lawyers. The three-year statute of limitations passed in May 1989, prohibiting any future claims.

The decision to quietly settle the two claims with relatively small payments was a wise one. It's not hard to imagine a jury determining that the weather only partially explained the sinking and deaths of May 14. As with all catastrophes, there was no one thing that went wrong.

Certainly, the chief cause of this one was the small but intense squall that, by pure chance, overwhelmed the *Pride*. Sugar estimated that the wind reached at least sixty knots, more than he had experienced at sea before and fierce enough to knock down many sailboats. While the wind may indeed have been at least that strong, the Coast Guard's analysis and the designer's own statements made clear that the *Pride* would have faced serious problems when hit from the side with winds of forty to fifty knots. Storms with winds that strong are unusual in the Sargasso Sea in mid-May, some might say freaky. But they are bizarre only in their timing, not in the fact that they appear. Indeed, the *Pride* had run into winds of forty, fifty, or even sixty knots at least a few times during its nine years of sailing. The challenge was to be prepared and the *Pride* could certainly have been better prepared:

• The knockdown may have been unavoidable, given the unexpected strength of the wind and the sailing decisions made by the crew, but the fact that it sank in a few minutes was the direct result of design decisions made a decade earlier. A schooner with watertight compartments may well have stayed on the surface considerably longer, and there's no doubt that a knocked-down boat on its side would have been far more useful to the twelve frantic crew members than no boat. There's wisdom in the old warning: *Don't leave the boat until the boat leaves you.* The squall lasted only about fifteen minutes. Had the crew been able to ride it out by clinging to the knocked-down *Pride*, they may have had time to send out a distress signal and to abandon ship with appropriate supplies and equipment, perhaps including the deck boats. Even with the bulkheads, the *Pride* may have sunk eventually, given its many openings and holes, but it's all but certain that more than eight of the crew would have made it home.

After the disaster, some people who sailed on the *Pride* said they were surprised the boat sank as quickly as it did.

"It never even crossed our minds that it would happen so fast. Now you think how naïve we were," Gail Shawe said later. "We never thought there would be no time to do anything." In retrospect, that attitude certainly seemed naïve. Since the *Pride* had no watertight compartments and often sailed with a hatch open, it would have been miraculous for the ship *not* to sink like a stone in the event of a knockdown.

• The open aft companionway played a crucial role in the sinking. With the crew not expecting a wind strong enough to cause a knockdown, they left the passageway open to provide quick access to the aft cabin's navigational equipment. In retrospect, it was a major misjudgment. However, the fact that it was offset to the port side was less important. If the hatch had been on the ship's center line, it probably would have flooded anyway, once the *Pride* was on its side.

• While it was simply bad luck that one of the life rafts was torn in the rigging, the malfunctioning of the other one may have contributed to the death of Barry Duckworth. Although he was half-drowned when the others found him, he would have had a far greater chance of survival if he had been immediately hauled out of the saltwater and into one of the rafts.

Given his poor condition, Barry might not have survived in a raft for the nearly five days it took to be rescued. But that begs a second, related question about the *Pride*'s operation. The survivors would surely not have been adrift for those five days if the ship had installed on-deck saltwater-activated EPIRBs that would have broadcast a distress signal immediately. On the *Pride*, though, the EPIRBs were stowed in the cabin largely because they would have appeared anachronistic on deck.

• The *Pride*'s mission had outgrown the boat. Once the *Pride* was built, there were only so many things that could be done to improve the ship's stability, and yet the scope of its travels grew increasingly difficult. Before making his ocean crossing, Armin took some steps to lower the center of gravity, but decided not to take others, such as removing fuel and water from the deck or sailing without the top rig. He had little choice. To ensure the safety of the crew during long ocean passages, the boat required adequate sail power and adequate water and fuel, which had to be kept on deck given the lack of storage space on a vessel originally intended to sit at the dock. In other words, the *Pride* was not fully equipped for the ambitious trips imposed on the ship after its construction.

All those issues aside, one crucial question remains: Why was a sailboat clearly vulnerable to capsizing in a fifty-knot wind on the ocean in the first place? There's only one good answer, and it's a powerful one: that's what sailboats do.

For Jan Miles, the longtime *Pride* captain, the boat's equation

could be summed up this way: "You have romance, drive, and adventure versus reality. To have avoided any risks, we could only
have *not* built the boat, or not sailed the boat. Sailboats can be
tipped over, end of statement. Anybody who thinks they can go to
sea and not suffer a capsize is absolutely foolish. I was quite comfortable with going across the Atlantic on her."

Many others were too. Sugar and Leslie knew exactly what they
were sailing and went anyway. Armin had doubts but put them
aside for a last turn at the helm. And Barry Duckworth, a newcomer, grasped the *Pride*'s vulnerability, but shrugged it off with
the fatalism of a sea-wise old salt.

"Oh, well," he said when asked about the chance of a disaster.
The risk, he figured, was part of the allure. Indeed, what was more
thrilling than setting sail and taking the wild black mare for a gallop
across the waves?

James Chesney nearly died on the *Pride* but holds no hard feelings. "It's nobody's fault. Yes, it was built for 1812. But boats built
today are going down, too. When you go out to sea, it's a big place
out there and the sea has all the power."

In the end, Chez is right. Nobody in particular was to blame for the
loss of the *Pride*, the deaths of four sailors, and the suffering of
eight others.

Yet it's also fair to say that many people could have prevented
the disaster. There were certainly warnings: the misadventures at
sea, the reluctant insurance companies, the questions about stability, and finally, the Baltic fiasco—a near-knockdown and two sailors
overboard. Again and again, though, ambition trumped caution and
nobody felt compelled to strike the sails and demand a rigorous
new accounting. With its low freeboard, internal ballast, and lack of
watertight integrity, this was a boat, after all, that even its creator
warned could be "extremely dangerous."

It seems impossible to conclude that the mundane payoff of
goodwill for the city of Baltimore was ever worth the risk of taking
such a vessel across the ocean. Yet many sensible people agreed
that it was, and for nine years nobody protested. Looking back with

the unforgiving insight of a grieving parent, Roma Schack understood exactly what happened with the people who loved this ship
called *Pride.*

"The sea," she said, "beguiled them all. It fooled the hell right
out of them."

CHAPTER 28

Spring 2003

The authorities may have deemed the sinking of the *Pride of Baltimore* an act of God, but the *Pride* organization decided not to take so many chances with divine luck the second time around. Even before the federal investigation of the sinking was finished, the organization began plans for a second boat and turned again to Tom Gillmer for the design. Melbourne Smith, the man most responsible for the look and feel of the first boat, was not invited back. He had burned his bridges during an acrimonious parting from the organization a decade earlier, and in any case, his purist desire for historical authenticity wasn't needed again.

The *Pride of Baltimore II* was commissioned in October 1988, two and a half years after the sinking. Most observers would notice few differences between the two schooners. Like the first, *Pride II* had raked masts, a black hull, and a dark green bottom. Instead of a broad white accent strip along her sides, *Pride II* had yellow.

But *Pride II* is a different and markedly safer ship, about 10 percent longer on deck but a full 50 percent heavier. She sits higher in the water and has a twenty-ton leaded keel for added stability below. Even with the extra weight, the second boat carries only 2 percent more sail area than the first. *Pride II* has twin engines powerful enough to push the schooner through almost any conditions.

The second time around, of course, there was no choice but to give the ship watertight bulkheads.

"All the things she is are things we all learned sailing the first *Pride*," said Peter Boudreau, who helped build and later captained the first boat, and supervised the building of the second.

The ship meets Coast Guard standards for carrying as many as six passengers; they sleep in comfortable bunks in two-person berths that line the main cabin. The crew of *Pride II*, meanwhile, sleeps in a stuffy warren of bunks not unlike those on the first boat. *Pride II* is not a pure replica of a nineteenth-century ship. The leaded keel, watertight compartments, and spacious cabin would not have been found in 1812. Nor would the large wooden wheel used to steer the boat, instead of the more unwieldy tiller found on the first *Pride*. But its sleek profile and expansive sails still capture the essence of the old boats, and she turns heads wherever she goes.

Despite the small salaries, dozens of mostly twenty-something sailors have signed on to crew *Pride II* over the years. Daniel Hornstein, the first mate in the fall of 2002, tried to explain the appeal. "You work all the time for little money. You don't control when you eat or when you get off the boat. You live in very cramped quarters and have to get along with people you may not like," he said during a stopover in the small Maryland town of Cambridge. But, he added: "It's probably the most memorable thing I'll ever do." Indeed, the day before I talked with Hornstein, the *Pride II* had made a thrilling run down the bay, sails bellied as it zigzagged easily through the southerly wind.

It was just another day on the water for a boat that has now sailed almost fifteen years—six more than the original—throughout North America, through Europe four times, and through much of Asia. Jan Miles stayed with the organization after the sinking and remains captain of *Pride II* today, one of the few human links between the two boats. He also met his future wife while sailing *Pride II*. The ship continues to sail the world, but fundraising remains a challenge and some of its most ardent supporters wonder how long *Pride II* can continue to work as a goodwill ambassador. When does even the best public relations idea go stale? One idea bandied about: placing the ship under glass at the water's edge, the same concept floated in the mid-1970s by Melbourne Smith for the first *Pride*.

The *Pride* organization celebrated twenty-five years of sailing in 2002 in a festive waterside party. Little was said about the sinking. The honoree that night was William Donald Schaefer, the former mayor of Baltimore, who went on to be governor of Maryland and then comptroller. He remembered the day the first *Pride* was launched: "I thought I would go out of my mind, I was so happy." I once asked him about the sinking of the first *Pride*. In the end, were the boat's successes worth all the pain? He sidestepped the impossible calculation to focus on the obvious benefits. "It did a lot for the city. People want to be proud of their city. It's our boat."

The *Pride of Baltimore* helped fuel a revival of interest in historic sailboats that remains strong today. Since the *Pride* was built, a steady stream of large sailboats has been launched, with varying degrees of historic authenticity. Many are involved in what has become a booming sail-training industry. By 2003, there were well over two hundred boats involved in licensed sail training and nearly all of them were built after the *Pride*. An ever-changing armada of these boats—schooners, ketches, sloops, and brigantines—travels from festival to festival, with stops in New York and Boston, but also in Cleveland and Muskegon, Michigan. With few exceptions, though, these ships, unlike the *Pride*, have been built to meet Coast Guard specifications for carrying passengers or sailing trainees.

The loss of the *Pride* had a modest impact on federal regulations. Under prodding from the NTSB, the Coast Guard pushed for a change in the law to require un-inspected vessels—the *Pride*'s category—to carry certain navigational and lifesaving equipment; the legislation, though, died in Congress. However, in 1993 Congress did enact another change initially recommended by the NTSB by requiring un-inspected vessels to carry EPIRBs during ocean or coastwise sailing. The Coast Guard rejected the NTSB's recommendation to require that un-inspected vessels stow life preservers on deck; they were concerned that the preservers could be washed overboard in heavy weather.

The *Pride* loss also prompted many sailing organizations to institute rigorous communication schedules while their ships are sailing to ensure that they avoid the *Pride* survivors' experience. While the lack of a fixed communication schedule with the home office did not contribute to the loss of life, it may well have extended the amount of time the survivors spent on the life raft.

Jennifer Lamb stuck to the plans she discussed with Armin in 1986. Still deep in mourning, she began a physical therapy program in Baltimore only days after the wrenching memorial service at Fort McHenry. She continued to work on boats but only doing day sails out of the Inner Harbor. In a final blow that summer, many of the belongings she left on *Te Vega* when she made her emergency exit in Bermuda burned up in a car fire before they could be returned to her.

Seven months after the sinking, Jennifer volunteered to answer phones at a Baltimore telethon to raise money for the second *Pride*. Among the many *Pride* alumni who showed up at the television studio to help was Mark Bolster, a veteran from the boat's early years. The two, who had never met before, hit it off and later married— yet another couple brought together by the *Pride*. Today, they live in a Baltimore suburb and Jennifer continues to sail for fun on the Chesapeake Bay, often with Sue Burton Hughes, who survived the Baltic scare with her in August 1985.

Dan Parrott, who helped pull Sarah Fox out of the water that day, sailed for years and met the woman he would marry on *Pride of Baltimore II*. After serving as a captain of *Pride II* for four years, he left the organization at the end of 2002 to teach seamanship, navigation, and captaining in Maine. As for Fox, she decided there was something special about the other man who pulled her out of the water, Rob Whalen. The two married and live in Rhode Island.

Gail Shawe, who had planned on leaving the *Pride* organization after the European trip in 1986, agreed to stay on to lead the rebuilding effort. The emotions of the loss of the boat were slow to fade. "For me, it was just below the surface for years. You become a lot more nervous about the forces of nature and how people tend to be so careless about taking risks."

And Arne Rostad, the skipper of the *Toro Horten*, continued to

sail on merchant vessels. Years later, he wrote to Sugar and Leslie
to tell them he had made yet another rescue at sea, this one of
refugee boat people trying to reach the United States.

Creating the *Pride* helped Melbourne Smith emerge as a major figure in the world of historic sailboats. Among the vessels he had a
hand in later were the *Spirit of Massachusetts*, the *Niagara*, the
Californian and the *Lynx*. The seventy-three-year-old designer lives
outside Annapolis and continues to work on what would be his grandest project: the *Sea Witch*, a re-creation of a nineteenth-century
American clipper ship, a project that could cost twenty million dollars to build. The enormous 1,100-ton ship would be constructed as
authentically as possible, with kerosene lamps, for example, instead of electric lights.

Smith's eyes twinkled as he recounted stories about building
and sailing the *Pride*—heady times that required him and his crew
to improvise as they constructed the first Baltimore clipper in more
than a century. Smith said he had no regrets about how the *Pride*
was designed or built. Risk, he said with no hesitation, is part of
sailing.

"There's no end of safety stuff you could do, but that's not really
sailing the boat," Smith said. "You tell everybody ahead of time,
'this is dangerous but it's fun.'"

To be sure, Smith did just that. From the very beginning, he
warned everyone that the boat he had in mind demanded careful
attention. After the disaster, he was also one of the first to criticize
the way the boat was handled on her last journey. The topmasts
should have been stowed on deck for a trip up the Atlantic, he said
confidently. "That would have made a lot of difference."

Tom Gillmer, the *Pride*'s architect, now in his nineties, lives in a
cozy house that overlooks the busy Annapolis harbor and is filled
with models and photographs of vessels he designed. His own
small sailboat, which he also designed, is docked right outside the
back door. The former Naval Academy professor moves slowly and

hears poorly, but maintains an air of formality, dressing in a blue blazer, dark tie, and button-down shirt for interviews. When I came to see him nearly seventeen years after the sinking, Gillmer had a question: "Are you going to condemn me?"

There's something in the question that suggested he expected it. Yet he was determined to put the loss of the *Pride* in context, noting that the boat simply went the way of many of her ancestors. "There were a lot of these Baltimore clippers that never got to their destination and nobody knows what happened; they just disappeared," Gillmer said. "That's one of the problems; they sank. They carried too much sail for their watertight integrity."

As for the *Pride* itself, Gillmer said he cannot recall the details of her stability and the inclining tests he performed. In retrospect, though, he said he would have done things differently.

"The *Pride* was practically finished before they decided to sail it. I thought it was going to be a dockside amusement," he said. "The original idea of *Pride* was that it was going to be an exhibit and not go to sea. If I had known that it was going to go to sea I probably would have done the same thing I did with *Pride II.*"

So, should it have gone offshore? "I don't think I would have recommended it go to sea," Gillmer said, taking off his round bifocals and rubbing his eyes. "But nobody asked me. They took it."

Like seemingly everyone else involved in the creation and loss of the *Pride of Baltimore*, he had no inclination to take any responsibility for the loss of life.

"I have," Gillmer said, "a clear conscience about that boat."

EPILOGUE

Each May, a small group gathers in Baltimore's Inner Harbor to observe the anniversary of the sinking of the *Pride*. The short program takes place at the *Pride* memorial: a sturdy ship's mast angling out of the ground with the names of the four who perished engraved in stone nearby. While the eight survivors developed seemingly unbreakable bonds during their ordeal, as a group they have not stayed close. According to several of the eight survivors, there has been at least one significant squabble, with Susie Huesman suggesting that Sugar Flanagan and Leslie McNish secretly secured a payout from the *Pride* organization—an unfounded assertion.

The last time all eight were together was at Sugar and Leslie's wedding more than seventeen years ago.

After recovering from what he calls his "trench body" in the spring of 1986, James Chesney returned to Maine to resume his carpentry work. But he stayed in touch with Suzy Winter, the young woman from the *Pride* office who greeted him on his return from Puerto Rico and later helped him find new glasses and get medical treatment. That summer, the *Pride* organization, with no boat and therefore little need for a public relations person, laid off Suzy. Soon after, Chez called with a rash proposition. *We'll never know whether this relationship was meant to be unless we give it a real try,* he told her. *Come up to Maine.*

The offer came from a man she barely knew, but somehow it sounded right and she headed to Maine. Three years later, the two were married on the *Pride of Baltimore II* in a ceremony in Camden, Maine. Jan Miles made sure the boat got there in time for the ceremony, despite an onslaught of bad weather brought on by Hurricane Hugo. Suzy got dressed for the ceremony in the captain's cabin. For the processional, she emerged up the aft companionway, comparable to the opening Chez managed to swim out of as the *Pride* sank. Today, the couple and their two children live on Vashon Island, a fog-draped outpost in Puget Sound just west of Seattle.

Now a full-time carpenter, Chez has a small scar on his lower back, a reminder of where the label in his gray shorts pressed firmly against his skin for more than four days in the life raft. "A lot of people have said, 'Boy, how unlucky you were to sink like that,'" Chez said. "Actually, I wasn't unlucky. I was hugely lucky. I made it through. In my eyes, I didn't suffer."

A few years ago, he bought a twenty-eight-foot San Juan sailboat, which is about a third of the length of the *Pride* but actually has more headroom below. By his own admission, Chez is a conservative sailor and watches with amazement as other sailboats blast around Puget Sound on windy days at steep angles of heel.

Of the eight survivors, Dan Krachuk may have gone through the roughest emotional patch, according to people associated with the *Pride*. He has continued to work on the water for much of the time since 1986, including five years on merchant marine vessels. In brief conversations, Krachuk expressed misgivings about the time he has spent at sea.

"As far as I'm concerned, if I had to do it all over again, I wouldn't [have] set foot on that boat," he said. The seafaring lifestyle, he added, has been rough. "Here it is fifteen years later and I'm still eating red beans and rice." It's hard, he says, to give away his memories of the *Pride* to a writer. "This is my story. It's very personal to me. It's the greatest thing I have in my life. Whether I see it as an accomplishment or not, I'm not quite sure."

Like Dan, Susie Huesman was deeply bruised by the *Pride* loss and the memory of being sucked down by the sinking ship. She has wrestled with guilt stemming from the deaths of Nina, Barry, Vinny, and Armin, and for a while became extra-cautious in her day-to-day life. In New York City not long after the disaster, she was riding an elevator in a friend's apartment building when she blurted out, "Are there stairs to get out of here in case there's a fire?" She was, in her own words, "a mess."

Susie stayed in the Baltimore area and helped build *Pride of Baltimore II*. Over time, she grew sharply critical of the organization in the wake of the tragedy, accusing the *Pride* organization of using the eight survivors as little more than public relations props. At the same time, she has expressed deep affection for the ship itself.

"I understand that I was taking risks," she told an interviewer once. "Now I didn't count on getting hit by a freak wind shear, but it happened. We sailed *Pride* for the same reason that people climb mountains. If the object were just to get to the top of the mountain, you would take a helicopter. You would get there the quickest way possible, with the least amount of risk. But that's not the reason people climb mountains or sail on *Pride*. We assume some risks, but the benefit of the experience is worth it for us."

Huesman earned a law degree, got married, and worked for a while in her father's law firm in Towson, Maryland. Both she and Krachuk declined to talk about their experiences for this book.

Joe McGeady spent time at home after the sinking but soon headed back to sea with Sugar and Leslie on the *Californian*. Eventually he returned to Baltimore to settle down and today works in the marine construction and transportation field. McGeady has four children and occasionally takes part in *Pride* official functions. Now in his forties, McGeady bears none of the resentment some of the *Pride* survivors carry. "I'm done with this," he said. "People went out of their way to treat us well."

McGeady does carry one nagging doubt about his own actions during the noontime blur on May 14. With the boat capsizing, McGeady did help others free themselves from their harnesses, but he wasted little time in climbing up to the bulwarks and heading aft. Moments later he was in the water, swimming to one of the life rafts.

He has gone over it in his head many, many times: *Why did I leave the boat—and the others—so quickly?* Barry, the non-swimmer, surely could have used a hand. His self-doubt seems misplaced; a person's first instinct is to survive and McGeady certainly helped the others by reaching one of the life rafts and making sure it didn't blow away. But, still, McGeady will continue to wonder if he somehow shirked his duty. "That's my curse to bear," he told me.

Robert Foster sailed for a while after the loss of the *Pride*, but eventually returned to merchant-marine work. He spent more than four years on ships in the United States, the Caribbean, and Central America, eventually reaching the rank of first mate. For many years, he also operated a charter sailing business on the Chesapeake Bay, where he first learned to sail. In 1992, he began work for the military's sea-lift command in Washington, D.C., and remains there today. He lives near where he grew up, in the Virginia suburbs of Washington; he and his wife have two children.

His sudden celebrity, in 1986, came with some guilt. After all, Foster became a media star after having served on the *Pride* for only two months. "Other guys had spent so much time on the boat but never got the attention. I had some guilty feelings about that."

Still intrigued with sailing after the *Pride*, Scott Jeffrey took various jobs on the water after the sinking, first in Maryland and then later on the schooner *Ernestina* in New England. However, after a couple of years he gave up professional sailing, got married, and today teaches geography at a community college in Baltimore. He co-owns a twenty-four-foot sailboat.

Nearly twenty years after he walked onto the *Pride* for the first time, Jeffrey's hair remains blond, his eyes still a vivid blue. He can easily recall the long-faded euphoria that settled in after the rescue, but he dismisses any suggestion that surviving such a disaster has somehow allowed him to accept life's harder moments with more patience. These days, the fact that he was part of the *Pride* story poses a dilemma. "I might be in front of the class talking about something, and I'll want to tell the story," Jeffrey said. "It elevates me in a way. But at the same time, it's very private."

* * *

Looking for a reliable way to continue sailing and living together, Sugar Flanagan and Leslie McNish decided to purchase a boat of their own a year after the sinking. They borrowed money from Leslie's family and purchased *Alcyone*, a sixty-five-foot, gaff-rigged topmast schooner built in 1956. They have lived ever since on the lovely wooden sailboat, which they keep in a sheltered marina in the cozy town of Port Townsend, Washington, amid fishing boats and otters. Their two children, Alyce Irie and Darby, born in 1991 and 1994, have lived on the boat their entire lives. In the fall of 2002, the four of them completed a two-year around-the-world trip on *Alcyone*. When not on extended cruises, the couple leads charters and sailing classes on *Alcyone*, which can carry six passengers. While in Port Townsend, their lives have a traditional shape: horseback riding lessons, birthday parties, and trips to the video store in the family's Volvo station wagon.

One of the small dories aboard *Alcyone* is named *Nina*; she was launched on May 14, 1998, the twelfth anniversary of the sinking. A picture of the *Pride* with all sails up hangs on one wall of the tiny cabin, amid masks, shells, and weavings the family has collected on its world travels. Other reminders of the *Pride* sneak up on Sugar. The nerve endings in his lower back were damaged by sitting in cold water for several days, and even today, he gets uncomfortable little sensations there. Sometimes he reaches for a particular tool only to realize, "Oh, yeah. That was on *Pride*."

Then there were the times—at least a half-dozen over the years—when someone brought up the sinking of the *Pride*, explaining to Sugar what happened without realizing his role. Often, these self-appointed experts point fingers at the crew. But Sugar and Leslie remain convinced that nobody did anything wrong the day of the sinking. The ship was in good shape; the sails were trimmed appropriately. The intense, unforeseen wind caused the problems.

"The squall made the circumstances," Leslie told me one evening as we sat around the small galley table on *Alcyone*. "All we did was respond. We went from one step to the next." Leslie had no illusions about the *Pride* and its inherent limitations. Those were part of the thrill. "She was what she was. We knew what we were sailing."

Sugar said he holds no regrets and no guilt. "I feel good that there wasn't much we could have done differently," he said. He did his job that day, letting out the main sheet, but it was simply too late to change the course of the disaster.

Like the *Pride*, *Alcyone* does not have watertight bulkheads and one of its hatches is slightly off-center, neither of which fazes its owners. The *Pride* sinking, though, has made them more cautious at sea. "In hindsight, in strong weather like that, I reduce sail way down" Flanagan said. "If the weather's screwy, reduce more than what you'd need for that weather."

A few months after the loss of the *Pride*, someone from the organization called Bob Jewett at his secluded log house in Delaware, offering to reimburse him for his stepson Barry's lost belongings, including his treasured tools. The insurance would pay for it. Jewett smiled and said, "No thanks. Barry wouldn't want that." Nor did Jewett entertain the notion of suing the *Pride* organization. He said Barry was aware of the *Pride*'s safety risks and accepted them.

In his cluttered pickup truck Jewett keeps Barry's nice set of chisels, a set of ten that now has eight, the other two having disappeared with the *Pride*. Down a winding path from the house, through a shady grove of maple, gum, oak, dogwood, and poplar, the foundation for Barry's meditation hut sits the way he left it in March 1986. Jewett goes there once in a while and whacks down the weeds. He and his other kids used to talk about finishing the project but never got around to it. Somehow it seems appropriate the way it is—an unfinished memorial to a life cut short.

When her mother died from cancer in May 1988, two years after the loss of the *Pride*, Roma Schack finally knew what to do with the foul-weather gear Robert and Chez returned to her. Before laying her mother to rest, Roma draped the yellow pants and top over her feet in the coffin. In her mind, her mother and daughter are buried together in Rosedale Cemetery, in Linden, New Jersey.

It took much longer for Roma to put aside the anger that Nina's death brought on—emotions that helped fuel her determined effort to change the name of the second boat. She thought often of her motherly phone call to Gail Shawe in early 1986, demanding to know what the *Pride* organization would offer her daughter after the European trip was canceled. Was it somehow Roma's fault that Nina sailed on the *Pride*? In the year after the sinking, as Roma learned more about the *Pride*'s shortcomings, she grew angrier. Her request to address the *Pride* board was refused. "I wanted to say that you simply must have safety measures to prevent this stuff," she recalled later. "How could you possibly let this happen?"

When the legal claim against the *Pride* organization was settled, Roma used the proceeds to establish a scholarship fund at the Bryn Mawr School in Baltimore. She also donated the money that the *Pride* organization paid for Nina's wages and lost belongings. A Bryn Mawr alumna living in Florida astonished Roma by contributing an unsolicited gift of more than sixty thousand dollars to the fund. It has helped pay tuition for several girls.

Roma, who now uses her maiden name of Foti, lives in Bloomington, Minnesota, near her son, Lawrence, and his two young daughters. In the corner of her living room, Roma has set up a display of Nina's sailing knife with pictures of Barry, Armin, and, of course, Vinny. Her battles with the *Pride* organization are long behind her and Roma has attempted to move on. She figures it serves no purpose to continue blaming anyone for the deaths.

"I just don't want to be mad at anybody."

In West Redding, Connecticut, a dark gray piece of granite sits next to the deck in front of Maria and Victor Lazzaro's home. The stone, picked from the beach in Maine where Vinny spent summers with the Outward Bound program, is rough on one side and smooth on the other, "just like Vincent." Next to it is a smaller, rounded stone; it is for Nina. The Lazzaros used to mark May 14 with a trip to the beach in Connecticut, where they and their two children made bouquets of lilacs and tossed them into the Long Island Sound, but the tradition has lapsed.

The Lazzaros wish they knew more about the final minutes of the lives of their son and Nina.

There's a consensus that once the boat was pushed over, Vinny ran forward on the *Pride*'s starboard bulwarks, moving in the opposite direction of the others. Nobody on board can explain his rush forward, other than to surmise he was trying to reach Nina. From his perch in the deflating life raft, Scott Jeffrey briefly saw them over the waves, moving toward each other. They met, he said, in a quick embrace, like a woman hugging a companion before hopping in a cab.

One can imagine that Vinny, a strong six-footer who had nonchalantly lived through the sinking of a fishing boat the previous year, would surely have remained calmer than the petite woman who had no experience with ocean storms. Did he get dragged down by a struggling Nina, the two of them drowning together? Perhaps they became separated and Vinny swam off to look for the rafts or something else. The only facts, of course, are that neither made it. The rest is unanswerable.

Victor Lazzaro, a lanky, soft-spoken architect, sometimes lies awake at night trying to piece it all together. It's perplexing that Vinny, a strong swimmer with a cool head, didn't make it to where the eight others had gathered. "There weren't vast bodies of waters between them," he said. "Vincent must have made the effort to find something they could use."

The Lazzaros did not find out about Scott's momentary sighting of their son until months after the survivors returned. They are still concerned that somebody was withholding important information from them about their son's last minutes. The concern is imperfectly formed, but still wholly understandable. A second, perhaps more troubling notion has also stayed with the Lazzaros—that somehow they indirectly contributed to their son's death. There are those moments, they say, when they blame themselves for not trying to stop him from going to sea on the historic sailboat.

Victor Lazzaro thinks back to the conversation he had with Vinny about the *Pride* in late 1985, the one in which he said the schooner looked awfully top-heavy. Despite his misgivings, Victor

Lazzaro seconded the idea of sailing on the boat. "I told him it would be an adventure."

Armin died without a will, which was no surprise to those who knew him, but sorting through the finances of a man with few land-side attachments proved to be straightforward. Living frugally, Armin had banked seventeen thousand dollars, a respectable figure given the low pay he was earning but still modest enough to startle his financially comfortable father. His estate received another twelve thousand dollars from the *Pride* organization to cover wages and possessions lost in the sinking, including his watch and brass sextant. But aside from a small car he had purchased the year before, Armin's probate papers listed no other assets. Everything of any value went down with the *Pride*.

The federal investigators cleared Armin of responsibility for the loss of the *Pride*. But that hasn't stopped others from second-guessing his sailing that day. With the wind picking up and storm clouds threatening in the east, Armin dropped two sails, and he and Sugar discussed dropping even more. But they ran out of time and the wind smashed into the boat at almost a ninety-degree angle—the angle most likely to cause a knockdown. Armin tried to turn off the wind for what would have been a white-knuckled gallop westward. But it was too late.

Some who have sailed the *Pride* contend that turning upwind would have been the better option, given the sails Armin had up. The *Pride*'s mainsail tended to act as a "wind rudder" by pushing the boat around and into the wind. When Armin tried to turn the schooner to port—or off the wind—the mainsail would have fought against the action of the rudder by pushing the bow into the wind. Armin wanted to go downwind, but the boat probably tried to go up.

Years earlier, Daniel Moreland took the opposite tack when the *Pride* got hit by a nasty squall a few hundred miles to the south in the Caribbean. That night, Moreland loosened the foresails and turned the *Pride* into the wind. The boat took a wicked pounding but survived.

Some have also questioned Armin's choice of sails that day: a "split rig" with the mainsail flying aft and the staysail at the bow. Some veteran sailors believe the ship would have had a better chance had Armin kept the foresail up instead of the mainsail. With the foresail and staysail up at the bow, the *Pride* would have had more "pull" instead of "push," and, therefore, a better chance of turning off the wind and running.

Did Armin wait too long to drop more sail? In hindsight, yes. Was his decision to run the right one? That question cannot be answered. Trying to run didn't work, but we also don't know if turning into the wind might have.

In any case, it's important to remember that Armin was apparently blindsided by the actual force of the squall. Had he known what was bearing down from the east, he would certainly have taken other steps. In that light, none of his decisions were wrong.

Finally, though, there are those who wonder if Armin, a cerebral sailor, was handicapped that day by something harder to identify. Tom Gillmer recalls that Armin peppered him with questions about the *Pride*'s sailing ability before the European trip. "We made it," he scribbled on a postcard to Gillmer after arriving in Barbados in the spring of 1986. Gillmer thought there was a sense of relief in the note, and in the architect's eyes, "Armin was a good sailor but he was a little bit afraid of the ship."

Roger Long, the Maine naval architect, wonders if he somehow played a role in the *Pride* disaster. It was his analysis, after all, that stirred up so many questions in Armin's mind about the boat's actual stability. Could that lack of certainty have led to indecision? It's a question Long has often thought about.

"She got caught in a very vulnerable position," Long points out about the *Pride*'s last moments. "Maybe my discussions with Armin put so much doubt in his mind that he couldn't decide what to do."

The story concludes with an unforgettable image: Armin Elsaesser swimming over the waves away from his lost ship, his crew, and his only chance for survival: the life rafts. He swam purposefully perhaps forty to fifty feet away when the others spotted him. Their screams went unheard, or at least unanswered.

Did he not realize where the rafts were? Given the disorienting conditions raging at the time, it's certainly possible. But unlike Vinny, Barry, and Nina, he had been near the group of survivors in the immediate aftermath of the storm, yelling for everyone to go to the life rafts. Yet, even as the eight came together, he swam away. Had he looked in their direction, Armin would have seen the surviving crew members. But he didn't turn.

Without enough facts to explain his puzzling final moments, others have imposed their own interpretations. There are two camps.

One includes a variety of people, all of whom were far from the Sargasso Sea on May 14, 1986, and all of whom believe that this captain chose to go down with his ship. Paul Esbensen, who headed the investigation for the NTSB, is now retired and lives on Maryland's Eastern Shore in a house with a view of the Chesapeake Bay. In May 1986, after talking privately with the survivors when they returned to Baltimore, he concluded that Armin made a selfless decision to ensure his crew had a better chance of survival. "He swam away from the raft because he didn't want to take a place on the raft," Esbensen said. "That is what I understand: he swam away from the wreck because he knew there wasn't room for him."

Roma Foti met Armin only once but considered him a mature, responsible man—one capable of making a life-and-death decision to sacrifice himself for the benefit of others. "I felt he assessed the situation. He knew there was only one life raft and he knew he couldn't be on the life raft. I believe he swam away."

Bob Jewett, Barry's stepfather, agrees. After visits from some of the surviving crew, he was left with the firm impression that Armin surrendered his own life. It's a romantic image that somehow bolsters his view of the tragedy.

"I've always thought that was one of the most beautiful things I ever heard in my life," Jewett said in an interview. "It makes you shake your head and say, 'Oh my God.'"

Generally speaking, the sailors with Armin that day in the Atlantic don't have much use for the idea that he made a conscious decision to give up his life to help them. For one thing, Armin had no way of knowing that only one of the life rafts was operable; the others didn't determine that until the day after the sinking.

Nor are they inclined to believe that losing his ship compelled him to swim away in a fit of despair. Jeff Bolster, Armin's good friend and crew mate from the *Westward*, rejects any suggestion that Armin committed suicide. "I never, ever, ever for one minute thought that he was depressed or heartbroken. I don't think that he would have done that," Bolster told me during an e-mail interview.

What Bolster and the six surviving *Pride* crew members interviewed for this book tend to believe is that Armin saw something in the water, something beyond the waves that nobody else could see. Perhaps he spotted Vinny struggling, or he may have set off to grab a water jug or other supplies. Once he was in the teeth of the storm, the waves could have overwhelmed him.

That's Joe McGeady's best guess. But he can't rule out the more romantic notion that Armin was too heartbroken to go on. Indeed, the thought of floating off alone to short-circuit the agony occurred to Joe that day.

"The fact that he had lost a vessel and people had drowned might have ruined him. It might ruin anybody," Joe theorized one night over dinner at a harbor-front restaurant. "I always thought Armin would have been romantic enough to go down with the ship."

Perhaps there's a middle-ground explanation that allows Armin to be both human and heroic at once. As his own heartfelt letters made clear, Armin had an overwhelming sense of responsibility for both the boat and the crew. *The prospect of losing a life fills me with the most horrible dread,* he told Jennifer five months earlier.

Picture the moment when the *Pride* began to sink, righting itself as it dropped—its masts, spars, and pennants disappearing into the ocean. For nine months, he had lived with the memories of the near-disaster in the Baltic. Now, suddenly, the ship was gone and his eleven sailors were fighting for their lives. Such a catastrophe could crush any captain's spirit, but at the same time make him desperate to make amends. Half an ocean away, Jennifer knew intuitively that Armin could not have survived such a blow. He would not have given up without trying to account for every sailor and every last supply.

We can surely imagine the captain of the lost *Pride* slicing over the waves, his heart racing, a dreadful sense of failure tearing at his soul. His eyes scan the churning sea for something—*anything*—that might begin to redeem the loss. Whatever he sees over the waves, whether real or imagined, surely is worth trying to reach.

AUTHOR'S NOTE

In writing this account, I drew heavily from Armin Elsaesser's writings and letters, as well as ship's logs written by several *Pride* sailors over the years. I relied on a wide array of other documents, including the *Pride of Baltimore* Inc.'s files, Charles Center-Inner Harbor Management Inc.'s records, Coast Guard and National Transportation Safety Board records, and papers held in the Baltimore City archives, as well as hundreds of newspaper and magazine articles and the books cited in the bibliography.

But the book was based largely on interviews I did with more than sixty people, including six of the eight people who survived the loss of the *Pride of Baltimore*.

It was no surprise that after so many years certain memories had faded. In other instances, memories conflicted with written records made at the time. In those cases, I generally relied on the written records. At least one participant confirmed the wording of all dialogue recounted in the book. If a participant could not recall the wording of a conversation with certainty, I used italics to indicate the approximate wording. Similarly, characters' thoughts are set off in italics.

The four and a half days the *Pride* survivors spent on the life raft proved especially difficult to re-create chronologically. Each of the events on the raft was described to me by at least one survivor. However, memories conflicted as to which day or night a handful of events took place. In such cases I weighed the various recollections and adopted the one that seemed strongest or most consistent with other memories. In each case, I am confident I stayed true to the memories of those involved.

Tom Waldron
Baltimore, Maryland
Spring 2003

ACKNOWLEDGMENTS

I must thank so many people who helped me with this book.

First, I offer my deepest appreciation to relatives of the four sailors who died in the *Pride* sinking. They reopened a painful part of their lives for me.

Ford Elsaesser went to great trouble to provide a wealth of information about his older brother. Roma Foti and Maria and Victor Lazzaro spent many hours telling me about Nina and Vincent, and offered me valuable materials. And Bob Jewett and Moss Willow graciously provided rich memories and materials from Barry's life.

There are several lovely tributes to the four lost sailors, including the official *Pride* memorial on the south shore of the Inner Harbor in Baltimore. A garden on the campus of the city's Bryn Mawr School bears Nina Schack's name, as does the scholarship fund established there. A friend of Armin's established a fund in his honor with the Sea Education Association to support students doing maritime research. And all four are remembered with a memorial in the basement of the Seamen's Bethel in New Bedford, Massachusetts.

Six of the *Pride* survivors took a chance on me and shared their memories. Without their voices, of course, this story could not have been told. So I extend a special thanks to Sugar Flanagan, Joseph McGeady, Leslie McNish, Robert Foster, Scott Jeffrey, and James

Chesney for the many hours they gave me. I hope I have done justice to their story of loss and survival.

And special thanks to Jennifer Lamb Bolster, who could not have been more generous discussing a bittersweet chapter in her life.

Jan Miles was astute, passionate, and patient throughout this project. And a special salute to the late M. Eamonn McGeady, who also encouraged me early on and whose name is appropriately honored on *Pride of Baltimore II*.

I appreciate the cooperation of Gail Shawe, Thomas Gillmer, and Melbourne Smith, as well as the many *Pride* sailors and builders who shared their memories. Thanks to Rob Whalen, Sarah Fox Whalen, Sue Burton Hughes, Leroy Surosky, Peter Boudreau, Chris Rowsom, Steve Wedlock, Daniel Moreland, Ellen Huebsch Anderson, Allen Rawl, Lew Beck, Andy Davis, Steve Bunker, and Kate Boone.

Special thanks to Dan Parrott, a keen observer and writer, and to Roger Long, Eliza Hitchcock, Al Nejmeh, Peg Brandon, Kim Pedersen, Jeff Bolster, Kelly Baumgartner, Suzy Shaw of SOBO Video Productions, and Craig and Susan Pendleton.

My appreciation also extends to Mario Schack, Lawrence Schack, Alex Elsaesser, Laura Groseclose, Barbara White, Kai Lassen, Don Witten, Ann-Wallis White, Gregg Swanzey, Nadine Bloch, Emily McGeady, Pete Lesher, Tom Hollowak, Tom Weschler, Bill Tower, and Cynthia Parsons.

Martin Millspaugh, Al Copp, Bob Embry, Charles Tomlinson, and Tom Todd shared their knowledge of the development of downtown Baltimore and the genesis of the *Pride*. Special thanks to Jay Scattergood.

I received firsthand insight into tall-ship sailing in September 2002, thanks to Jan Miles and the crew of the *Pride of Baltimore II*: Daniel Hornstein, Justin Cathcart, Greg Bailey, Alex Ott, Jocelyn Lohse, Chris Martin, Chris Whitlock, Diane Sternberg, Krysta Tyburski, Jamie Wasser, and Daphne Glover.

I also appreciate the cooperation I received from the Board of Directors of Pride of Baltimore Inc., especially members Charles E. "Pete" Partridge Jr. and Chris Hartman. Current and former employees Linda E. Christenson, Dale Hilliard, and Susan Winter Chesney were also helpful, as was Paul Mullen. Thanks also to William Donald Schaefer and Michael Golden, current and former Coast Guard officials John Maxham, Howard Chatterton, and Michael Brown, and Paul Esbensen and Leon Katcharian from the NTSB.

And I must extend thanks to former colleagues and competitors at the *Baltimore Sun, Evening Sun* and *News American,* and the *Boston Globe,* whose stories about the *Pride* from the 1970s and 1980s were extremely valuable, particularly Liz Bowie, Tom Horton, Frank D. Roylance, Ann LoLordo, Joel McCord, Dan Rodricks, Carl Schoettler, and Steve McKerrow.

A small group of friends gave me patient encouragement and feedback, particularly William F. Zorzi Jr., Dan "It's Only a Suggestion" Fesperman, and Judy Oppenheimer. Thanks to Ann LaFarge of Kensington Books; Elizabeth Frost-Knappman of New England Publishing Associates literary agency; three fine artists, Ann Feild, J. Brough Schamp, and Greg Pease; Ann Waldron and, of course, Stephanie.

And finally, high fives to Ben and Henry Waldron, two very cool guys who always remembered not to mess up the towering piles of papers in the office.

BIBLIOGRAPHY

"Baltimore: A Living Renaissance." Edited by Lenora Heilig Nast, Laurence N. Krause, R. C. Monk, Baltimore: Historic Baltimore Society Inc., 1982.

Callahan, Steven. *Adrift: Seventy-six Days Lost at Sea*. New York: Houghton Mifflin, 1986.

Chapelle, Howard Irving. *The Baltimore Clipper: Its Origin and Development*. New York: Dover Publications, 1988 edition.

Cranwell, John Philips and William Bowers Crane. *Men of Marque*. New York: W. W. Norton & Co., 1940.

Footner, Geoffrey M. *Tidewater Triumph: The Development and Worldwide Success of the Chesapeake Bay Pilot Schooner*. Centreville, Md.: Tidewater Publishers, 1998.

Gillmer, Thomas C. *Pride of Baltimore: The Story of the Baltimore Clippers*. Camden, Maine.: International Marine, 1992.

Giorgetti, Franco. *Sailing Ships*. New York: MetroBooks, 2001.

Grayson, Stan. "Replica Ships." *The Nautical Quarterly*, No. 35, Autumn 1986.

Henderson, Richard "Jud." *Chesapeake Sails: A History of Yachting on the Bay*. Centreville, Md.: Tidewater Publishers, 1999.

Keith, Robert C. *Baltimore Harbor: A Picture History*. Baltimore: The Johns Hopkins University Press, 1991 edition.

Kiley, Deborah Scaling and Meg Noonan. *Untamed Seas: One Woman's True Story of Shipwreck and Survival*. New York: Houghton Mifflin, 1994.

Olson, Sherry H. *Baltimore: The Building of an American City*. Baltimore: The Johns Hopkins University Press, 1998 edition.

Parrott, Daniel S. *Tall Ships Down*. Camden Maine: International Marine/McGraw-Hill, 2003.

Pease, Greg, "Sailing with Pride." Baltimore: Baumgartner Publishing, 1990.

"Pride of Baltimore," Baltimore Operation Sail Ltd., 1977.

Smith, C. Fraser, *William Donald Schaefer: A Political Biography*. Baltimore: The Johns Hopkins University Press, 1999.

Travers, Paul J. *The Patapsco: Baltimore's River of History*. Centreville, Md.: Tidewater Publishers, 1990.

INDEX

BALTIMORE CLIPPER SCHOONER

DRAWN TO 1:32 SCALE

FOR THE INTERNATIONAL HISTORICAL WATER CRAFT SOCIETY INC.

REFERENCE DESIGN Nº 301

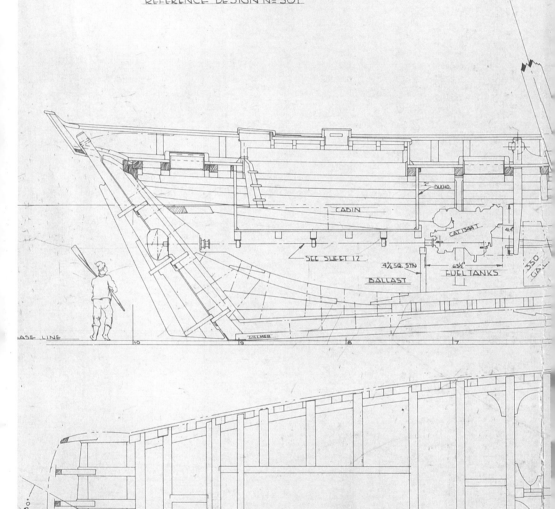

CABIN

2" BLKHD.

CAT 3A4T

SEE SHEET 12

3½ SQ. STN

BALLAST

FUEL TANKS

6¾"

4½"

350 GAL.

BASE LINE

GILLMER

10   9   8   7

30°

DECK BEAM SPACING